Trauma, Dissociation and M

C000095649

Trauma, Dissociation and Multiplicity provides psychoanalytic insights into dissociation, in particular dissociative identity disorder (DID), and offers a variety of responses to the questions of self, identity and dissociation. With contributions from a range of clinicians from both America and Europe, areas of discussion include:

- the concept of dissociation and the current lack of understanding on this topic
- the verbal language of trauma and dissociation
- the meaning of children's art
- the dissociative defence from the average to the extreme
- pioneering new theoretical concepts on multiple bodies.

This book brings together latest findings from research and neuroscience as well as examples from clinical practice and includes work from survivor-writers. As such, this book will be of interest to specialists in the field of dissociation as well as psychoanalysts, both experienced and in training.

This book follows on from Valerie Sinason's *Attachment, Trauma and Multiplicity* 2nd edition and represents a confident theoretical step forward.

Valerie Sinason is a child, adolescent and adult psychotherapist and adult psychoanalyst. She is Director of the Clinic for Dissociative Studies, President of the Institute for Psychotherapy and Disability (IPD) and Hon Consultant Psychotherapist for the University of Cape Town Child Guidance Clinic.

Contributors: Philip M. Bromberg, Richard A. Chefetz, Dick Corstens, John Kent, Phil Mollon, Mary Sue Moore, John Morton, Andrew Moskowitz, Ellert R.S. Nijenhuis, Susie Orbach, Valerie Sinason, Margaret Wilkinson, Carole, David, Jo, The Poet, Pumpkin, Rainbow Crewe and Mary Bach-Loreaux

Trauma, Dissociation and Multiplicity

Working on identity and selves

Edited by Valerie Sinason

Routledge
Taylor & Francis Group

LONDON AND NEW YORK

First published 2012
by Routledge
27 Church Road, Hove, East Sussex BN3 2FA

Simultaneously published in the USA and Canada
by Routledge
711 Third Avenue, New York NY 10017

Routledge is an imprint of the Taylor & Francis Group, an Informa business

British Library Cataloguing in Publication Data
A catalogue record for this book is available from the British Library

Library of Congress Cataloging-in-Publication Data
Trauma, dissociation, and multiplicity : working on identity and selves /
edited by Valerie Sinason.
     p. ; cm.
  Includes bibliographical references.
 ISBN 978-0-415-49816-6 (hbk) – ISBN 978-0-415-55425-1 (pbk.)
   1. Dissociative disorders. 2. Post-traumatic stress disorder. I. Sinason,
Valerie, 1946-
   [DNLM: 1. Dissociative Disorders. 2. Self Concept. 3. Stress Disorders,
Post-Traumatic. WM 173.6]
  RC553.D5T72 2012
   616.85'23–dc22

                                                                    2011007414

ISBN: 978-0-415-49816-6 (hbk)
ISBN: 978-0-415-55425-1 (pbk)
ISBN: 978-0-203-15728-2 (ebk)

Typeset in Times by Garfield Morgan, Swansea, West Glamorgan
Paperback cover design by Hybert Design
Printed and bound in Great Britain by TJ International Ltd, Padstow,
Cornwall

Contents

Notes on contributors

Philip M. Bromberg is a training and supervising analyst and faculty member of the William Alanson White Psychoanalytic Institute, and Clinical Professor of Psychology at the New York University Postdoctoral Program in Psychotherapy and Psychoanalysis. He is emeritus co-editor-in-chief of *Contemporary Psychoanalysis* and an editorial board member of *Psychoanalytic Dialogues*, *Journal of the American Academy of Psychoanalysis*, and *Psychoanalytic Inquiry*. In addition to his numerous journal articles, he is most widely recognized as author of *Standing in the Spaces: Essays on Clinical Process, Trauma, and Dissociation* (Analytic Press, 1998) and *Awakening the Dreamer: Clinical Journeys* (Analytic Press, 2006). For over three decades he has written extensively concerning human mental development and the patient–therapist relationship, presenting an interpersonal/relational point of view that emphasizes self-organization, states of consciousness, dissociation, and the relationship between self-coherence and multiple self-states.

Carole, David, Jo, The Poet, Pumpkin, Rainbow Crewe and Mary Bach-Loreaux are courageous women and men who have survived extreme abuse by means of DID. Mary Bach-Loreaux is also a poet and visual artist.

Richard A. Chefetz, MD is a psychiatrist in private practice in Washington, DC. He was president of the International Society for the Study of Trauma and Dissociation (2002–3), founder and chair of its Dissociative Disorders Psychotherapy Training Program, and a distinguished visiting lecturer at the William Alanson White Institute of Psychiatry, Psychoanalysis, and Psychology. He is also a faculty member at the Washington School of Psychiatry's Advanced Psychotherapy Training Program, the Institute of Contemporary Psychotherapy and Psychoanalysis, and the Washington Center for Psychoanalysis: New Directions in Psychoanalysis, and Modern Perspectives in Psychotherapy. He is also a certified consultant at the American Society of Clinical Hypnosis, and is trained in Level I and II EMDR. He was editor of 'Dissociative disorders: An expanding window into the psychobiology of mind' for *Psychiatric Clinics of North America* (March 2006), 'Neuroscientific and therapeutic advances in dissociative disorders', *Psychiatric Annals* (August 2005) and 'Multimodal treatment of complex dissociative disorders', *Psychoanalytic Inquiry* (20:2, 2000), as well as numerous journal articles on psychoanalytic perspectives on trauma and dissociation. An affect theorist, he is currently at work on a book that shows how affect theory coherently links the world of traumatology and psychoanalysis.

Mary Sue Moore, PhD is a clinical psychologist, psychotherapist and educator in Colorado. She has taught and participated in a variety of clinical research projects in the USA, UK and Australia since the mid-1980s. Her research has focused on attachment theory and the impact of trauma on the developing brain. From 1986 to 1988, Mary Sue undertook a Fulbright Research Fellowship in London, where she worked with John Bowlby at the Tavistock Clinic. Moving to Boulder in 1989, she worked as a clinician and consultant at the Mental Health Center of Boulder County while continuing her teaching and research in England. In 1999, she helped found the Boulder Institute for Psychotherapy and Research (BIPR), where she is pursuing long-standing educational, research and clinical training interests. She is also completing a book for Analytic Press, *Reflections of Self*, on the impact of trauma in children's drawings.

John Morton, PhD, Acad. Eur., OBE works at the Institute for Cognitive Neuroscience, University College London. He worked at the Medical Research Council's (MRC) Applied Psychology Unit in Cambridge for many years, specializing in theories of cognitive function with a particular interest in reading and memory. He then became director of the MRC Cognitive Development Unit in London where, among other things, he studied memory in young children. His work is in the information processing tradition, with an emphasis on empirical testing of his ideas. He was chair of the British Psychological Society's Working Party on Recovered Memories, and has received a variety of awards for his work, including the Neuronal Plasticity Prize of La Fondation Ipsen. His books include *Biology and Cognitive Development: The Case of Face Recognition* (Blackwell, 1991, with M.H. Johnson) and *Understanding Developmental Disorders: A Causal Modelling Approach* (Blackwell, 2004).

Andrew Moskowitz, PhD is an American-trained clinical psychologist who has held academic positions in New Zealand and the UK. He is currently Professor of Clinical Psychology at Aarhus University in Denmark. He has been working for years on the interface between dissociation and psychosis, considering in various publications the historical roots in Janet and the allied dissociationists for the original concept of schizophrenia, and exploring traumatic and dissociation bases for a wide range of psychotic symptoms, including catatonia, delusional mood, thought disorder and auditory hallucinations. These explorations culminated in the acclaimed edited book *Psychosis, Trauma and Dissociation: Emerging Perspectives on Severe Psychopathology* (Wiley, 2008). His articles include 'Auditory hallucinations: Psychotic symptom or dissociative experience?' (2007, with Dirk Corstens), '"Scared stiff": Catatonia as an evolutionary-based fear response' (2004) and 'Are psychotic symptoms traumatic in origin and dissociative in kind?' (2009).

Ellert R.S. Nijenhuis, PhD is a clinical psychologist, psychotherapist and researcher. He received his PhD, with the highest honours, at the Medical Department of the Vrije Universiteit Amsterdam for his book: *Somatoform Dissociation: Phenomena, Measurement, and Theoretical Issues* (reprinted by Norton, 2004). In 1998 the International Society for the Study of Dissociation (ISST-D) granted him the Morton Prince Award for Scientific Excellence for his scientific contributions; in 2000 the Pierre Janet Writing Award; and in 2002 the status of Fellow for his outstanding contributions to the diagnosis, treatment, research, and education in dissociative disorders. He works at the Outpatient Department of Psychiatry of Mental Health Care Drenthe, Assen, The Netherlands, where he engages in the diagnosis and treatment of severely traumatized patients, and chairs the Trauma Committee. He performs his original scientific research at this hospital, and collaborates with the universities of Groningen, Utrecht, Amsterdam, Zurich, and Saarbrücken. His innovating empirical and experimental research addresses the psychology and psychobiology of chronic traumatization and dissociation. He has written many clinical and scientific articles, book chapters, and some books, he is a reviewer of several professional journals, and provides presentations and workshops at many international conferences. In 2003, he was granted the closing plenary at the International Society for Traumatic Stress Studies (Chicago) addressing the emerging psychobiology of trauma-related dissociation and dissociative disorders. He is a director of the Executive Council of the International Society for the Study of Dissociation (ISSD) and co-director of the Centre of the Study of Chronic Traumatization at the ISSD.

Susie Orbach is a psychoanalyst and writer. She co-founded the Women's Therapy Centre in London in 1976 and the Women's Therapy Centre Institute in New York in 1981. Her numerous publications include the classic *Fat is a Feminist Issue* (Paddington Press, 1978), along with other such influential texts as *Hunger Strike* (Faber & Faber, 1986), *The Impossibility of Sex* (Allen Lane, 1999) and *Bodies* (Profile, 2009), which proposes new theory on how we acquire a body. She is a founder member of ANTIDOTE (working for emotional literacy) and Psychotherapists and Counsellors for Social Responsibility and is convener of Anybody (www.any-body.org), an organization campaigning for body diversity. She is currently chair of the Relational School in the UK and has a clinical practice seeing individuals and couples.

Valerie Sinason, PhD is a poet, writer, child psychotherapist, adult psycho-analyst and adult attachment-based psychotherapist registered with the United Kingdom Council for Psychotherapy (UKCP) and British Psychoanalytic Council (BPC). She works especially in the field of intel-lectual disability and trauma. She was a consultant psychotherapist at the Tavistock Clinic for almost twenty years as well as holding a three-year consultant post at both the Anna Freud Centre and the Portman Clinic. She worked at St George's Hospital Medical School in the Mental Health Unit for sixteen years and is currently director of the Clinic for Dissociative Studies. She has written and published widely. Her books include *Treating Survivors of Satanist Abuse* (Routledge, 1994), *Memory in Dispute* (Karnac, 1997) and the newly revised second editions of *Mental Handicap and the Human Condition: An Analytic Approach to Intellectual Disability* (Free Association, 2010) and *Attachment, Trauma and Multiplicity: Working with Multiple Personality Disorder* (Routledge, 2010). She is also a widely published poet. She is president of the Institute for Psychotherapy and Disability and Honorary Consultant Psycho-therapist at Cape Town Child Guidance Clinic.

Margaret Wilkinson is a professional member of the Society of Analytical Psychology (SAP) and of the West Midlands Institute for Psychother-apy, and a member of the editorial board of the *Journal of Analytical Psychology*. She teaches neuroscience research reading seminars for the Northern School of Child and Adolescent Psychotherapy and at the SAP. She lectures internationally on contemporary neurobiology and its relevance to clinical practice. She is the author of numerous papers and two books, *Coming into Mind: The Mind-Brain Relationship: A Jungian Clinical Perspective* (Routledge, 2006) and *Changing Minds in Therapy* (Norton, 2010). She is in private practice in North Derbyshire, England.

Acknowledgements

Thanks to Erasmis Kidd and Joanne Forshaw at Routledge for providing me with a space in which the words of all the authors could be held and read and for making that space as containing and attractive as possible and for believing in this project, including the second edition of *Attachment, Trauma and Multiplicity*.

To Beric Livingstone, for shepherding the book through its stages and liaising and caring about the Clinic, its members and all communications.

To my husband David Leevers and our respective children and grand-children, who enrich our lives.

To Graeme Galton, Cate Potter, Jeremy Glyde and Michael Curtis for help in keeping the workplace running smoothly enough for me to have the space to write and edit, and to Adah Sachs, Ena Walker, Lynn Greenwood, Liz Lloyd, Zoe Hawton, Julian Turner, Judy Williams, Arnon Bentovim, Phil Mollon, Pat Frankish, Rajnesh Attavar, Nikki Scheiner, Orit Badouk-Epstein, Rachel Wingfield, Emerald Davies, Sue Cross, Sue Cook, Joan Coleman, Sandra Buck and RAINS, Sheila Hollins and Alan Corbett for clinical thinking.

To First Person Plural, NAPAC, Survivors Trust, One in Four, The Paracelsus Trust, Susan McPherson, Richard and Xenia Bowlby, Deborah Briggs, Juliet Hopkins, Moira Walker, Venetia Young, ESTD and ISSTD, the UKCP Diversity committee, Pearl King, the Bowlby Centre, IPD and the BACP ethics committee for clinical thinking, work and stimulating discussions.

To Philip Stokoe for crucial ongoing supervision that understands the complexities of outer reality as well as the internal world of trauma, and to Susie Orbach and Brett Kahr for clinical consultation.

And finally and most importantly, to the contributors to this book for allowing their work to be shared and included here, and all those survivors with DID whose courage and understanding has altered the universe for those around them.

Contain me. I cannot
Hold such knowledge.
It makes me the vessel
For all the bodies and missing
Ones from the sea,
Tossed ashore
Like sea glass
With only a tenth
Of the hardness.
Cup in your hands
My skinlessness
Hold my trembling hand
                    Mary Bach-Loreaux

Introduction

Valerie Sinason

I am alone so there are four of us
Gaston Bachelard[1]

The newborn baby lies in a cradle and all the admiring relatives gather round to look. 'She has her mother's eyes', says one, 'and her father's nose', says another, 'and her grandmother's fingers', 'and her aunt's temperament'. According to the particular characteristics of the family, projections of positive, negative or mixed kinds are made. In the first moments of entering the outside world, the newborn babe is clothed and embedded in the cultural, physical, emotional, genetic, environmental, political and religious wishes and assumptions of her ancestors. Each movement, change of emotional and physical state is ascribed a particular meaning. The current (and past) family members compete for genetic ascendancy and so the baby grows with her multiplicity of states and identifications and the ongoing multiple intersubjectivities and co-creating of relationships.

Plurality of a mixed kind can be seen in the popular nineteenth-century English nursery rhyme with its sugary awareness of plurality 'What are little girls made of?' and its contrasting negative 'What are little boys made of?', which has delighted (and worried) many small children who puzzle over the huge issues of plural human existence. What is an I? Who am I? Is there such a thing? What do I consist of? Biology and medicine have taught us the name of the internal muscles and organs and drawn the paths of cells and chromosomes, but where does the magic ingredient come from that says what selves are?

Religions have made this inquiry the core of their teaching with a multiplicity of responses, not so different from international cross-cultural philosophy and psychology, ranging from non-self to multiplicity of selves to single thinking self. The German philosopher Thomas Metzinger (2009: 17) hypothesises that religious human beings from earlier periods of history may even have experienced their religions and deities in a different way which might be inaccessible to those in a technological age. Identity and states of consciousness and the nature of consciousness are part of the territory covered by philosophy and religion with psychiatry, psychology and psychoanalysis following not so long after in the twentieth century.

When children, adolescents and adults ask for help as family, friends, colleagues or clients, they pose existential problems we may not have come to any conclusions about. This means that not only do they fail to be understood and helped, but also, to cover up our own existential fears, their emotional existence or existences are denied, disavowed and dissociated from. A 2 year old can exhaust the intellectual capacities of a postgraduate parent by asking about moon and stars and repeating the question 'Why?' or 'How?' Adolescent Hamlets agonise over existential meaning. Old-age Lears ponder attachment, senility and death. Each age group tries again to navigate the deep issues of identity, loss and transformation.

With the level of dissociation that comes from trauma (as opposed to the universal ordinary experiences of dissociation), the questions of identity become even more pressing. A further problem enters the field here. Psychoanalysts and their multi-professional colleagues have largely not been trained in understanding dissociation. As Werner Bohleber (2010), the German intellectual and psychoanalyst, comments, 'The concept of dissociation was long banned from the body of psychoanalytic theory. Trauma research has brought about its gradual return'. He wishes for dissociation to be 'removed from its marginal position as a clinical phenomenon and once again be integrated into the body of psychoanalytic theory' (Bohleber 2010: 148, 149).

While the first and revised editions of *Attachment, Trauma and Multiplicity: Working with Dissociative Identity Disorder* (Sinason 2002, 2010) had the aim of helping British clinicians enter this clinical field in which they lag behind European and American colleagues, this new book represents a more confident theoretical step forward.

Theoreticians and clinicians of all backgrounds are ethically encouraged to look at their contexts of competence and take part in continuing professional development to ensure that lapses in understanding are as minimised as possible. Ignorance is no defence in law and, increasingly, advocacy groups representing clients are ensuring that health service commissioners refer to specialist centres that understand dissociation. World-renowned researcher-clinicians such as Professor Peter Fonagy of University College London and a Patron of the Clinic for Dissociative Studies have confirmed the high aetiology of childhood abuse and disorganised attachments in the creation of Dissociative Identity Disorder over ten years ago. The beginner stage has now passed.

In this book, a range of thinkers, who are also clinicians, provide their responses to the questions of self, identity and dissociation. Authors may or may not agree with each other or the editor or only in part: that is the demanding multiplicity on offer for the reader to explore and reflect. The editor herself subscribes to the theoretical model that states integration is at best 'a harmonious interaction among the multiple self-states' (Howell 2005: 12).

There is a tension that runs throughout the book between having dissociative experiences as part of the human condition for all and focusing on the experiences at the end of the spectrum where dissociative identity disorders intensify and highlight the meaning of identity. There is a danger that in looking at the universal aspects of human existence we could appear to be minimising the particular existential pain of those at the extreme end. Similarly, in focusing on the experience rather than the causes, we could be in danger of pathologising creative defences.

Psychoanalyst and psychologist Dr Phil Mollon starts us off with an historical tour of the concept of dissociation and the reason for the current lack of teaching and understanding on this topic. Dr Andrew Moskowitz, Dirk Corstens and John Kent highlight the universality of hearing voices, a crucial subject given the way voice-hearers can be so misunderstood and misdiagnosed. Psychoanalyst and editor Dr Valerie Sinason looks at the verbal language of trauma and dissociation showing how misinterpreted torture victims, ritual abuse survivors, people with intellectual disability and others can be.

Dr Mary Sue Moore has spent her professional lifetime analysing the meaning of children's art and here she provides new insights on the dissociative brain as seen through drawings. UCL Professor of Psychology John Morton looks at the meaning of amnesia between states and illustrates what a true level of deep structural dissociation tells us about memory. Jungian analyst Margaret Wilkinson looks at the origin and nature of the dissociative defence from the average to the extreme, bringing in the latest findings from neuroscience as well as examples from clinical practice. Professor Susie Orbach provides pioneering new theoretical concepts in her ongoing work on multiple bodies.

The seminal Dutch thinker, Professor Ellert Nijenhuis, knighted by Queen Juliana of the Netherlands for his services to the country over his theoretical and clinical advances for people with dissociative disorders, draws on the active field of consciousness studies to offer a major lengthy philosophical and clinical chapter on the meaning of consciousness and self consciousness in dissociative disorders. He particularly focuses on the work of Thomas Metzinger.

Thomas Metzinger is currently director of the Theoretical Philosophy Group at the Department of Philosophy at the Johannes Gutenberg University of Mainz and co-founder of the Association for the Scientific Study of Consciousness. He brings his philosophical and linguistic skills to bear on the issues of mind and consciousness. His 2003 monograph *Being No-One*, as well as *The Ego Tunnel, The Science of the Mind and the Myth of the*

Self (2009) claim that no such things as selves exist in the world: only phenomenal selves as they are consciously experienced.

The final chapter – and the only one that has been published before – is the seminal two-part discussion between Richard A. Chefetz and Philip M. Bromberg. A major paper, which is also Bromberg's only published discussion on extreme dissociation, it continues to provide a state-of-the-art debate on the meaning of dissociation for all and the levels of dissociation that lead to dissociative identity disorder.

Interspersed between the chapters are reflections on identity and dissociation from lived experience of DID. These survivor-writers have chosen to go under the names of Jo, Carole, David, The Poet, Mary Bach-Loreaux, Rainbow Crewe and Pumpkin.

While the original major theoretical and clinical research came from and continues to come from the United States (Kluft, Putnam, Ross, Van der Kolk, Lanius among others), there has been a growing interconnected European development as well, and this book aims to represent and embody the best of both.

These chapters are demanding. They are, as stated, not a first introduction to clinical work. The chapters by Nijenhuis and Bromberg and Chefetz are also unusually rich and long. However, now the European Society for the Study of Trauma and Dissociation (ESTD) exists alongside the American-based International Society for the Study of Trauma and Dissociation (ISSTD) there is a greater chance for major theoretical developments which will then inform clinical and social changes.

With thanks to all the courageous men, women and children who show us how DID can bear witness not only to suffering of an extreme level but also to creativity and resilience and greater understanding. Thanks to them we are allowed to learn about our own multiplicity and reflect on what is universal as well as to experience gratitude that after having endured so much there is still the emotional generosity to be willing to reach out and teach others.

Note

1 From *The Poetics of Reverie* by Gaston Bachelard, translated by Daniel Russell, copyright © 1969 by Grossman Publishers, Inc. Orig. Copyright © 1960 by Pressus Universitaires de France. Used by permission of Viking Penguin, a division of Penguin Group (USA) Inc.

References

Bohleber, W. (2010) *Destructiveness, Intersubjectivity, and Trauma: The Identity Crisis of Modern Psychoanalysis*. London: Karnac.

Howell, E.F. (2005) *The Dissociative Mind*. Hillsdale, NJ: Analytic Press.

Metzinger, T. (2003) *Being No One: The Self-Model Theory of Subjectivity*. Cambridge, MA: MIT Press.

Metzinger, T. (2009) *The Ego Tunnel: The Science of the Mind and the Myth of the Self*. New York: Basic Books.

Sinason, V. (ed.) (2002) *Attachment, Trauma and Multiplicity: Working with Dissociative Identity Disorder*. London: Routledge.

Sinason, V. (ed.) (2011) *Attachment, Trauma and Multiplicity: Working with Dissociative Identity Disorder*, 2nd edn. London: Routledge.

No one has been trained in this because if they were they would have to face our reality, our torture and it is much better to hate the victim or lock them up and see them as abnormal than to realise we are the shadow side of your normality. Our normality is your worst nightmare. We live your nightmare. What psychotherapy training wants to hear about that? What historian of theories cares about that?

Carole

Chapter 1

The foreclosure of dissociation within psychoanalysis

Phil Mollon

There is a paradox in the origin of psychoanalysis. The most famous case depicting the 'talking cure', that of Anna O, a patient treated by Josef Breuer, is one that clearly displays dissociation as a prominent feature – and yet this characteristic does not find a place in Freud's theorising about repression and the unconscious. This is because the division between conscious and unconscious mind, and a process of 'repression', which banishes unwanted contents of the mind to the unconscious, does not accommodate dissociation of the mind into alternate states of *consciousness*. As a result, psychoanalysts have, for decades, been puzzled by, and unable to conceptualise coherently, the widespread phenomenon of dissociation. Without the cognitive tools to think about dissociation, its presence has tended to be ignored, overlooked, or scotomised by psychoanalysts. It has, in short, been foreclosed from psychoanalytic perception and discourse.

Anna O was described as presenting two states of consciousness, rather than a tension between a conscious and an unconscious mind:

> Throughout her entire illness her two states of consciousness existed side by side: the primary one in which she was quite normal psychically, and the second one which may well be likened to a dream in view of its wealth of imaginative products and hallucinations, its large gaps in memory and the lack of inhibition and control in its associations . . . [T]he patient's mental condition was entirely dependent upon the intrusion of this secondary state into the normal one . . . It is hard to avoid expressing the situation by saying that the patient was split into two personalities of which one was mentally normal and the other insane.
>
> (Breuer and Freud 1893–5: 45)

In contrast to Freud's theory of psychoneuroses of defence – whereby repressed mental contents (unacceptable desires) are repressed and banished to the unconscious mind, subsequently finding disguised expression in symptoms, dreams, parapraxes, and free-associations – Breuer's case of Anna O presented alternate states of consciousness, each being incompatible with the other. One was 'normal' and the other dreamlike – her illness seeming to consist of the intrusion of the dreamlike state into her 'normal' state. In addition, a third state (or part) of the mind is indicated in the following comment:

> Nevertheless, though her two states were thus sharply separated, not only did the secondary state intrude into the first one, but – and this was at all events frequently true, and even when she was in a very bad condition – a clear-sighted and calm observer sat, as she put it, in a corner of her brain and looked on at all the mad business.
>
> (Breuer and Freud 1893–5: 46)

The presence of a clear-sighted observer has been noted in other conditions where consciousness is split into several states or parts. On recovering from a schizophrenic psychosis, a patient may report an awareness of a sane but helpless part of the mind observing the madness. Freud himself, in his last book, *An Outline of Psycho-Analysis* (1940a), described this process in states of psychosis:

> one learns from patients after their recovery that at the time in some corner of their mind (as they put it) there was a normal person hidden who, like a detached spectator, watched the hubbub of illness go past him . . . Two psychical attitudes have been performed instead of a single one – one, the normal one, which takes account of reality, and another which under the influence of the instincts detaches the ego from reality. The two exist along side of each other.
>
> (Freud 1940a: 202)

This is also a common feature of Dissociative Identity Disorder. Some alters may appear unaware of the existence of others within the system, but there may be at least one alter that has an overview of the entire internal system, and who can provide a helpful and sane perspective.

While some (more neurotically organised) patients may present phenomena indicative of their being unconscious of the source of troublesome feelings, those whose minds are organised dissociatively display something more along the lines of a *constellation of consciousnesses* competing for temporary executive control – like a meeting of people who are each striving for their time with the microphone.

The first use of the term 'unconscious' in a psychoanalytic context was in Breuer's description of Anna O – but, ironically, in a sentence where it makes little sense. He wrote:

> Every one of her hypnoses in the evening afforded evidence that the patient was entirely clear and well-ordered in her mind and normal as regards her feeling and volition so long as none of the products of her secondary state was acting as a stimulus 'in the unconscious'.
>
> (Breuer and Freud 1893–5: 45)

Breuer is not referring here to an unconscious part of the mind, but to an alternative consciousness. The sentence is actually more coherent if the phrase 'in the unconscious' is omitted. As the editor, Strachey, suggests, the reference to 'the unconscious' seems to be placed there as a gesture towards the theory of repression and the unconscious of his co-author Freud.

Hysteria resulting from blocked excitation

Breuer explains his view that hysteria occurs when a quantum of excitation is prevented from normal release. He gives an example of a 12-year-old boy who developed a difficulty in swallowing and a headache, refusing food and vomiting when it was pressed on him. No clear explanation was initially forthcoming. Eventually, 'in response to strong appeals from his clever and energetic mother', he tearfully recounted the following. On his way home from school, he had visited a public toilet where 'a man had held out his penis to him and asked him to take it into his mouth'. The boy had run away in terror and from that point had been ill. However, as soon as he had 'made his confession', he completely recovered. Breuer notes that to produce the hysteria several factors were involved: 'the boy's innate neurotic nature, his severe fright, the irruption of sexuality in its crudest form into his childish temperament, and . . . disgust.' He adds the crucial point that 'The illness owed its persistence to the boy's silence, which prevented the excitation from finding its normal outlet' (Breuer and Freud 1893–5: 212).

Hypnoid states versus Freud's theory of repression

Breuer's further discussion includes an account of Freud's theory of defence hysteria, whereby a troubling idea is repressed, thereby preventing a normal 'wearing-away' of the excitation or affect. However, he then went on to refer to another kind of idea whose associated excitation or affect is not worn away:

> This may happen not because one does not want to remember the idea, but because one cannot remember it: because it originally emerged and was endowed with affect in states in respect of which there is amnesia in waking consciousness – that is, in hypnosis or in states similar to it.
>
> (Breuer and Freud 1893–5: 214)

Breuer quotes some earlier comments by Moebius, who had been trying to understand how it is that an idea can generate somatic phenomena, such as found in hysteria. He had reasoned:

> The necessary condition for the (pathogenic) operation of ideas is, on the one hand, an innate – that is, hysterical – disposition and, on the other, a special frame of mind. We can only form an imprecise idea of this frame of mind. It must resemble a state of hypnosis, it must correspond to some kind of vacancy of consciousness in which an emerging idea meets with no resistance from any other – in which, so to speak, the field is clear for the first comer. We know that a state of this kind can be brought about not only by hypnotism but by emotional shock (fright, anger, etc.) and by exhausting factors (sleeplessness, hunger, and so on).
>
> (Moebius 1894, quoted in Breuer and Freud 1893–5: 215)

While disagreeing with the implication of a 'vacant' state of mind,[1] Breuer emphasises the importance of 'hypnoid states': 'most especially, in the amnesia that accompanies them and in their power to bring about the splitting of the mind', Breuer states his view that hypnoid states may play a part even in those hysterical conditions where Freud had found 'the deliberate amnesia of defence' (Breuer and Freud 1893–5: 216). He describes the hypnoid states as 'dream-like' and subject to amnesia in the subject's normal consciousness. Crucially, he notes that they are protected from correction by reality:

> The amnesia withdraws the psychical products of these states . . . from any correction during waking thought; and since in auto-hypnosis criticism and supervision by reference to other ideas is diminished . . . the wildest delusions may arise from it and remain untouched for long periods.
>
> (Breuer and Freud 1893–5: 216)

Breuer argued that 'hysterical conversion' takes place more easily in a hypnoid state, in the same way that hallucinations and bodily movements occur in response to suggested ideas during hypnosis. He reasoned that 'pathogenic autohypnosis' may come about in some people 'by affect being introduced into a habitual reverie' – a condition in which there is first an 'absence of mind', such that the 'flow of ideas grows gradually slower and at last almost stagnates; but the affective idea and its affect remain active, and so consequently does the great quantity of excitation which is not being used up functionally' (Breuer and Freud 1893–5: 218–19).

Breuer then goes on to make a point about the possible role of fear and shock in generating pathogenic hypnoid states:

> Since fright inhibits the flow of ideas at the very same time at which an affective idea (of danger) is very active, it offers a complete parallel to a reverie charged with affect; and since the recollection of the affective idea, which is constantly being renewed, keeps on re-establishing this state of mind, 'hypnoid fright' comes into being, in which conversion is either brought about or stabilized. Here we have the incubation stage of 'traumatic hysteria' in the strict sense of the word.
>
> (Breuer and Freud 1893–5: 219–220)

Thus Breuer postulates that trauma creates fright, which inhibits the flow of ideas, and thereby establishes a hypnoid state – one which is re-established every time there is a recollection of the emotionally charged idea. This is very close to modern views of trauma creating dissociative states that are combined with intrusive recollections, or reliving, of the trauma. In the intrusive reliving states, the person may lose contact with present reality, experiencing a past trauma as if it were happening in the present. Current therapies for traumatic stress involve enabling the person to access the distressing recollections, while simultaneously bringing these into contact with present reality (e.g. Foa and Kozak 1985). Indeed, Breuer and Freud describe how their patient's symptoms

> immediately and permanently disappeared when we had succeeded in bringing clearly to light the memory of the event by which they were provoked and in arousing their accompanying affect, and when the patient had described that event in the greatest possible detail and had put the affect into words.
>
> (Breuer and Freud 1893–5: 6)

Similarly, they describe, in a manner essentially identical to the formulations of contemporary cognitive-behavioural theorists, how traumatic memories retain their pathogenic potency because of cognitive-emotional avoidance, which prevents extinction of the anxiety:

> It may be said that the ideas which have become pathological have persisted with such freshness and affective strength because they have been denied the normal wearing-away processes by means of abreaction and reproduction in states of uninhibited association.
>
> (Breuer and Freud 1893–5: 11)

The pathogenic ideas are excluded from being 'worn away' by association with other ideas either because 'the patient is determined to forget the distressing experiences and accordingly excludes them as far as possible from association' (Freud's theory of repression as a defence) or because 'there is no extensive associative connection between the normal state of consciousness and the pathological ones in which the ideas made their appearance.' (Breuer's theory of hypnoid states) (Breuer and Freud 1893–5: 11).

Breuer and Freud agree with their contemporaries, Binet and Janet, that 'what lies at the centre of hysteria is a splitting off of a portion of psychical activity' – but Breuer notes that the phenomena those authors report 'deserve to be described as a splitting not merely of psychical activity but of consciousness' (Breuer and Freud 1893–5: 227, 229):

> As we know, these observers have succeeded in getting into contact with their patients' 'subconsciousness', with the portion of psychical activity of which the conscious waking ego knows nothing; and they have been able in some of their cases to demonstrate the presence of all the psychical functions, including self-consciousness, in that portion, since it has access to the memory of earlier psychical events. This half of a mind is therefore quite complete and conscious in itself. In our cases the part of the mind which is split off is 'thrust into darkness', as the Titans are imprisoned in the crater of Etna, and can shake the earth but can never emerge into the light of day. In Janet's cases the division of the realm of the mind has been a total one.
>
> (Breuer and Freud 1893–5: 229)

While the *Studies on Hysteria* is written jointly by Breuer and Freud, and each attempts to accommodate the views of the other, there are clear differences in emphasis between the two. Breuer places crucial importance on hypnoid states, the presence of distinctly different states of mind alternating with the 'normal' state, whereas Freud focuses on his notion of 'defence' and repression as a basis for the 'strangulation of affect' which leads to hysterical 'conversion' (of the affect into a somatic symptom).

Freud's model of the psychodynamic mind

For Freud, 'defence' employed by the psychodynamic mind in a state of conflict is the basis of hysteria (and other conditions of mental pathology):

> I have shown how, in the course of our therapeutic work, we have been led to the view that hysteria originates through the repression of an incompatible idea from a motive of defence. On this view, the repressed idea would persist as a memory trace that is weak (has little intensity), while the affect that is torn from it would be used for a somatic intervention. (That is, the excitation is 'converted'.) It would seem, then, that the idea becomes the cause of morbid symptoms – that is to say, becomes pathogenic. A hysteria exhibiting this psychical mechanism may be given the name of 'defence hysteria'.
>
> (Breuer and Freud 1893–5: 285)

Freud saw the essence of the therapeutic task as simple – one of allowing the patient to talk of the troubling episode with an expression of the appropriate emotion:

> the patient only gets free from the hysterical symptom by reproducing the pathogenic impressions that caused it and by giving utterance to them with an expression of affect, and thus the therapeutic task *consists solely in inducing him to do so*; when once this task has been accomplished there is nothing left for the physician to correct or remove.
>
> (Breuer and Freud 1893–5: 283)

However, he noticed that the patient is often reluctant to reveal or speak of the experiences and thoughts that had given rise to the distress that is now converted into a somatic symptom. He found that he had to *work* to encourage the patient to reveal these matters – and this fact led to his recognition of the phenomenon of *resistance* and *defence*:

> the situation led me at once to the theory that by means of my psychical work I had to overcome a psychical force in the patients which was opposed to the pathogenic ideas becoming conscious (being remembered). A new understanding seemed to open before my eyes when it occurred to me that this must no doubt be the same psychical force that had played a part in the generating of the hysterical symptom and had at that time prevented the pathogenic idea from becoming conscious. What kind of force could one suppose was operative here, and what motive could have put it into operation? . . . I recognised a universal characteristic of such ideas: they were all of a distressing nature, calculated to arouse the affects of shame, of self-reproach and of psychical pain, and the feeling of being harmed; they were all of a kind that one would prefer not to have experienced, that one would rather forget. From all this there arose, as it were automatically, the thought of *defence*.
>
> (Breuer and Freud 1893–5: 269)

Thus Freud began to formulate his model of a psychodynamic mind in conflict. Within this framework he saw no need for the concept of hypnoid states.[2]

Layering and stratification within the psychodynamic mind

In the same text, Freud goes on to discuss in some detail, and using a variety of metaphors, how the 'pathogenic material' is layered and stratified within the mind. He notes first that the pathogenic psychical material which has ostensibly been forgotten, which is not at the ego's disposal and which plays no part in associ-ation and memory, nevertheless in some fashion lies ready to hand and in correct and proper order. It is only a matter of removing the resistances that bar the way to the material.

(Breuer and Freud 1893–5: 287)

He then states that rather than there being a single traumatic memory and pathogenic idea as the nucleus of the symptom, there are often 'successions of partial traumas and concatenations of pathogenic trains of thought'. Nevertheless, there might be a nucleus where the trauma or pathogenic idea 'has found its purest manifestation', around which is 'an incredibly profuse amount of other mnemic material which has to be worked through in the analysis' (Breuer and Freud 1893–5: 288). Partly this material is arranged in a linear chronological order, but also as 'themes . . . stratified concentric-ally round the pathogenic nucleus . . . the degree of resistance . . . increases in proportion as the strata are nearer to the nucleus.' Freud further notes that the more peripheral strata of psychical material contains content that is easily conscious, while the deeper strata contains 'memories which the patient disavows even in reproducing them' (Breuer and Freud 1893–5: 289). A third aspect of the arrangement of the material is via a 'logical thread which reaches as far as the nucleus and tends to take an irregular and twisting path', one which if represented by a diagram

would have to be indicated by a broken line which would pass along the most roundabout paths from the surface to the deepest layers and back, yet would in general advance from the periphery to the central nucleus . . . a line resembling the zig-zag line in the solution of a Knight's Move problem.

(Breuer and Freud 1893–5: 289)

Freud reasons that the pathogenic material operates like a foreign body and that the treatment is akin to removing this foreign body – but with the complication that the psychical material cannot cleanly be 'extirpated from the ego' since 'its external strata pass over in every direction into the portions of the normal ego' (Breuer and Freud 1893–5: 290). Moreover, in working through a 'complicated and multidimensional organisation' of pathogenic material, only one element at a time 'can enter ego conscious-ness'. He observes that 'we should rightly ask how a camel like this got through the eye of the needle' and refers to the 'defile of consciousness'. As a result of this process, 'the whole spatially-extended mass of psychogenic material is in this way drawn through a narrow cleft and thus arrives in consciousness cut up, as it were, into pieces or strips.' The psychoanalyst's task, he argues, is 'to put these together once more into the organisation which he presumes to have existed' (Breuer and Freud 1893–5: 291).

The process of reaching the 'nucleus of the pathogenic organisation' cannot be carried out directly and linearly, since even if the material were reached it would be of no value to the patient, who 'would not be psychologically changed by it' (Breuer and Freud 1893–5: 292). Work has to begin at the periphery, asking the patient to speak of what he or she knows and remembers, while gradually helping him or her to advance *radially*, during which process the patient will generate much *peripheral* material at each strata. However, the free communications of the patient will not alone lead to the required depths. Indeed it will be 'as though we were standing before a wall which shuts out every prospect and prevents us from having any idea whether there is anything behind it, and if so, what'. The psychoanalyst must 'examine with a critical eye' the account given by the patient to 'discover the gaps and imperfections in it' and the 'lacunas which are often covered by "false connections"' (Breuer and Freud 1893–5: 293, 294).

Freud's remarkable account of the psychodynamic mind, using processes of 'defence' to protect consciousness from ideas of a distressing nature, lay the groundwork for the development of psychoanalysis – a method of unravelling, of *analysing*, the complex mass of pathogenic psychical material, that has penetrated, in a cancer-like fashion, deeply into the surrounding layers of the otherwise healthy ego. He describes the *work* of the analyst, in helping the patient overcome *resistance*, tracking the myriad pathways of the psychical material, and detecting the lacunae and 'false connections', including transference of material to the image of the physician. This, in essence, remained the basis of Freud's method, and of those analysts who followed his principles (although many did not, as evidenced in the 'controversial discussions' during the 1940s: King and Steiner 1991).

Neurotic versus dissociative minds

Freud's formulation and technical method works well for those patients whose minds are organised on a 'neurotic' basis. The Freudian model of neurosis is as follows: first, a mind is in conflict; second, the mind attempts to protect consciousness from thoughts and associated emotions that would give rise to distress (shame, guilt, mental pain, or fears of being harmed); third, the attempt at defence interferes with optimum functioning (inhibitions) and the warded off (strangulated) affect is expressed in disguised or displaced form (as symptoms). While this model can be elaborated in terms of complexities of internal structures, nature of the 'instincts', etc., this remains the essence.

The Freudian model of neurosis does not work well for those whose minds are organised dissociatively. In dissociative organisations we may encounter not a gradual emergence of stratified material, shredded into strips as it passes through the 'defile of consciousness', but sudden and complete *shifts of consciousness* with elaborate mental content fully available in a seemingly complete form and without disguise. The defensive strategy, if there is one,[3] involves keeping the different states of consciousness separate, and at times the creation of alternative and more palatable 'realities'. For these dissociative conditions, Breuer's account of hypnoid states (as well as the related formulations of Moebius and Binet and Janet) seems much more apt. Not only does the concept of hypnoid states contain the idea of distinct and separate states of mind, but also it retains a connection to the phenomena of hypnosis. Any clinician who is familiar with dissociative identity disorders will appreciate that many aspects of these presentations contain elements akin to hypnotic processes, whereby normal aspects of reality and logic are suspended (Mollon 1996). For example, the different alters of a person with DID may consider they are separate people existing within the same body, each having a different name. One alter may appear to believe that it would be possible to kill off another alter through destroying the body, as if not appreciating the shared inhabiting of the same vessel. In the case of one person with DID, an alter asserted that her parents lived in one country and were wonderful people, while those of another alter lived in a different country and were terrible people. Commonly, child states of mind and identity may emerge, appearing to believe they are still existing in some traumatic episode, or series of episodes, from years ago. All such typical DID phenomena follow the 'logic' of hypnosis, and autohypnosis – precisely the processes Breuer drew attention to. As Breuer noted, trauma and shock may induce 'hypnoid fright', blocking the normal associative processes that would bring an experience or idea into contact with other ideas and with reality. Breuer's formulations could have laid the basis for a good understanding of how trauma gives rise to hypnoid states and dissociation. The legitimate and respectful perspective of DID as a severe form of hysteria induced by trauma, along the lines outlined by Breuer, could have been developed. With the triumph of the Freudian model of neurosis, based on repression, the understanding of hysteria, based on dissociation, was lost – both hysteria and DID becoming seen implicitly as invalid conditions, ones that did not *really exist*.

Splitting of the mind versus gradations of consciousness

As the Breuer model faded, the emphasis upon 'splitting' (a topic cited fifteen times in the index to Breuer and Freud) also receded. Freud's model of the neurotically structured mind – with its layering and stratification of pathological material extending complex filaments into the otherwise healthy tissue of the ego – does not suggest splitting or other sharp differentiations of mental states. Rather, it implies *gradations* of consciousness, with disguise and complicated pathways of thought designed to prevent access of repressed material to consciousness. Of course, there is no reason why aspects of the Freudian repression/defence model and the Breuerian hypnoid states/dissociation model might not apply within the same patient. Nevertheless, to the extent that psychoanalysts have been schooled in a neurosis model, they may lack the conceptual tools to identify and work with dissociative states. Falling back on Kleinian (1946) notions of splitting in *phantasy* (between emotionally 'good' and 'bad' aspects) is of no help, since this does not grasp the *splitting of the functioning mind* in the context of hypnoid states. A psychoanalyst with no way of thinking of dissociation and hypnoid states may fall into three particular errors: first, assuming that he or she is speaking to the same person on different occasions, or at different moments, when in fact different identity states, with radically different perspectives and attitudes, may be being addressed; second, assuming that allusions to severe abuse might be dreamlike metaphors, when they could be literal accounts of actual events; third, failing to grasp the 'hypnoid logic' of some dissociative states of mind. While the 'primary process' mode of thought of the unconscious mind, discovered so brilliantly by Freud (1900), is the relevant material for analysis in neurotic organisations, hypnoid logic underpins the psychic material of DID.

Having been foreclosed from the main body of Freudian psychoanalysis, it is as if splitting of the mind and dissociation have kept trying to find their way back in. Freud himself returned to the notion of splitting in a paper outlining how an acknowledgement of the reality that women do not possess a penis may exist in one part of the mind, while in another part of the mind there persists an incompatible belief that they do (Freud 1940b). Somewhat later, Fairbairn (1949), who worked with patients who had been sexually abused and also wrote his masters thesis on multiple personality disorder, began to develop a theory of personality based on internalised relationships and splitting of the ego. Noting the presence of splitting in schizophrenic and other primitive states of mind, he reasoned that

> a theory of personality based upon the conception of splitting of the ego would appear to be more fundamental than one based on Freud's conception of the repression of impulses by an unsplit ego. The theory which I now envisage is, of course, obviously adapted to explain such extreme manifestations as are found in cases of multiple personality; but, as Janet has pointed out, these extreme manifestations are only exaggerated examples of the dissociation phenomena characteristic of hysteria.
>
> (Fairbairn 1949: 159)

Still later, Kernberg (1975) proposed splitting of the ego as a key feature of borderline personality organisation, the crucial defence being one of keeping dissociated states of mind and identity separate. Similarly, Kohut (1971) wrote of the combination of 'vertical' and 'horizontal' splits in narcissistic conditions. Then, in 1981, Grotstein made an important contribution in which he stated

> the analyses of narcissistic, borderline, and even neurotic cases have caused me to increasingly regard the phenomenon of splitting from the vantage point of dissociation and to suggest that the phenomenon of dissociation of personalities is more widespread and universal than has hitherto been thought.
>
> (Grotstein 1981: 111)

Reintroducing and integrating the concept of dissociation (and hypnoid states) fully into psychoanalysis requires some considerable work – although much has already been done (e.g. Bromberg 1998; Howell 2005). Meanwhile, acknowledging the lacuna left by the writing out of dissociation at the origin of psychoanalysis can at least allow an awareness of the problem.

Notes

1 I once asked a patient with DID how she created a new personality. She replied somewhat along the following lines: 'when something bad is happening, I withdraw further and further from it – until there is just a space where I used to be – and in that space a new personality forms'.
2 In his paper 'On the history of the psycho-analytic movement', Freud (1914) explicitly repudiated the concept of hypnoid states. Dismissing Breuer's theory as 'still to some extent physiological' he explained that 'everywhere I seemed to discern motives and tendencies analogous to those of everyday life' and that while he 'made a shortlived attempt to allow the two mechanisms a separate existence side by side' before long 'my "defence" theory took up its stand opposite his "hypnoid" one' (Freud 1914: 11).
3 Reports from some patients, and some texts (e.g. Phillips and O'Brien 1995; Thomas 2008) suggest the possibility that certain kinds of organisations, with perhaps varying motivations, have made malign use of psychological methods, in order to induce dissociation deliberately through a combination of trauma and hypnosis.

References

Breuer, J. and Freud, S. (1893–5) *Studies in Hysteria*. In *Standard Edition of the Complete Psychological Works of Sigmund Freud, II*. London: Hogarth Press.

Bromberg, P.M. (1998) *Standing in the Spaces: Essays on Clinical Process, Trauma, and Dissociation*. Hillsdale, NJ: Analytic Press.

Fairbairn, W.R.D. (1949) Steps in the development of an object-relations theory of the personality. In Fairbairn (1952) *Psychoanalytic Studies of the Personality*. London: Routledge & Kegan Paul.

Foa, E.B. and Kozak, M.J. (1985) Treatment of anxiety disorders: Implications for psychopathology. In A.H. Tuma and J.D. Maser (eds) *Anxiety and the Anxiety Disorders*. Hillsdale, NJ: Lawrence Erlbaum.

Freud, S. (1900) The interpretation of dreams. In *Standard Edition of the Complete Psychological Works of Sigmund Freud*, IV & V. London: Hogarth Press.

Freud, S. (1914) On the history of the psycho-analytic movement. In *Standard Edition of the Complete Psychological Works of Sigmund Freud, XIV*. London: Hogarth Press.

Freud, S. (1940a) *An Outline of Psycho-Analysis*. In *Standard Edition of the Complete Psychological Works of Sigmund Freud, XXIII*. London: Hogarth Press.

Freud, S. (1940b) Splitting of the ego in the process of defence. In *Standard Edition of the Complete Psychological Works of Sigmund Freud, XXIII*. London: Hogarth Press.

Grotstein, J. (1981) *Splitting and Projective Identification*. New York: Aronson.

Howell, E.F. (2005) *The Dissociative Mind*. New York: Routledge.

Kernberg, O. (1975) *Borderline Conditions and Pathological Narcissism*. New York: Aronson.

King, P. and Steiner, R. (1991) *The Freud–Klein Controversies 1941–45*. London: Routledge.

Klein, M. (1946) Notes on some schizoid mechanisms. In Klein (1975) *Envy and Gratitude and Other Works, 1946–1963*. London: Hogarth Press.

Kohut, H. (1971) *The Analysis of the Self*. New York: International Universities Press.

Mollon, P. (1996) *Multiple Selves, Multiple Voices: Working with Trauma, Violation, and Dissociation*. Chichester: Wiley.

Phillips, M. and O'Brien, C. (1995) *Trance Formation of America*. Las Vegas, CA: Reality Marketing.

Thomas, G. (2008) *Secrets and Lies: A History of CIA Mind Control and Germ Warfare*. London: JR Books.

We all know about that joke – the neurotic builds castles in the air, the psychotic moves in and the psychiatrist takes the rent. Same with bloody voices. Tell someone you hear them and they call you schizophrenic, or they say you have imaginary friends or try and shut them up with drugs. Someone else gets the money or the power and our words are sectionable. Like being a prophet or a heretic.

Carole

Chapter 2

What can auditory hallucinations tell us about the dissociative nature of personality?

Andrew Moskowitz, Dirk Corstens and John Kent

For most of the past half century, auditory hallucinations (hearing voices) have been viewed by the psychiatric community (along with much of the general public) as synonymous with madness. The image of someone talking to themselves, as portrayed in movies and in the media, has become shorthand for mental illness. Indeed, since 1980, one can receive a diagnosis of schizophrenia in most parts of the world solely on the basis of hearing a voice commenting on one's behaviour or hearing two or more voices conversing with each other. And yet it has been known for well over 150 years (Berrios and Dening 1996) and confirmed with a spate of recent research studies that many people who hear voices are more accurately diagnosed with post-traumatic stress disorder (PTSD) than with schizophrenia, and even more never come to the attention of mental health professionals, suffer psychiatric distress or report any (other) symptom of mental illness (Moskowitz and Corstens 2007). The mainstream response to this is to insist that 'psychotic' voices differ from those that are post-traumatic in nature or present in non-clinical populations – and that only the former are 'true' hallucinations in contrast to the 'pseudo-hallucinations' heard by the other two groups. But this distinction is deeply problematic: every attempt to parse 'pseudo' (auditory) hallucinations from 'true' hallucinations on the basis of some reported characteristic of the voice (most often perceived location) has failed, leading some commentators to refer to pseudo-hallucinations as a 'joker in the diagnostic game' (Berrios and Dening 1996). Such a joker, Berrios and Dening (1996: 761) propose, is often used to 'call into question the genuineness of some true hallucinatory experiences' when the clinician wishes, for other reasons, to avoid some diagnostic label.

The traditional psychiatric perspective is to view the above as a problem – namely, how a core symptom of schizophrenia can be experienced by other diagnostic groups and by the general population in a form that is not readily distinguished from a 'psychotic' symptom. An alternative perspective, however, which we have advocated (Moskowitz and Corstens 2007), is to view auditory hallucinations or hearing voices as a common human experience, often precipitated by crises or traumas, which is essentially dissociative in nature. From this perspective, the commonality between the voice experience of persons in the general community and those diagnosed as schizophrenic is not problematic; rather the problem becomes how to ascertain the factors that determine whether a particular voice hearer becomes distressed by their voices or becomes engaged with mental health services.

Building on this second perspective, we argue in this chapter that the experience of hearing voices helps to illuminate the essentially dissociative nature of normal human personality. In doing so, we are advocating the view that the significant dissociation underlying the experience of hearing voices and dissociative disorders are not uniquely the result of traumatic experiences, but build on the schisms, *subpersonalities* or *selves* present (but typically overlooked) in normal personality. Trauma, however, helps to make the invisible visible, by embodying these subpersonalities, making them more independent and giving them a voice that can be heard like any other voice. In making this connection, we discuss the ideas proposed by Hal and Sidra Stone since the 1980s, which have become known as the *Voice Dialogue* or *Psychology of the Selves* approach.

This chapter is structured in the following way. First, we begin by reviewing the research on auditory hallucinations and hearing voices in the community and in psychiatric groups, summarising material covered in our 2007 paper (Moskowitz and Corstens 2007) and updating it with new relevant studies. This review supports our position that the voices heard by persons in the community are not different in essence from those heard by psychiatric patients and are best characterised as dissociative in nature. Then we consider the ideas of Hal and Sidra Stone about the nature of personality, including their concepts of primary and disowned selves and disowned instinctual energies. These ideas can be linked back to the research on hearing voices, and can also help us to understand why some voices are attacking and abusive in nature, and how they can be transformed back into more constructive parts of the personality. As an illustration, we discuss in detail one particular self, familiar to most of us, that the Stones have deemed the 'inner critic'; the devastating effects of childhood abuse and the disowning of instinctual energies on this self is discussed. An example is presented of how such a 'killer' critic, heard by a voice-hearer treated by one of us, can be transformed back into an ally. Finally, we discuss the implications of this position for future research and clinical work with persons who hear voices. For space considerations, we will not be reviewing relevant psychoanalytic perspectives on this material here; the interested reader may wish to consult prior publications for such perspectives (Moskowitz et al. 2008, 2009).

The experience of hearing voices

Prevalence in the general population

Since the landmark nineteenth-century England-based *Society for Psychical Research* study (Sidgewick et al. 1894), which interviewed more than 17,000 persons, there have been many studies on voice hearing in the general community, at least nine of which (mostly published since 2000) have been designed to assess the prevalence of voice hearing (reviewed in Moskowitz and Corstens 2007). The results indicate that between 1 and 13 per cent of the general population (figures are higher for adolescents than adults) in the Western world hear voices other than when they are falling asleep or waking up, and more than simply their name being called.

To examine this issue in more detail, we consider the most recent study, Pearson et al. (2008), conducted since our 2007 review was published. This study examined the prevalence and experience of voice hearing in 500 adolescents and adults in the UK, using an instrument previously used in two US studies (Barrett and Etheridge 1992; Posey and Losch 1983–4). This instrument includes questions on hearing one's name, hearing voices when falling asleep or waking up, and hearing one's own thoughts. In our 2007 review, we sought to use a narrow definition of voice hearing, and thus excluded such experiences. However, for illustrative purposes it is worth noting that Pearson et al. (2008) found these experiences commonly reported in both of their samples (more than 40 per cent heard their own thoughts spoken aloud), at rates that were not significantly different from those reported in the prior two US studies (correlations between the studies were 0.90 or greater). They also found that 10 per cent of their adolescents and 5 per cent of their adults reported having a 'current' imaginary companion; 17 per cent of adolescents and 8 per cent of adults had 'talked with a dead relative', and 7.5 per cent of the adults (the question was not asked of adolescents) had 'heard God's voice'. About half of all reported hallucinations occurred 'regularly'. Pearson et al. (2008: 637) concluded that auditory hallucinations were 'a part of average development during the whole life cycle', and that the link to psychopathology had primarily to do with the interpretation of, or reaction to, the voices. This is the position that has espoused by Romme and Escher (1989) for many years, as well as cognitive-behavioural therapists such as Anthony Morrison (1998).

Consistent with the above, in three studies in which levels of (psychiatric) distress or contact with mental health services was assessed (Johns et al. 2002; Tien 1991; Van Os et al. 2000), only a minority of voice hearers – between one-fifth and one-third – reported such difficulties. Thus, it appears that most persons who hear voices in the community are *not* psychiatric patients. What can be made of this?

Pseudo-hallucinations – an invalid concept?

While recognising that persons in the community also hear voices, psycho-pathologists have attempted to salvage the notion of auditory hallucinations as a psychiatric symptom by insisting that voices heard by non-patients (and voices which were 'trauma-based') differed in significant ways from voices heard by persons with schizophrenia – that the former were in fact 'pseudo' and not 'real' hallucinations. While this notion has a lengthy history, most contemporary versions of the concept date from Jaspers (1963). Jaspers claimed that pseudo-hallucinations were similar to true hallucinations in that they both had 'full, fresh sensory elements' and could not be voluntarily controlled, but differed from the latter in that they were experienced in 'inner subjective space' and did not appear concretely real. True hallucinations, in contrast, were experienced in 'external objective space' and did appear concretely real. Another criterion proposed for distinguishing 'true' from 'pseudo' hallucinations has been 'insight' (Hare 1973), but as this is not an experienced characteristic of the hallucinations, and is typically interpreted as whether or not the person recognises the voice as a symptom of a mental illness, it will be ignored here.

Most persons can readily report whether the voices they hear appear to be localised within their head or are heard through their ears – sometimes the apparent location of a voice changes (Nayani and David 1996). However, there appears to be no reliable clinical correlate of perceived location (Copolov et al. 2004), and the experienced 'reality' of internal voices is not rated lower than that of external voices (Oulis et al. 1995; Yee et al. 1995). Indeed, one large-scale study of this issue was called 'On the non-significance of internal versus external auditory hallucinations' (Copolov et al. 2004). As reviewed in Moskowitz and Corstens (2007), there is no evidence that perceived external location is more strongly associated with a diagnosis of schizophrenia than with another diagnosis (post-traumatic stress disorder or dissociative identity disorder). Between 31 per cent and 61 per cent of persons diagnosed schizophrenic hear exclusively external voices, as compared to 56 per cent of non-schizophrenic psychiatric patients, 27 per cent of those with dissociative disorders, and 40 per cent of non-patients (Moskowitz and Corstens 2007). Because of evidence such as this, the editors of the DSM-IV removed the previous comment in the manual that 'externally perceived' hallucinations were characteristic of schizophrenia (American Psychiatric Association (APA) 1994). Further, the specific voices still considered 'pathognomic' for schizophrenia (voices 'commenting' on one's behaviour or two or more voices conversing with one another) are common not only in dissociative identity disorder (Kluft 1987) but also in persons hearing voices in the general community (Honig et al. 1998).

Two important studies comparing diagnostic groups have been conducted since the completion of our 2007 paper – Scott et al. (2007) and Dorahy et al. (2009). The results are consistent with the above and are discussed in detail. Scott et al. (2007) compared voices heard by 20 adolescents with PTSD and 18 adolescents diagnosed with a psychotic disorder. They found auditory hallucinations to be common in both groups, present in more than 85 per cent of each diagnosis. Voices commenting on one's behaviour or conversing with one another were equally as prevalent in both groups; also, persons hearing only externally localised hallucinations, while relatively few, were equally prevalent in both groups (10 and 16.7 per cent). Experiencing *only* internally located voices were more common in the PTSD group than in the psychosis groups (35 versus 11.1 per cent), but experiencing internal voices overall was equally common (70 versus 72.2 per cent), as the psychosis group more commonly heard *both* internal and external voices (61.1 per cent) than did the PTSD group (35 per cent). Scott et al. (2007) also noted that, in less than one-third of the PTSD hallucinating group, did the hallucinations reflect the trauma in content. They concluded that the 'prevalence, form and content of hallucinations experienced by adolescents with PTSD were not distinguishable from those experienced by adolescents with psychotic disorder' (Scott et al. 2007: 46).

Dorahy et al. (2009) compared voices heard by adult patients with dissociative identity disorder (*n* = 34) and schizophrenia (*n* = 30), in one of the few carefully designed studies using reliable diagnostic instruments. While the diagnostic groups did not significantly differ in perceived location, *only* external voices were experienced by a minority of the schizophrenia group (18 per cent), but by none of the DID group. Both external and internal voices were reported by half of the DID group, and by 20 per cent of the schizophrenia group. Strikingly, in contrast to the Scott et al. (2007) study, more than half of the schizophrenia group (59 per cent) reported only internal voices compared to 50 per cent of the DID group. As has previously been reported, Dorahy et al. (2009) found voices commenting and voices conversing to be *more* common in DID than in schizophrenia – the former twice as common in DID (55 versus 27 per cent) and the latter more than five times as common (79 per cent in DID compared to 15 per cent in schizophrenia).

Both studies are consistent with prior research, arguing strongly that the perceived location of voices has little diagnostic relevance, and thus that the concept of 'pseudo-hallucinations' lacks validity (Moskowitz and Corstens 2007). The type of auditory hallucinations currently emphasised in the DSM-IV criteria for schizophrenia are *not* more common in schizophrenia than in other diagnoses, and are likely to lead to misdiagnosis and inappropriate treatment. So, if voices are common not only in schizophrenia but also in post-traumatic disorders, and occur as well in the general population (following a trauma or serious crisis in 70 per cent of the cases: Romme and Escher 1989), how can we understand their presence?

Auditory hallucinations, trauma and dissociation

Moskowitz and Corstens (2007: 58) have previously argued that there is only one 'type' of auditory hallucination (AH), which is best conceptualised as 'dissociative experiences which appear in individuals predisposed, for reasons not yet clear, to hear voices when under stress'. The evidence connecting auditory hallucinations to both trauma and dissociation is strong. Traumatic or highly stressful experiences precede the development of AH in the vast majority of voice hearers (Heins et al. 1990; Romme and Escher 1989) and childhood trauma appears more strongly related to hearing voices than to other 'psychotic' symptoms (Ensink 1992; Read et al. 2003; Ross et al. 1994). Strong correlations between dissociation and hearing voices in clinical and non-patient populations have now been found in a number of studies, reviewed by Moskowitz and Corstens (2007), even after controlling for other relevant variables such as schizotypy and trauma. Studies published since the review are consistent with viewing auditory hallucinations as dissociative experiences. For example, Perona-Garcelán et al. (2008) found depersonalisation scores derived from the Dissociative Experiences Scale to be the only variable predictive of auditory hallucinations (with a robust partial correlation of 0.795). They concluded that dissociation was a 'relevant factor in understanding the hallucinatory phenomenon' (Perona-Garcelán et al. 2008: 195).

The presence of voices in a wide range of persons suggests that they are best viewed not only as dissociative phenomena, but also as essentially normal experiences. Indeed, we would suggest that voice hearing is directly related to the experience of subpersonalities or selves which occurs in a treatment approach for non-patients known as Voice Dialogue, to which we now turn.

Voice dialogue – do any of us have just one self?

In the 1980s, two American psychologists, Hal and Sidra Stone, developed a therapeutic approach and a psychological theory based around recognising and engaging with an individual's subpersonalities or selves. Their approach, which came out of their own personal work with each other, resulted in an initial book entitled *Embracing Our Selves: The Voice Dialogue Manual* (1989), and was followed by a series of books by themselves and others. This approach assumes that none of us in fact has one monolithic personality, despite the illusion that we do, but rather that we all have a number of selves developed from a very early age to protect feelings of vulnerability or, if you will, a vulnerable self.

The Stones make some basic assumptions. The first – backed up by much cognitive and biological research – is that a child is an aware and sentient being from a very early age. The fact that autobiographical memory cannot typically be demonstrated until around the age of 2 years – when the part of the brain known as the hippocampus has fully developed – has obscured this essential fact. So, not only are we dependent on care and very vulnerable in the first few years of life, but also we are well aware of this. Psychologically, our primary task becomes to learn how to protect this vulnerability, and the Stones suggest that we do so by noticing what sort of behaviours and actions please those around us, particularly our parents, on whom we must depend to get our basic needs met.

Second, the Stones assume that the job of protecting this vulnerability leads to the development of several parts, subpersonalities or selves – not simply the adoption of certain behaviours and the de-emphasis of other behaviours. Why such behaviours should coalesce into subpersonalities or selves is not immediately clear, but this is an assumption that has been adopted by many theorists – from Freud and Jung to Eric Berne's Transactional Analysis ('parent', 'child' and 'adult') and most recently Jeffrey Young in the modes of his Schema-Focused Therapy (Young et al. 2003).

Some of these selves – supported by (implicit and explicit) rules in our family and in our culture – tend to become those that we identify with, such as one dedicated to 'pleasing others' ('be nice to others and you won't get hurt'), 'perfectionism', etc. Importantly, some selves or patterns of behaviour – often natural aggression or even assertiveness – are discouraged and become 'disowned'. As we develop, we find a set of selves which the Stones have called 'primary selves', who more or less run our lives. Typically, we are not aware of these selves as such, but believe that 'I' am making decisions about my life. In reality, the Stones would say, it is our operating ego which in fact consists of a set of selves, closely working together. Opposing these selves are those which are 'disowned'; these are the parts of us that our primary selves do not accept and would like to get rid of. However, the Stones insist that one must recognise and accept *all* of our selves, and not try to make any go away – though they are at pains to note that recognising and accepting does not have to mean acting them out in our daily lives. Ignoring certain aspects of our behaviour and wishing that they were not there simply makes them fester and, under some circumstances, grow stronger. The Stones's approach involves helping us to become aware of all aspects of our personality – all of our selves to use their language – so that we can make informed decisions about how to act in certain situations. They refer to this process as the creation of an 'aware ego', in contrast to an 'operating ego' which has been taken over by a group of primary selves, and lacks awareness of this. Thus, a third assumption that is made in Voice Dialogue is that no part or self is a 'problem' – 'problems' arise only when selves are ignored, shunned or not accepted. Psychological development results from recognising all of our selves and dealing with them in one way or another. This leads to the development of an 'aware ego' which is not a structure per se, but a process of becoming aware of the 'tension of opposites' which is inherent in each of us and in life itself.

An additional assumption that the Stones make is that we all come into the world with certain instinctual energies – aggression or sexuality, for example. When these energies are also disowned, as they frequently are, they can become even more powerful – the Stones refer to them as 'daemonic' under these circumstances. When this occurs they may provide fuel for a part most of us are familiar with – the *inner critic* – which acts as sort of a policeman to the primary selves, providing guidance as to what 'should' and 'should not' be done in our life and in our relationships with others. This inner critic, however, can become destructive and abusive in the context of a history of childhood abuse and particularly when instinctual energies have been disowned. In persons who actually hear voices, the inner critic is commonly experienced as a hostile, punitive or relentless force, which sometimes drives self-harming or even suicidal behaviours. However, if the underlying anxiety of such a voice can be identified and respected the 'killer' critic can be rehabilitated and turned to an ally that helps in protecting the vulnerable self.

The 'killer' critic

In their 1993 book, *Embracing your Inner Critic: Turning Self-criticism into a Creative Asset*, the Stones discuss the effect that childhood abuse can have on the development of the inner critic, turning it, in some cases, into an 'inner abuser' of the vulnerable child. This phenomenon has been long documented, and is well recognised by clinicians working with abuse survivors as 'identification with the perpetrator'. This is the part that blames the person themselves (or the body specifically) for the abuse and that drives self-harming or suicidal behaviours as a way of dealing with overwhelming guilt and shame. The secrecy this 'killer' critic insists on not only perpetuates the abuse, but also blocks effective treatment.

> If this need for secrecy blocks you, then the entire cycle of (inner) child abuse remains out of reach. You cannot let others hear your Critic so that they might help you. You cannot gain access to your Aware Ego, which might be able to see things differently and would most certainly have others tools at its disposal. *You are left alone with your shameful secrets, which grow ever more fetid in the dark closets of your psyche, and a Critic who keeps reminding you how truly disgusting they are.*
> (Stone and Stone 1993: 82, emphasis added)

Should this Critic also be fed by disowned instinctual energies, as often occurs, it can become even more powerful and destructive:

it is often the case that powerful feelings, emotions, and instinctual energies are blocked from moving out into the world. What happens then is that instead of providing us with power in the world, these energies turn sour, begin to fester, and over time become more and more potent and negative inside of us. Ultimately, this disowned mass of instinctuality becomes a killer energy that spills over onto another track, the Inner Critic track, and comes back at us. Thus the Inner Critic is infused with all the power and rage of these disowned energies.

(Stone and Stone 1993: 85)

The development of a killer critic, and its ultimate transformation and rehabilitation, can be seen in the following clinical vignette.

Case vignette: 'Maggie'

Maggie is the pseudonym for a young mother that AM worked with over a period of several years. She had been sexually abused as a child by an adult male along with several accomplices – one of whom was female. She also grew up in a culture that strongly de-emphasised aggressive behaviour – particularly for girls. She had completely disowned her aggressiveness after attacking one of her caretakers, who had inadvertently forced her to see one of her abusers.

Maggie heard many voices, both male and female, adult and child, and was initially diagnosed with schizophrenia when we began our work together. The work was tumultuous, with several crises along the way and hospitalisations. Over time, after putting AM through some 'tests' to make sure that he was not like the 'other men', this voice (which was initially identified with the adult woman who was involved in the abuse – she was a witness and encouraged the men in their actions) began to be engaged in therapy. The work was conducted very much along the lines of Voice Dialogue, with a neutral, curious and respectful attitude toward all voices, regardless of how destructive they initially appeared to be. Over a period of several months, this voice, which in the beginning called itself 'the Accuser', changed dramatically. She revealed that she had actually been present prior to the abuse at age 8, but had had 'little to do' before then. After the abuse, however, she became highly critical and abusive toward Maggie, blaming her for what had happened and repeating many of the sadistic, sexual comments from the perpetrators. She also was very critical of Maggie's parenting. When engaged, however, with respect, tolerance and – particularly – patience, the 'Accuser' began to change from a part singling out Maggie for punishment, to a part concerned with her 'flaws', her weaknesses. As the Stones described the Inner Critic, it became clear that this part was very anxious that others would criticise or blame Maggie – perhaps even take away her son if her parenting was found wanting. Her criticism reflected an underlying anxiety which was identified. In light of this, a name change was negotiated – initially to the 'Critic', and ultimately to the 'Protector'.

While Maggie heard the voice of the Protector regularly, she was never able to respond to it – out of fear. In a sense, the therapist AM served as a form of bridge, a surrogate Aware Ego *for* Maggie, until Maggie and the Protector could deal directly with one another. This did occur toward the end of the treatment, and now the Protector is a valued – though perhaps not cherished – voice for Maggie. As in standard Voice Dialogue, there was no attempt made to 'get rid' of any of the voices; Maggie continues to hear all of her voices, but they have changed dramatically. Several that were previously identified with her abusers are now clearly recognised as important, valued parts of her self.

Conclusion

Hearing a voice is a very dramatic experience – shocking when it first occurs, and yet research suggests that it is not nearly as uncommon as we have been led to believe. Voices are heard by many persons in the community who otherwise do not meet diagnostic criteria for any form of mental illness, and their experience of voices is not different in essence from the voices heard by persons diagnosed with a mental disorder. The differences lie primarily in the emotional reaction to the voices and the sense of control over them (Moskowitz and Corstens 2007). Further, while voices are common after trauma, the content of the voices does not always directly reflect the traumatic event – in fact it usually doesn't (Scott et al. 2007) – and essential characteristics of auditory hallucinations, including perceived source location, do not differ among persons diagnosed with PTSD, Dissociative Identity Disorder (DID) and schizophrenia. Indeed, the specific types of auditory hallucinations considered typical of schizophrenia – voices commenting and conversing – are *more* common in DID (Dorahy et al. 2009). Finally, the evidence that voices are related to traumatic experiences and are essentially dissociative in nature is robust.

All of the above leads us to conclude that auditory hallucinations are essentially normal phenomena, which are best characterised as dissociative in nature. Because of how dramatic and unusual they appear, we have overlooked their continuity with normal personality, a continuity that clearly can be seen by comparing the experience of hearing voices with the Voice Dialogue approach to working with non-psychiatric patients. While the parts of ourselves that are directly addressed through the Voice

Dialogue process are not normally *heard* as voices, they appear – in every other respect – to be identical with voices heard by persons experiencing auditory hallucinations. The content of such voices, as illustrated in the case vignette presented above, is well explained by the Stones's discussion of the 'Killer Critic', particularly with regard to the impact of childhood abuse and the disowning of instinctual energies. Perhaps the time is right for us to stop viewing voice hearing as a symptom of mental illness but rather as an overt manifestation of the (usually) hidden multidimensionality of all of us. Is it time for us to recognise that we all, to paraphrase Walt Whitman, 'contain multitudes'?

References

American Psychiatric Association (APA) (1994) *Diagnostic and Statistical Manual of Mental Disorders*, 4th edn. Washington, DC: APA.

Barrett, T.R. and Etheridge, J.B. (1992) Verbal hallucinations in normals. I: People who hear voices. *Applied Cognitive Psychology*, 6: 379–87.

Berrios, G.E. and Dening, T.R. (1996) Pseudohallucinations: A conceptual history. *Psychological Medicine*, 26: 753–63.

Carlson, E.B. and Putnam, F.W. (1986) Development, reliability, and validity of a dissociation scale. *Journal of Nervous and Mental Disease*, 174: 727–33.

Copolov, D.L., Trauer, T. and Mackinnon, A. (2004) On the non-significance of internal versus external auditory hallucinations. *Schizophrenia Research*, 69: 1–6.

Dorahy, M.J., Shannon, C., Seagar, L., Corr, M., Stewart, K., Hanna, D., Mulholland, C. and Middleton, W. (2009) Auditory hallucinations in dissociative identity disorder and schizophrenia with and without a childhood trauma history: Similarities and differences. *Journal of Nervous and Mental Disease*, 197: 892–8.

Ensink, B.J. (1992) *Confusing Realities: A Study on Child Sexual Abuse and Psychiatric Symptoms*. Amsterdam: VU Press.

Hare, E.H. (1973) A short note on pseudo-hallucinations. *British Journal of Psychiatry*, 122: 469–76.

Heins, T., Gray, A. and Tennant, M. (1990) Persisting hallucinations following childhood sexual abuse. *Australian and New Zealand Journal of Psychiatry*, 24: 561–5.

Honig, A., Romme, M.A.J., Ensink, B.J., Escher, S.D.M.A.C., Pennings, M.H.A. and deVries, M.W. (1998) Auditory hallucinations: A comparison between patients and nonpatients. *Journal of Nervous and Mental Disease*, 186: 646–51.

Jaspers, K. (1963) *General Psychopathology*, trans. J. Hoenig and M.W. Hamilton. Manchester: Manchester University Press (original publication date 1913).

Johns, L.C., Nazroo, J.Y., Bebbington, P. and Kuipers, E. (2002) Occurrence of hallucinatory experiences in a community sample and ethnic variations. *British Journal of Psychiatry*, 180: 174–8.

Kluft, R.P. (1987) First-rank symptoms as a diagnostic clue to multiple personality disorder. *American Journal of Psychiatry*, 144: 293–8.

Morrison, A.P. (1998) A cognitive analysis of the maintenance of auditory hallucinations: Are voices to schizophrenia what bodily sensations are to panic? *Behavioural and Cognitive Psychotherapy*, 26: 289–302.

Moskowitz, A. and Corstens, D. (2007) Auditory hallucinations: Psychotic symptom or dissociative experience? *Journal of Psychological Trauma*, 6 (2–3): 35–63.

Moskowitz, A., Schäfer, I. and Dorahy, M.J. (eds) (2008) *Psychosis, Trauma and Dissociation: Emerging Perspectives on Severe Psychopathology*. Chichester: Wiley.

Moskowitz, A., Read, J., Farrelly, S., Rudegeair, T. and Williams, O. (2009) Are psychotic symptoms traumatic in origin and dissociative in kind? In P. Dell and J. O'Neil (eds) *Dissociation and the Dissociative Disorders: DSM-V and Beyond*. New York: Routledge.

Nayani, T.H. and David, A.S. (1996) The auditory hallucination: A phenomenological survey. *Psychological Medicine*, 26: 177–89.

Oulis, P.G., Mavreas, V.G., Mamounas, J.M. and Stefanis, C.N. (1995) Clinical characteristics of auditory hallucinations. *Acta Psychiatrica Scandinavica*, 92: 97–102.

Pearson, D., Smalley, M., Ainsworth, C., Cook, M., Boyle, J. and Flury, S. (2008) Auditory hallucinations in adolescent and adult students: Implications for continuums and adult pathology following child abuse. *Journal of Nervous and Mental Disease*, 196: 634–8.

Perona-Garcelán, S., Cuevas-Yust, C., García-Montes, J.M., Pérez-Álvarez, M., Ductor-Recuerda, M.J., Salas-Azcona, R., Gómez-Gómez, M.T. and Rodríguez-Martín, B. (2008) Relationship between self-focused attention and dissociation in patients with and without auditory hallucinations. *Journal of Nervous and Mental Disease*, 196: 190–7.

Posey, T.B. and Losch, M.E. (1983–4) Auditory hallucinations of hearing voices in 375 normal subjects. *Imagination, Cognition and Personality*, 3: 99–113.

Read, J., Agar, K., Argyle, N. and Aderhold, V. (2003) Sexual and physical abuse during childhood and adulthood as predictors of hallucinations, delusions and thought disorder. *Psychology and Psychotherapy: Theory, Research and Practice*, 76: 1–22.

Romme, M.A.J. and Escher, D.M.A.C. (1989) Hearing voices. *Schizophrenia Bulletin*, 15: 40–7.

Ross, C.A., Anderson, G. and Clark, P. (1994) Childhood abuse and the positive symptoms of schizophrenia. *Hospital and Community Psychiatry*, 45: 489–91.

Scott, J.G., Nurcombe, B., Sheridan, J. and McFarland, M. (2007) Hallucinations in adolescents with post-traumatic stress disorder and psychotic disorder. *Australasian Psychiatry*, 15: 44–8.

Sidgwick, H., Johnson, A., Myers, F.W.H., Podmore, F. and Sidgwick, E.M. (1894) Report on the census of hallucinations. *Proceedings of the Society for Psychical Research*, 26: 259–394.

Stone, H. and Stone, S. (1989) *Embracing Our Selves: The Voice Dialogue Manual*. Novato, CA: New World Library.

Stone, H. and Stone, S. (1993) *Embracing Your Inner Critic: Turning Self-Criticism into a Creative Asset*. New York: HarperCollins.

Tien, A.Y. (1991) Distributions of hallucinations in the population. *Social Psychiatry and Psychiatric Epidemiology*, 26: 287–92.

van Os, J., Hanssen, M., Bijl, R.V. and Ravelli, A. (2000) Strauss (1969) revisited: A psychosis continuum in the general population? *Schizophrenia Research*, 45: 11–20.

Yee, L., Korner, A.K., McSwiggan, S., Meares, R.A. and Stevenson, J. (2005) Persistent hallucinosis in borderline personality disorder. *Comprehensive Psychiatry*, 46: 147–54.

Young, J.E., Klosko, J.S. and Weishaar, M. (2003) *Schema Therapy: A Practitioner's Guide*. New York: Guilford.

If you no ow me you no love me.
                    Pumpkin (aged 2)

('Ow' means sexual abuse)

Endless monologue

I am an endless monologue
Done in choral voices
Forgetting to speak up or harmonise
Forgetting to be heard or take turns
What would happen if you were to listen?
Listen to me, listen to me
Endless monologue. Fractured speaker

Broken ear. Willing. So willing to hear
An endless monologue raspy with whispering
Sibilant with sighs and sights
A voice forbidden, telling secrets
Telling lies, telling tales, telling telling.
I am an endless monologue and walking
Between the hyphens and commas
Ellipsis, eclipses my lost lost voice
Uncertain and halting between the ands and the
Ohs, an endless monologue
Preaching hoping walking talking
Moving about with alabaster flasks
Hearing my tears speaking speaking
Out of the fears of a thousand shattering
Pieces of consciousness, voiceless
Yet I am an endless monologue
Falling falling calling you near

                                    Mary Bach-Loreaux

Chapter 3

The verbal language of trauma and dissociation

Valerie Sinason

Introduction

Psychoanalysis has always privileged the symbolic as the summit of linguistic and psychological development, with symbolic equation as a half-way stage down to the allegedly deep depletion of the literal (Segal 1979). As a poet, writer, psychoanalytic psychotherapist and psychoanalyst, I have always treasured the symbolic too. However, with a sample of severely traumatised patients with intellectual disabilities, post-traumatic states and dissociative disorders I have been learning of a place where 'literalism' is rich, truthful and holds a capacity for facing intolerable reality. In working with such patients, ordinary 'symbolic' language can be escapism. Indeed, it can be the therapist who resorts to symbolic language to evade the pain of the traumatic reality. On the other hand, I consider there a different order of symbolism inherent in the language of trauma that is being ignored. Language, after all, is inherently symbolic.

Case vignetts: Lorna

Lorna was removed from her multi-perpetrating abusive family at the age of 9. She had now spent two years in a school for emotionally disturbed children. She found it very painful to learn, checking out the meaning of every word said to her. Suddenly there was a violent incident. At the school end-of-term party she was offered a glass of lemonade. She smashed the glass to the floor with the liquid spoiling all her schoolwork and glass fragments covering the floor. She was inconsolable. 'I didn't think you did lemonade here,' she screamed.

In therapy it emerged that the drink of semen mixed with other fluids, that she was forced to drink in her family home, was called lemonade. On the rare occasions when she went to visit friends and they had lemonade, it was proof to her that her family was normal, that other people drank the same things even if it tasted different. It was only after eighteen months of a stable foster-placement that she suddenly become consciously aware that the word 'lemonade' could have a different meaning for other people. It could mean a fizzy drink that did not have any real lemon in it that was marketed by a range of brands in glass bottles, plastic bottles or cans, or a drink made with real lemons and water, or a drink her family made that was not a proper drink and which made her feel sick.

'Talk talk!' she shouted. 'All of you talk talk. You think you are speaking English. How do I know what language you are speaking. It is all different to me.'

Language, she had come to realise, was co-constructed in an attachment relationship. Even speaking the same ostensible language – English – the same word could have profoundly different meanings used by different people. All her upbringing up to the age of 9 had been with a family who consistently used words and bodies in a particular way. That was her language.

Her excellent class teacher found she made major progress in being taught French. Starting with a brand new language with a dictionary and books, she had a chance to hypervigilantly check things out that brought her high marks rather than emotional pain and shame.

It was not possible for Lorna to consider that there were only a few words her family had provided which had different meanings. After all, that was not true. Each week in therapy another word would appear. 'Cuddle' meant sexual intercourse, 'bath' meant being scrubbed ready for abuse, 'bedroom' meant a place of torture. Slowly we could all see that Lorna had been provided with a different language. Segal (1979) provides a psychoanalytic understanding of the relationality between baby and mother that co-constructs language.

> The infant has had an experience and the mother provides the words or phrase which binds this experience. It contains, encompasses and expresses the meaning. It provides a container for it. The infant can then internalise this word or phrase containing the meaning.
>
> (Segal 1979: 63)

Lorna is a bilingual child and as with any child who has to learn to be bilingual, she faced particular hurdles. For one language to be a language of abuse made her bilingual experiences even harder.

Amniocentesis

After several years of building up trust, a woman in a psychotherapy group for women with severe intellectual disabilities says 'I know the worst word in the world'. The other women in the group nod. My co-therapist and I look at each other with amazement. The women do not come from the same hospital. They are not friends outside of the group. The group, held for 90 minutes each week, is the only place they meet. We do not know this word.

'What is the word?' we ask.

One person cannot answer. The weight of the word is so huge that it needs all the women to say it.

'Am-'

'ni-'

'o-'

'cen-'

'tes-'

'is'

Amniocentesis.

For many adults, amniocentesis is a neutral word or term that signifies the act of checking whether an unborn baby is carrying any severe chromosomal disorder or has a severe learning disability. The word 'amniocentesis' literally means puncture of the amnon, the thin-walled sac of fluid in which a developing fetus is suspended during pregnancy. During the procedure amniotic fluid is withdrawn for testing by a needle which is guided by ultrasound images. The fetal cells in the sample of amniotic fluid are isolated and grown in order to provide enough genetic material for testing.

For someone with a severe intellectual disability, the word covers a meaning that is far more than that. Faced with a hidden societal eugenics' wish, people with an intellectual disability are very aware of a deeper meaning in the term, signifying their own destruction. It is rarely possible to consider amniocentesis as something that is to stop people like yourself from being born, rather than something to kill you even after you have been born, when you feel the full weight of societal death wishes towards you. This is even more powerful when you sense ambivalence in your family (Sinason 2010).

Similarly, for orthodox Roman Catholics who consider abortion to be against their religious belief system, the word can also mean far more than the medical procedure it is for those who wish to know if their fetus is carrying any chromosomal abnormalities or other genetic problems. While amniocentesis can be carried out without leading to a termination, it is largely seen as a transition to that possibility. This means that the word 'amniocentesis' has a very different meaning according to the belief system of the speaker or listener.

The politics of language therefore tells us that the minority in any culture will have the experience of being seen as 'primitive' or 'defensive' when words which convey profound meaning to them are seen as neutral by others.

In considering the meaning of the word 'amniocentesis', are we looking at something literal or symbolic? In needing a whole group to carry the burden of the word which has become a word of dread are the group to be perceived as having literal or symbolic language? What does it show about them? Is the language of trauma adequately respected or is it pathologised?

I found it interesting that the first example that came to my mind for this chapter involved something akin to death in that as Lacan says, 'Language names things and thus murders them as full presences, creating an alienation between the word and the thing' (Ragland-Sullivan and Bracher 1991: 4). The goal of language is to replace what is lost and Stern (1985: 163) from the start of his work emphasised that 'Language, then, causes a split in the experience of the self.'

Take a musical instrument. A lyre. For some it is an historic Greek instrument and has no other meaning. For others (E. Rhode 2003) it is a religious symbol with the seven strings representing the seven circles of heaven as a soul membrane. A photograph can be an ordinary object to millions around the world, something that can even be taken from a mobile phone. To others it is something that catches and steals the image of the soul.

Nothing is but culture, class, race and religion make it so!

Back-to-front story

Let me move to an example from a school for emotionally disturbed children where I was the psychotherapist.

Case vignetts: Dania

Mrs Mona Curtis (her chosen pseudonym) was a particularly fine foster-mother for traumatised children. She had an instinctive capacity to under-stand what language to use in reaching the most frozen or violent of children. At parents' evenings she would gently reprove us for praising her children's work. 'You ought to know by now they'd have to tear it all up after you went on and said how good it was'. Her special term of praise was 'a dab hand': 'Nina is a dab hand at craftwork', 'Joan is a dab hand at cooking'.

One term, Mrs Curtis came with a particularly troubled new child, Dania. She fluctuated between extremes of violence to moments of seductive excitement to silence to terror. We knew little about the home she had been removed from as, yet again, Mrs Curtis had been provided with a child with extreme behaviour and hints of extreme multi-perpetrator abuse and neglect. She was now to be put up for adoption after Mrs Curtis had helped to 'calm her down', although Mrs Curtis herself considered such a move unlikely to be successful. 'She's been hurt in a home by her nearest and dearest and a home is going to be too dangerous. She needs to stay fostered or be in a children's home. But they won't listen. She'll just get herself rejected and hurt herself more'.

Dania slowly settled in well. Her outbursts of violence gave her 'cool' in the eyes of some of the older children, who also felt protective to her in her more vulnerable states.

However, among many other lessons she taught me, there was something I kept coming back to. When I went to collect her from her classroom on one occasion, Dania pointed triumphantly and mockingly at her wall collage:

> 'Mona says I am a dab hand. Dab is Bad back-to-front. And I am bad. So my painting is bad and that means Dab. Because my Mummy uses back-to-front language. So I am a Bad-hand and Mummy and Daddy are right'.

I was immediately struck by her intelligence in finding a way of accepting praise without being disloyal to her family and wondered whether I could build on this.

I said I knew a story about that and asked if she would like to hear it in the therapy room. She nodded intently while muttering 'Lickle nicey nicey story to hurt a baby with' in a very different voice. I had described her as fragmented but I had no idea about dissociation in the 1980s.

I said if stories were used to hurt babies then how sensible of her not to listen. But I would tell this one and she could check it out.

> 'Once upon a time,' I began
> 'Upon?' sneered Dania, 'underneath more like', she added pointedly.
> 'OK,' I said. 'Once, underneath a time'
> 'underneath lots of times!' shouted Dania
> 'Once underneath lots of times there was a little girl called Bad.'

There was silence and she looked at me intently.

> 'Her Mum called her Bad, her Dad called her Bad'
> 'and her grandma and grandpa,' she called.
> 'Yes. And her grandma and grandpa. Everyone called her Bad. She did everything she could to please them but they said she was Bad and they hurt her and said they hurt her because she was Bad and they starved her because she was Bad. In the end she had so many bruises all over her because she was Bad that someone saw and took her away.'
> 'Because I was too bad for them,' said Dania sadly.

'And they took her to the back-to-front country where some words get spelled in opposite ways and things are different. So instead of saying she was Bad all the time they said she was a Dab hand at everything she did when she tried her best.'

'And they do,' said Dania wonderingly.

'And they are not lying people. When they say she is a dab hand at something they mean it just as her Mum and Dad in their back-to-front world meant it when they said she was Bad. So –'

Dania jumped up and down:

'So if we don't go back to the Badland we can stay being a Dab Hand but if we go back we are Bad again. But since I am back-to-front and front-to-back I can be Bad and a Dab Hand at the same time.'

'Exactly,' I said, feeling shocked at how many light years faster than me she was. It was to take twenty years for me to learn that when severe dissociation takes place and emotions are split from intellect, people can be logically way ahead!

A year later she could inform me, 'If I leave the Badlands and never go back I will miss my Mummy but if I say 'dab is bad' I still have her. But you know, those Badlands are Sadlands too.'

Dania taught me many things and this extract could be taken in many ways to cover the crucial fields of identification, attachment, shame, loyalty and trauma. However, I have included that particular extract as it highlights another problem at the core of this chapter. In the language of trauma, we know that the symbolic is unavailable and that literal thinking prevails. So many of us have written for so many years, on how the internalising of feeling bad is one of the most corrupting affects of abuse within an attachment relationship. There was no way Dania could question the behaviour of her family as yet, but perhaps she could understand a linguistic challenge that would allow her to not feel disloyal and accept the rules of a very different world.

Dania, I learned from her teacher, could not bear listening to any fairy tale or fable. Anything 'literal' she grasped immediately. Was my story to Dania literal or symbolic?

When the symbolic is a comic

When Anders Svensson and I began to work together on the first case of a woman with intellectual disability and a ritual abuse history we had ever encountered, we realised the way the therapist can want to put into the symbolic what is only too awful and literal (Sinason and Svensson 1994).

Patient: They gave me shit to eat.
Anders: They gave you horrible food.

In fact, the patient was speaking the literal truth.

Indeed, it is significantly missing from the therapeutic literature that while some traumatised patients might indeed be sticking to the literal (and denigrated for it), most therapists, at times, need to seek comfort in the symbolic to get away from the reality of lived trauma.

Case vignette: John

John was referred to a unit for extremely disturbed children because of his sexual attacks on female teachers. His mother loved him dearly but moved in and out of psychotic episodes and there was no father or other relative to help. There were concerns that his mother sexually abused him when she was in a psychotic state.

When he started to lick a furry toy dog between its back legs and said 'Erch!' week after week and showed enormous sexual disgust, I was able to consider sexual abuse by his psychotic mother. Weeks in which he made clear the dog was a bitch and the ways in which he treated female dolls and the female teachers made it possible for me to draw attention to his behaviour in a tentative way. 'You keep calling that dog a bitch and you call your teacher a bitch and maybe what you are doing with the dog makes you think of women.' John looked completely bored and registered nothing.

When he was moved to a foster home as a result of his mother's psychotic breakdown, they rang me up embarrassedly. 'We would like to see you to talk about something too difficult to say on the phone.' I wondered if this was going to be more about his mother. In fact, they came to tell me they had a family dog and John was trying to have sex with it.

In his sessions John could tell me it was much easier to talk about his mother 'fiddling' with him when she was mad. He knew other boys this had happened to. But he felt shamed and a freak about the sex she made him have with their dog.

This was only the 1980s but even so sex with animals can remain a more frightening taboo. I thought I was being carefully symbolic and tentative. The reality was far more literal and the literal was far more painful.

When fairy tales are literal

An extract from Round Up

Boys and girls come out to play
I call you up now
I am marking the register
Of broken nursery rhymes
Are you there?
Are you listening, dear dead ones?

Where is Eddy, Eddy
With his Brylcreem Ever-ready?

Prince Charming is in the night sky
He revs up on his two-wheeled steed
He revs up at the dead end of the world
His mother has smashed the glass slipper
Cinderella rocks her cold Borstal feet.

Boys and girls come out to play. . .

Sleeping Beauty burps
Under mountains of fat, rivers of gin
Her flesh cries out for silk and jewels
Her flesh cries out for the mouth of a king.
                              (Valerie Sinason 1986)

We could consider, as a staff group, that the familiar fairy tales in which a
princess finds her prince or is found by her prince would be meaningless for
a girl who has already become the queen by having a sexual link with her
father. In Oedipal language, the whole developmental symbolic aid that
fairy tales offer is ruined and destroyed when reality has altered the hidden
meaning. The princess has married the wicked king, and the queen has
disappeared or become a persecutor of the abused princess-daughter who
mirrors her own degraded experience.

The lucky loved little girl is sitting playing with a bride doll and a jewelled bag.
She is playing at weddings and brides and symbolically putting things inside of
her bag and taking them out. The bag is representing her vagina but she
herself does not consciously know how her imaginative play is aiding her
development. There is no such moment for the abused little girl. Playing with

a doll is mad for her. She has experienced, too young and wrongfully, the reality of a marital relationship.

Jack, whose father was in prison for killing his mother and attempting to kill him, did not want to read a fairy tale about a boy who kills a giant. The Oedipal help Jack the Giant-Killer can present does not exist when the reality is so awful.

Fairy tale narrative as a reflection of DID and trauma

When I began to read fairy tales more carefully, I became fascinated to consider how much dissociation and full-blown Dissociative Identity Disorder is represented in them as a falsely symbolic tale when reality is being represented.

For example, a princess or a prince, or a shepherd girl and boy (their more humble alter egos), walk into a forest to find a beautiful feast is set. This happens for Beauty too in the Beast's palace.

A woman with DID invites me to her home saying honestly she does not know if there will be any food. She has prepared a shopping list and will walk into a shop but she does not know if another alter will buy the things on the list and cook and prepare them. When I arrive at her house to see a beautifully prepared and arranged tea on the table, the woman looks at it with pleasure and amazement and says, 'It is like one of those fairy tales'.

Similarly, there are the tales in which someone suddenly finds themselves, through magic, in a completely different house, wood or country. How much are these ways of trying to make sense of the experience of dissociation in which one alter 'loses time' and comes to finding themselves wherever the last alter to walk the body reached. In the heart of what is considered symbolic there can therefore be something literal.

Language, loss and autism

As an infant school teacher I started out, as the custom was, with the children learning their own names first. Then came the flashcards 'mother' and 'father'. 'Please miss, my mother is my father,' cried one child desperately. How do you spell and learn the word 'father' if he is not there? What does the word mean? Following Lacan, Kristeva (1981) comments that the sign is given in the absence of something which makes it symbolic. 'They all replace or represent something that is absent, evoked by an intermediary, and, consequently, included in a system of exchange: in a communication' (Kristeva 1981: 3).

The pre-verbal child can possess a vast number of visual or musical concepts contained in the sound 'dere', 'dat'. Once words come in the child initially loses speed, all the vast repertoire of sensations diminishing into a small word, 'cat', 'dog'. Language builds on separation and loss.

> Steven, who had a severe intellectual disability and was autistic, pulled at his mouth with the effort of saying a sound. The sound, for him, together with the pulling of his lips, was his link with his mother. He experienced separation from her as black hole. (Tustin 1990), not just the fact of living away from her, but the earliest bodily sensations of weaning.

This takes us back to the origins of speech and the baby's awareness of sound and mouth. Such issues are crucial in work with autistic children where Marie Rhode (2003) shows the way in which words can be experienced as a physical link to the mother with all the traumatic issues of separation that implies. Indeed, Rhode points out:

> Words are not just symbols: they are sensory constructs with rhythmical and musical properties. These two aspects of language are perhaps most fruitfully integrated in poetic diction, which relies on the sound of words to produce a bodily and emotional impact just as their meaning produces a mental impact. Clinical work, on the other hand, and particularly work with autistic children, allows us to study the disjunction between form and meaning, or sound and sense.
>
> (Rhode 2003: 35)

Novelist William Golding (1980) expresses the physical aspects of uttering a word brilliantly.

> Not only did he clench his fists with the effort of speaking, he squinted. It seemed that a word was an object, a material object, round and smooth sometimes, a golfball of a thing that he could just about manage to get through his mouth, though it deformed his face in the passage.
>
> (Golding 1980: 19)

This is close to the Sudanese Bambaras, who consider language a physical element. The whole body including sexual organs participate in speech; to speak 'is to give birth'. There are rites for preparing the mouth to speak. We can also note the importance of the Judea-Christian tradition in which, in the beginning, was the Word. The literal and the litteral share many areas of thinking.

Work with autistic children can show us how problematic language becomes in a different way.

> A child had been told to go to the head teacher. He was busy and asked her to wait outside. She went outside into the playground where a teacher reprimanded her. 'But he told me to wait outside,' protested the autistic child, unaware of how her honest reply was inflaming her teacher. She did not have the social means to understand that 'outside' was an abbreviation for waiting outside of his room until he was free to see her.

This kind of apparent literalism can pose serious problems for children and adults whose autism has not been recognised and diagnosed (Alvarez and Reid 1999). David Leevers (personal communication) has commented on another aspect of this non-dialogue, that the rules of the majority versus minority apply here. The head teacher saw himself as inside in the place that linguistically mattered and had not understood what the child needed.

> Mary, who had severe intellectual disability as well as autism, saw anything old or damaged as representing disability and therefore something that had to be rejected. In one session, after I had had a cold, she rejected a female doll saying it was old and handicapped and ill and she had to get rid of it. I tentatively said, 'Perhaps you would like to get rid of me since I have got older and haven't been well with my cold.' 'No,' she said firmly, 'You are a person and that dolly is only a teddy'.

Schizophrenia

In looking at autism it is also worth noting the overlapping issues in terms of language and schizophrenia. In that clinical area metaphoric language has been set in opposition to literal language, although Chouvardas (1996) and Billow et al. (1997) dispute this. The language of schizophrenia can often resemble that of poetry, especially in the rich use of metaphor. Poetry is any imaginative, structured language that employs imagery, simile, or metaphor with an artistic aim in mind. Similarly Billow et al. (1997) found on measures of metaphoric, evocative, and idiomatic language, that the speech of patients with schizophrenia was similar to other groups. As expected, patients with schizophrenia were also verbally more autistic and tangential but not more concrete.

Language and dissociation

There are ways in which the emotional experience of trauma and dissociation has important overlaps with the work on autism. A language is called literal, let us remind ourselves, when what is meant to be conveyed is the same as what the word to word meaning is of what is said. In contrast in figurative language, the words are used to imply meaning which is other than their strict dictionary meaning.

Dissociation can mean the separation of feeling from intellect which can allow what Van der Hart et al. (2006) call the apparently normal part (ANP) of the personality, even with a severe intellectual disability, the logic of a barrister. Without the impact of feeling to slow down logical thinking, the person with a DID is a formidable barrister to work with, who picks up every linguistic contradiction or inconsistency.

There can be an apparent fierce adherence to what appears to be literal:

Therapist: I am afraid I cannot ring you at that time.
Patient: Why are you afraid?

When we consider the trauma of the DID person who is still being tortured and requires dissociation to survive, we can see that the word 'afraid' cannot be considered in a euphemistic way. Fear and terror are at the heart of trauma.

Conclusion

> Much Madness is divinest Sense –
> To a discerning Eye –
> Much Sense – the starkest Madness –
> . . .
> Demur – you're straightway dangerous –
> And handled with a Chain.
>   (Emily Dickinson 1830–86)

The American poet Emily Dickinson suffered from a violent father and a constricted life and education. Nevertheless she was able to write from this place. She is a forerunner of the psychoanalyst Bion's famous maxim that common sense is not common. She understood that the majority has the power to declare the minority mad.

I consider that language is one of the key ways that hierarchy and trauma reveal themselves. While we might all follow the Quaker humorous line that all the world is mad except for thee and me and even thee is a bit mad sometimes, the fact remains that the most severely hurt develop a different language from the luckier. The language of those injured in their upbringings (or downbringings) is a language that is either not recognised or pathologised.

I apologise to those I have hurt by naming minority diagnostic labels. My aim has not been to denigrate the language of others but indeed to observe the contradictions and paradoxes in all language. By listening more to whoever our own 'other' is our own language has a chance of being more complete.

References

Alvarez, A. and Reid, S. (eds) (1999) *Autism and Personality: Findings from the Tavistock Autism Workshop*. London: Routledge.

Billow, R., Rossman, J., Lewis, N., Goldman, D. and Raps, C. (1997) Observing expressive and deviant language in schizophrenia. *Metaphor and Symbol*, 12 (3): 205–16.

Chouvardas, J. (1996) The symbolic and literal in schizophrenic language. *Perspectives in Psychiatric Care*, 32 (2): 20–2.

Dickinson, E. (1998) *The Poems of Emily Dickinson*, Variorum Edition. Cambridge, MA: Harvard University Press.

Golding, W. (1980) *Darkness Visible*. London: Faber & Faber.

Kristeva, J. (1981) *Language, the Unknown: An Initiation into Linguistics*, trans. A.M. Menke. London: Harvester Wheatsheaf.

Ragland-Sullivan, E. and Bracher, M. (1991) Introduction. In Ragland-Sullivan and Bracher (eds) *Lacan and the Subject of Language*. London: Routledge.

Rhode, E. (2003) *Plato's Silence: A Study in the Imagination*. London: Apex One.

Rhode, M. (2003) Sensory aspects of language development in relation to primitive anxieties. *Infant Observation*, 6 (2): 12–32.

Rozewicz, T. (1995) In the midst of life. In H. Schiff (ed.) *Holocaust Poetry*. New York: St Martin's Griffin.

Segal, H. (1979) Notes on symbol formation. In Segal, *The Work of Hanna Segal: A Kleinian Approach to Clinical Practice*. London: Free Association Books.

Sinason, V. (1986) Roundup. In Sinason, *Inkstains and Stilettos*. West Kirby, UK: Headland.

Sinason, V. (2010) *Mental Handicap and the Human Condition: An Analytic Approach to Intellectual Disability*, 2nd edn. London: Free Association Books.

Sinason, V. and Svensson, A. (1994) Going through the fifth window. In V. Sinason (ed.) *Treating Survivors of Satanist Abuse*. London: Routledge.

Stern, D.N. (1985) *The Interpersonal World of the Infant: A View from Psychoanalysis and Developmental Psychology*. New York: Basic Books.

Tustin, F. (1990) *The Protective Shell in Children and Adults*. London: Karnac.

Van der Hart, O., Nijenhuis, E.R.S. and Steele, K. (2006) *The Haunted Self: Structural Dissociation and the Treatment of Chronic Traumatization*. New York: Norton.

Floating in soul clouds
Not hearing or seeing ourselves
Punishment
For knowing
And separating us
From all we know
And all who

The Poet

Chapter 4

Children's art and the dissociative brain

Mary Sue Moore

Introduction

There is substantial evidence that an individual's unique, interpersonal relationship history significantly impacts not only the specific *characteristics* included or omitted in one's drawing of a person, but also the *process* by which one creates the drawing (Coates and Moore 1997; Kaufman and Wohl 1992; Koppitz 1968; Malchiodi 1990; Moore 1994a, 1994b; Mortensen 1991). The areas of the brain that hold knowledge of relational experience are located predominantly in the right, but as an infant matures, also in the left hemisphere (Cozolino 2006; Schore 2003; Siegel 1999). In terms of what is communicated in a drawing when one *consciously* thinks about oneself, or a person in general, these areas are activated. Thus the task of thinking about or drawing a person elicits both conscious, declarative *and* nonconscious, procedural knowledge of self and other (Gallese et al. 2004; George and Solomon 1989; Grigsby and Stevens 2002; Lanius et al. 2003). The neurobiological impact of relational trauma as it is recorded in brain processes directly affects the quality and content of any individual's drawing of a person.

Why is a drawing of a person not a drawing of *a* person?

As a social species, we have evolved to learn as powerfully by *observing* others as through direct *personal experience* (Divino et al. 1992; Gallese et al. 2004; Grigsby and Hartlaub 1994; Rizzolatti et al. 2006). One result of this complexity in our development is that we commonly develop a primary concept of self by attempting to link and internally integrate various experiences of 'self-in-relation'. These are our internal working models (Bowlby 1969) based on procedural experience with our primary caregivers (Beebe and Lachmann 1994). Importantly, these original experiences of self are in relation not to just *any* other, but to a few different *specific* others (Bowlby 1980; Braten 1993). Thus, the same infant may show an insecure attachment behavior pattern with one parent, and a secure pattern with the other parent.

Specific attachment dyads may be classified, but as an individual matures she is always 'standing in the spaces' (Bromberg 1998) between potential self-states, one in relation to every important attachment figure – all of which is activated when we ask someone to draw a person.

The neurobiology of being-in-relation directly impacts capacity for self-expression in an attachment relationship, and in drawings

In the selective review below, I focus on the understanding we gain of the natural development of dissociative states which have powerfully informed my understanding of human figure drawings.

Experience of self as agent in attachment dyads depend upon the capacity to recognize – to know and be known by – the other

In Sander's (1964) early study of 7-day-old infants and their mothers, Sander describes how in the first week of the mother and baby's experience together a consistent routine for sleeping, bathing, diapering, and feeding was established. On the seventh day, the mother was given a woollen ski mask to wear while carrying out the routines, altering her face although not her eyes. The infant showed no difference while being routinely handled by mother. It was *only* when settling to feed, that the infant's habitual neuro-biological patterns of interaction were massively disrupted. The infant's act of *agency*, within the dyad, depended upon being with a known, familiar other. He could not suck and did not gaze directly at mother, but turned his head to see the mask face from several angles. Mother's familiar voice did not calm him enough to feed in the normal way.

Contingently visual responsive behaviors within the attachment dyad are crucial to the recognition of an-other and development of the capacity to have self agency in the dyad

In further similar studies (Stern 1985; Tronick 2001), the mother was instructed to suddenly stop interacting, and provide a non-responsive facial expression, but continue to face the infant. Infants tried to re-engage her. A majority protested and showed – sometimes extreme – distress.

Working with 6–8-week-old infants, Murray employed an innovative technique that allowed mother and baby to see and hear each other via an audio-video (AV) monitor, and to view the face of the other, in a manner very similar to what each would see in a normal face-to-face interaction. Infant responses gave stunningly clear evidence that within only a minute or two, the mother and infant were actively engaged in what was a typical interactive pattern for that particular dyad (Murray and Trevarthen 1985, 1986).

After the infant experienced interaction with the mother through the AV system, there was a brief period when the AV system was shut off. When the system was turned on again, the infant was shown an audio-video replay image of the mother's face filmed during a previous happy inter-action with the infant. Within a few seconds, each infant stopped looking at the smiling and speaking image of mother on the screen. *All* the infants looked away, with confused expressions on their faces, and only briefly looked back at the screen from the corner of their eyes. Gaze length toward the mother dropped to an average of 2–3 seconds. The infants showed distress, confusion and negative emotions but *only while looking away from* the mother's image on the screen; some grimaced, some frowned, and many showed distress. *Unlike* the infants in the other research studies who were in the same room and face to face with the mother who suddenly did not respond, Murray's infants did *not* show distress *or protest toward* the mother's face on the screen. All infant negative affect was directed away from the image of the mother. When looking briefly back at the screen with a goal to re-engage the mother, the infants showed only neutral or positive affect toward the mother's image.

After this experience, the infants once again were connected to the mother in real time, through the AV system, and both returned to typical, *contingent*, positive interactive behaviors.

Murray demonstrated with 6–8 week olds, as Sander had with 1-week-old infants, that the capacity to engage as an active participant – an *agent* – within a dyadic relationship, to ensure that survival needs are met, is possible only when there is an experience of *contingent responsiveness* on the part of the other. As a result of being unable to determine whether the observed *other* is familiar or strange, the innate reactions of protest (fight) or withdrawal (flee) are *not* possible. Instead, a third innate survival reaction is triggered: that of a dissociated (freeze) state. By contrast, in experiments where the mother and infant were actually face to face, extremely subtle facial changes shown by the mothers who were attempting to hold a 'still face' clearly conveyed to the infant the fact that mother *was still present*, if not responding. Thus, active behaviors were triggered in the infant, in an effort to re-establish the connection that was disrupted.

These specific findings regarding infant agency provide a key understand-ing implicit communication in human figure drawings: it becomes evident that there can be no self-as-agent activated when the other in the self-other relationship, is completely disconnected (dissociated) from the present, in which the self exists.

Human figure drawings reflect dissociative brain states as well as integrated brain process

All human figure drawings are a re-presentation of the experience of self and other at many levels, only some of which are symbolic (Burns 1987; Kaufman and Wohl 1992; Klepsch and Logie 1982; Lewis et al. 1997; Moore 1990a, 1994a; Wohl and Kaufman 1985). What is less well known is the fact that the quality of a drawing, similar to the quality of a rapid eye movement (REM) dream of a non-REM mentation during sleep, is directly dependent on the exact areas of the brain either activated or shut down, at the time the drawing is created or the dream dreamt (Hartmann 1984; Moore 1998). Functional MRI brain scans and EEGs reveal the altered brain activation states involved in dissociative versus integrative processing of information (Conway 1994; Lanius et al. 2003).

Without brain scan or EEG process, can we recognize dissociative process in the human figure drawing of a child or adult with a documented history of interpersonal trauma? Below are the drawings of four 5–6-year-old girls, three of whom were diagnosed with dissociative psychopathology, the fourth having no known history of interpersonal trauma. Each child was asked to draw the best picture of a whole person they could. Each had a pencil with an eraser, and complied with the request comfortably, carefully drawing a whole person.

Dissociative drawings are unique to the individual's dyadic history

Figures 4.1 to 4.3 are examples of drawings of a person by young girls who habitually showed episodes of dissociation when triggered by memories of family trauma and loss. Figure 4.1 was drawn by a 5½-year-old child whose father had died of sudden heart failure two years previously. Her mother had been severely depressed since that time.

Figure 4.1

Figure 4.2 was drawn by a 7-year-old child who had been removed from her biological family at age 3, after extensive physical abuse by the parents was documented. Subsequently, she had been placed in seven foster homes.

Figure 4.2

Figure 4.3 was drawn by a 6½-year-old girl who had been habitually abused both physically and sexually, from infancy.

Figure 4.3

As children, in terms of personality, these three young girls were as different as their drawings are. That is important to remember, because when identifying indicators of dissociation, I stress the fact that every drawing will be a reflection of a known or unknown specific dyadic interpersonal history. Thus, while some drawings are similar, no two will be identical.

Importantly, the same is true for those identifying 'disorganized' behaviors in Strange Situation videos (Ainsworth et al. 1978). Children in attachments with parents who have unresolved interpersonal trauma in their own history show brief, involuntary, highly reactive or dissociative behaviors that are unique to the experience of trauma *within the dyad*. This is why it is difficult to give generalizable examples of 'dissociative indicators' in drawings (Moore 2007, in preparation).

In my years of studying the human figure drawings (HFDs) of children and adults who have documented dissociative episodes, I have found that rather than creating figures with a separate, two-dimensional body, head and limbs, as would be typical of most individuals of any age who are asked to draw a whole person, the HFDs of these individuals are often drawn using a single line to trace the form of the figure or with empty nondescript units placed where a person's limbs would be. I have come to refer to these drawings as 'cookie cutter' or 'rag doll' drawings (Moore 1994a, 1994b). These drawings re-present not a live, vital sense of self-in-relation to a specific other, but the 'idea' of a person, as a concept or an inanimate object drawn on paper, seen from the outside not from the inside. You will see that while this description fits one or more of the drawings, none of the HFDs could be 'predicted' either from the child's history, or the above description.

For comparison, Figure 4.4 is an example of a 'vitalized' drawing of a person, done by a 5-year-old girl with no known history of interpersonal trauma. Her figure is wearing specific items of clothing, identifiable items of jewelry, and her 'glancing eyes' give a sense of the drawing having a kind of vitality, despite obvious distorted aspects to the drawing that indicate the age of the child drawing (Harris 1963; Koppitz 1968).

Figure 4.4

The issue of age appropriateness in a person drawing has been recognized as being a potential indicator of trauma in an individual's history (Moore 1990b). Figures 4.1 to 4.3 above, when scored for developmental age using either the Koppitz (1968) or the Goodenough-Harris scales (Harris 1963), reflect a developmental age more commensurate with each child's history of interpersonal trauma, than her chronological age at the time she did the drawing, again, despite the widely differing appearance of the drawings.

What keeps behavior in a dissociated state, or drawings from dissociative individuals from being predictable?

Look back at the drawings of a person in Figures 4.1 to 4.4 above. As you look at each of the drawings, I would like you to consider your answer to each of these questions:

- What is your physiological response to each of the drawings, individually?
- If you have more of a feeling response than a thinking one, where do you feel it in your body?
- Do you feel anything at all when looking at some of the drawings?
- Judging only from these drawings, which child would you most like to meet?
- Which would you prefer – or least prefer – to have referred as a client?
- Do any of the drawings make you feel disturbed or vaguely frightened?

The questions I am asking are about reactions to drawings that are often from our right hemisphere, responding to the communication from another person's (in this case the artist's) right hemisphere when in a dissociative state. Our innate reactive survival system is alerting us to an interpersonal situation – that is what looking at a human figure drawings triggers in our brains – where there may be unpredictability or even danger. When we cannot make 'sense' of a drawing, when it does not conform to our left-hemisphere knowledge of what a person looks like, or when it leaves us feeling unmoved or cut off, we are feeling some of what the particular artist creating that unique drawing has felt. Human figure drawings carry the potential to alter a *viewer's* neurobiology, by communicating simultaneously to one's reflective, neocortex, as well as mid-brain and brainstem areas especially in the right hemisphere, linking our interpretive self, and our non-interpretive, procedurally developed self-in-relation, affective state.

Traumatic attachment dyads show involuntary reactively contingent and organized behavior when a survival threat is perceived

If the person acting 'at' a child is unknown or unknowable, his or her perception of danger overrides any organized pattern of behavior learned from and based on familiarity. Children in relationships with adults who have chronic dissociative episodes cannot avoid developing dissociative relational behaviors themselves, as part of a procedurally learned attachment pattern (Lyons-Ruth 2001, 2003; Sinason 1994, 1998). When a distressed infant repeatedly confronts a parent who is in a dissociated state, 'repair' of the derailed interaction cannot occur. When dissociation is frequently triggered in interaction with the child, his 'familiar mother' is replaced suddenly, distressingly by someone who looks like mother, but is 'not mother'. The earlier in life the child learns procedurally that direct expression of distress towards the mother is futile, the greater the likelihood that the infant or child's own parasympathetic nervous system will be triggered, in order to decrease the experience of fear or anger. The infant's body will *likely* become the container of somatic symptoms of blocked negative emotions: despair, arousal and anger. Thus, we can see the beginnings of chronic stress, physical anxiety and arousal becoming a connected, self-organizing 'procedural' pattern expressing the capacity to disengage psychologically from interpersonal interaction. Children born to mothers with extreme forms of dissociative identity disorder are therefore very vulnerable.

Dissociative escape when there is no escape within the traumatic attachment relationship

When in extreme fear, or dissociative states, it is not uncommon for individuals to have the experience of being removed from their own body, so that they feel nothing. Often, after near death experiences, individuals report having the experience of being above the scene where their body remains, near to death. There is ample evidence from clinical reports from adults traumatized as children, that when abuse is chronic and or sadistic, there is often a report of the dissociative experience of suddenly looking down from above the scene where abusive acts are being perpetrated on themselves as a child.

Collecting drawings from children with abuse histories over the years, I found that in many instances, very young children drew a scene viewed from above, but did not comment on it. This is highly unusual for young children, as normal development of an aerial perspective normally occurs in late latency or early adolescence. It is clear, however, that the innate dissociative capacity to cut off all sensation from the body when in inescapable pain, is available to all humans as a survival mechanism that is triggered by terror, not thought about.

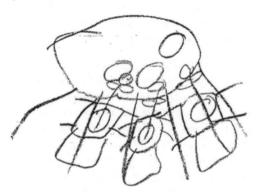

Figure 4.5

Figure 4.5 represents the family drawing of one of the children who drew the earlier human figures. When drawn it was not immediately clear that she had heard the request to draw her family doing something together. Finishing, she said, 'We're at dinner.' Her early history included having been removed from her family of origin when she was found tied into a highchair and being force fed until she vomited. She was 2 years old at the time.

Dissociative states as non-conscious communicative states

Dissociation is *not* a completely non-communicative state, as we once assumed. There is a non-declarative, non-conscious, right-brain to right-brain sharing of knowledge in the non-verbal dissociative state (Bromberg 1991; Chefetz and Bromberg 2004; Ginot 2007; Schore 2002). Our sense that the other is not present with us, paying attention to what is happening in the here and now, is accurate, but only our here-and-now-focused left hemisphere will be disorganized.

Figure 4.6

In conclusion, in Figures 4.5 to 4.8, I have included a second drawing by each of the children whose human figure drawings were represented in Figures 4.1 to 4.4. I have purposely not yet indicated which child drew which second picture. Had you guessed? It has been my experience that it is very difficult, when working with a person of any age with a history of interpersonal trauma to predict what a family drawing will look like, even after seeing a drawing of a person by that individual. In the case of the little girl whose father had died (Figures 4.1 and 4.6), we see that she simply repeated the same undifferentiated shape she had drawn for her person, and added two more overlapping copies of the shape. She did not comment on her drawing, but just before giving her drawing to the examiner, she took the eraser and partially erased one.

And the child who drew her 'family eating dinner' (Figure 4.5) was the one who created a classic 'rag doll' in Figure 4.2. After her abusive infancy, she had been passed from foster-family to foster-family, where further abuse had occurred. She had almost no sense of herself as a person. But being asked to draw her family triggered traumatic abuse that she did not remember consciously. Her bland description of her drawing did not lessen the impact of the image on those who saw what she had drawn.

Figure 4.7

The child who drew the person in Figure 4.7, who is not known to have family trauma or dissociate when stressed, drew a figure that I imagine is identifiable to most readers. It is a 'predictable' person, drawn in the style of her original human figure; however, in this picture, where the family was all to be included, her self drawing is without hands. Finishing this drawing she said, 'Whoops! There isn't room for anyone else!' The difference between these two similar drawings (Figures 4.4 and 4.7) and the dupli-cated, identical 'idea of a person' images drawn by the child whose father had died, is the 'vitality' in the bodies. In Figures 4.1 and 4.6, people are shapes, not individuals. By contrast, in Figure 4.7, we see that this 5-year-old child has again created a person, body part by body part, put clothes on over the limbs and trunk, and given the face an expression. I am sorry there was not room for her family members (all five of them) to fit into the drawing, because we might imagine that each one would be created in a likeness of that individual.

The final drawing included here (Figure 4.8) is a drawing of a whole person, spontaneously volunteered by the child. It was the first drawing done since the original one (Figure 4.3). The child had been in psycho-therapy once weekly for ten months, since the assessment drawing was done. This is not a family drawing. As she finished, she handed it to her therapist, announcing, 'It's me!' A call to her teacher by the therapist revealed the fact that in the ten months she had gone from being a non-reader to a reader, and the school psychologist-administered IQ test had shown a score 29 points above the one she was given at the time of her first drawing. She was still capable of going into extreme dissociative states when she was frightened by something unpredictable in the school or home environment, but she had found a state of herself as an agent, in relationships at school and in therapy. Her human figure drawings let us know that.

Figure 4.8

References

Ainsworth, M.D.S., Blehar, M.C., Waters, E. and Wall, S. (1978) *Patterns of Attachment: A Psychological Study of the Strange Situation*. Hillsdale, NJ: Lawrence Erlbaum.

Beebe, B. and Lachmann, F. (1994) Representation and internalization in infancy: Three principles of salience. *Psychoanalytic Psychology*, 11 (2): 127–65.

Bowlby, J. (1969) *Attachment and Loss*. Volume 1: *Attachment*. London: Hogarth Press and Institute of Psycho-Analysis.

Bowlby, J. (1980) *Attachment and Loss*. Volume 3: *Loss: Sadness and Depression*. London: Hogarth Press and Institute of Psycho-Analysis.

Braten, S. (1993) Infant attachment and self-organization in light of this thesis: Born with the other in mind. In I.L. Gomnaes and E. Osborne (eds) *Making Links: How Children Learn*. Oslo: Yrkeslitteratur.

Bromberg, P.M. (1991) On knowing one's patient inside out: The aesthetics of unconscious communication. *Psychoanalytic Dialogues*, 1 (4): 399–422.

Bromberg, P.M. (1998) *Standing in the Spaces: Essays on Clinical Process, Trauma and Dissociation*. Hillsdale, NJ: Analytic Press.

Burns, R. (1987) *Kinetic-House-Tree-Person Drawings (K-H-T-P): An Interpretive Manual*. New York: Brunner/Mazel.

Chefetz, R.A. and Bromberg, P.M. (2004) Talking with 'Me' and 'Not-Me': A dialogue. *Contemporary Psychoanalysis*, 40: 409–64.

Coates, S.W. and Moore, M.S. (1997) The complexity of early trauma: Representation and transformation. *Psychoanalytic Inquiry*, 17: 286–311.

Conway, A. (1994) Trans-formations of abuse. In V. Sinason (ed.) *Treating Survivors of Satanic Abuse*. London: Routledge.

Cozolino, L. (2006) *The Neuroscience of Human Relationships: Attachment and the Developing Brain*. New York: Norton.

Divino, C., Mrazek, D. and Klinnert, M. (1992) Development of affect, affect regulation and attachment in infancy. Paper presented at the World Association for Infant Psychiatry and Allied Disciplines.

Gallese, V., Keysers, C. and Rizzolatti, G. (2004) A unifying view of the basis of social cognition. *Trends in Cognitive Science*, 8: 396–403.

George, C. and Solomon, J. (1989) Internal working models of caregiving and security of attachment at age six. *Infant Mental Health Journal*, 10 (3): 222–37.

Ginot, E. (2007) Intersubjectivity and neuroscience: Understanding enactments and their therapeutic significance within emerging paradigms. *Psychoanalytic Psychology*, 24 (2): 317–32.

Grigsby, J. and Hartlaub, G. (1994) Procedural learning and the development and stability of character. *Perceptual and Motor Skills*, 79: 355–70.

Grigsby, J. and Stevens, D. (2002) Memory, neurodynamics, and human relationships. *Psychiatry*, 65 (1): 13–34.

Harris, D. (1963) *Children's Drawings as Measures of Intellectual Maturity: A Revision and Extension of the Goodenough Draw-A-Man Test*. New York: Harcourt Brace.

Hartmann, E. (1984) *The Nightmare: The Psychology and Biology of Terrifying Dreams*. New York: Basic Books.

Kaufman, B. and Wohl, A. (1992) *Casualties of Childhood: A Developmental Perspective on Sexual Abuse Using Projective Drawings*. New York: Brunner/Mazel.

Klepsch, M. and Logie, L. (1982) *Children Draw and Tell: An Introduction to the Projective Uses of Children's Human Figure Drawings*. New York: Brunner/Mazel.

Koppitz, E. (1968) *Psychological Evaluation of Children's Human Figure Drawings*. New York: Grune & Stratton.

Lanius, R., Hopper, J.A. and Menon, R.S. (2003) Individual differences in a husband and wife who developed PTSD after a motor vehicle accident: A functional MRI case study. *American Journal of Psychiatry*, 160 (4): 667–9.

Lewis, M.L., Osofsky, J.D. and Moore, M.S. (1997) Violent cities, violent streets: Children draw their neighborhoods. In J.D. Osofsky (ed.) *Children in a Violent Society*. New York: Guilford.

Lyons-Ruth, K. (2001) The two-person construction of defenses: Disorganized attachment strategies, unintegrated mental states, and hostile/helpless relational processes. *Psychologist-Psychoanalyst*, 21: 40–5.

Lyons-Ruth, K. (2003) Dissociation and the parent–infant dialogue: A longitudinal perspective from attachment research. *Journal of the American Psychoanalytic Association*, 51: 883–911.

Malchiodi, C. (1990) *Breaking the Silence: Art Therapy with Children from Violent Homes*. New York: Brunner/Mazel.

Moore, M.S. (1990a) Common cognitive features of dreams and drawings after trauma. Paper presented at the New South Wales Institute of Psychotherapy Training Programme, Australia.

Moore, M.S. (1990b) Understanding children's drawings: Developmental and emotional indicators in children's human figure drawings. *Journal of Educational Therapy*, 3 (2): 35–47.

Moore, M.S. (1994a) Common characteristics in the drawings of ritually abused children and adults. In V. Sinason (ed.) *Treating Survivors of Satanic Ritual Abuse*. London: Routledge.

Moore, M.S. (1994b) Reflections of self: The use of drawings in evaluating and treating physically ill children. In A. Erskine and D. Judd (eds) *The Imaginative Body: Treating Physically Ill Patients in Psychotherapy*. London: Whurr.

Moore, M.S. (1998) How can we remember, but be unable to recall? The complex functions of multimodular memory. In V. Sinason (ed.) *Memory in Dispute*. London: Karnac.

Moore, M.S. (2007) Clinical commentary: Child with neglect and abuse history. *Journal of Child Psychotherapy*, 33 (2): 247–52.

Moore, M.S. (in preparation) Reflections of self: The impact of trauma in children's drawings.

Mortensen, K.V. (1991) *Form and Content in Children's Human Figure Drawings: Development, Sex Differences, and Body Experience*. New York: New York University Press.

Murray, L. and Trevarthen, C.B. (1985) Emotional regulation of interactions between two-month olds and their mothers. In T. Field and N. Fox (eds) *Social Perception in Infants*. Norwood, NJ: Ablex.

Murray, L. and Trevarthen, C.B. (1986) The infant's role in mother–infant communication. *Journal of Child Language*, 13: 15–29.

Rizzolatti, G., Fogassi, L. and Gallese, V. (2006) Mirrors in the mind. *Scientific American*, November: 54–69.

Sander, L. (1964) Adaptive relationships in early mother–child interaction. *Journal of American Academy of Child Psychiatry*, 3: 231–64.

Schore, A.N. (2002) Dysregulation of the right brain: A fundamental mechanism of traumatic attachment and the psychopathogenesis of posttraumatic stress disorder. *Australian and New Zealand Journal of Psychiatry*, 36 (1): 9–30.

Schore, A.N. (2003) Early relational trauma, disorganized attachment, and the development of a predisposition to violence. In D. Siegel and M. Solomon (eds) *Healing Trauma: Attachment, Mind Body, and Brain*. New York: Norton.

Siegel, D.J. (1999) *The Developing Mind: Toward a Neurobiology of Interpersonal Experience*. New York: Guilford.

Sinason, V. (ed.) (1994) *Treating Survivors of Satanist Abuse*. London: Routledge.

Sinason, V. (ed.) (1998) *Memory in Dispute*. London: Karnac.

Stern, D.N. (1985) *The Interpersonal World of the Infant: A View from Psychoanalysis and Developmental Psychology*. New York: Basic Books.

Tronick, E.Z. (2001) Emotional connections and dyadic consciousness in infant–mother and patient–therapist interactions. *Psychoanalytic Dialogues*, 11: 187–94.

Wohl, A. and Kaufman, B. (1985) *Silent Screams and Hidden Cries: An Interpretation of Artwork by Children from Violent Homes*. New York: Brunner/Mazel.

well this day   i falter on the edge of my own encounter   over ridden by myself   her-self .   where will I go   i don't know   will I emerge as the self
Jo, I cannot say.   I fear we have gone too far...........too far into the abyss of my
mind   to her   or is it her-self   coming to my-self.........it feels it cannot ever be
born.......................like two separate pieces of hot metal to solder together..........and
that   that is   beyond screams   beyond sufferance

Jo

Chapter 5

Memory and the dissociative brain

John Morton

The DSM criteria for Dissociative Identity Disorder (DID) includes four components (American Psychiatric Association 1994):

- The presence of two or more distinct identities or personality states.
- At least two of these personality states recurrently take control of the person's behaviour.
- Inability to recall important personal information.
- The problem is not due to substances or a general medical condition.

In this chapter I restrict myself to exploring the nature of the amnesia which is reported between personality states in most people who are diagnosed with DID. Note that this is not an explicit diagnostic criterion, although such amnesia features strongly in the public view of DID, particularly in the form of the fugue-like conditions depicted in films of the condition, such as *The Three Faces of Eve* (1957). Typically, when one personality state, or 'alter', takes over from another, they have no idea what happened just before. They report having lost time, and often will have no idea where they are or how they got there. However, this is not a universal feature of DID. It happens that with certain individuals with DID, one personality state can retrieve what happened when another was in control. In other cases we have what is described as 'co-consciousness' where one personality state can apparently monitor what is happening when another personality state is in control and, in certain circumstances, can take over the conversation.

A further feature of inter-state amnesia is that it appears to be restricted to certain kinds of material. Dorahy (2001) summarises the current research. He concludes: 'research suggests that amnesic barriers between alter personalities are typically impervious to explicit stimuli, as well as conceptually driven implicit stimuli. Autobiographical memory deficits are also experimentally evident in DID' (Dorahy 2001: 771). The focus here will be on explicit stimuli.

The Headed Records framework

In this discussion of inter-state amnesia, the distinction between *dissociation* and *repression* features strongly. The contrast between the two terms bears a family resemblance to their use in other contexts, but is specifically anchored within a particular cognitive psychological framework, that of Headed Records (Morton et al. 1985). I first describe the framework and then return to dissociation and repression.

Headed Records (HR) is a framework for describing the retrieval of individual event representations. 'Record' is the term used to describe mental representations of events. The foundation blocks for the development of the framework were Tulving's (1983) encoding specificity principle and the principles of context-dependent memory and state-dependent learning. The most important principle is that people can remember more about an episode when they are in the same context as they were during the episode itself. This context includes both external and internal factors. To take the external factors first, Godden and Baddeley (1975) looked at deep sea divers. The divers were asked to learn lists of words either on the beach or in 15 feet of water. They were then asked to recall the lists either in the same or in the opposite environment. There was no general effect of the environment, but there was a 40 per cent loss in recall if the learning and recall were in different environments. In a similar fashion, Wilkinson (1988) found that 6-year-old children remembered what had happened on a walk the previous day much better when they were out again on the walk than when they were questioned in a room at school. This also applied to material that was not directly cued by features of the environment (for example, the song they sang in a particular spot).

As an example of the effect of the internal environment, an experiment by Storm and Caird (1967) demonstrated a state-dependent effect in a serial learning task with chronic alcoholic subjects. Subjects learned a list of twelve two-syllable common nouns under the influence of alcohol or without any alcohol. Forty-eight hours later subjects were tested by having them relearn the same list again either under the influence of alcohol or not. Retention was worse in the groups whose relearning state differed from their learning state. In a similar vein, Goodwin et al. (1969) reported a decrement on a number of memory tasks if the subject's state, drunk or sober, was different on learning and recall occasions. These authors also reported examples of alcoholic subjects secreting money and alcohol when drunk, which they were unable to find when sober. However, they managed to recall the hiding places when they were on their next binge. It has also been shown that memory for events is better when the subject is in the same mood as they were at the time of the original event (J.E. Eich 1980; Teasdale and Russell 1983). Baddeley (1990) discusses the experimental work underlying these concepts.

Schacter et al. (1982) treat personal identity in a similar way to external context. They studied a fugue patient, PN, who effectively had access only to autobiographical memory of events that occurred during a period of his life when he had the nickname 'Lumberjack'. Schacter et al. (1982) invoked Estes' (1972) notion of hierarchically organised 'control elements' that can activate or inhibit specific kinds of information that are nested under them. They speculated that the name is 'the ultimate control element' that gave PN access to his 'Lumberjack' days. We can use the general principle here without the particular theory, and suppose that 'self', through the name, acted as a context in a similar way to place or mood in facilitating recall of autobiographical memories. However, while place and mood influence the likelihood of recall, the self cue sometimes seems able to act in an all-or-nothing fashion.

Retrieval and forgetting in the Headed Records framework

Normally, when we take part in an event, we encode information about the event, its context and the outcome. Such information is stored in memory. The function of these memories is to enable us to anticipate and recognise a similar event next time it occurs and plan our actions accordingly. We will also be able to produce a representation of it on a subsequent occasion (recall). Morton et al. (1985) talk about a memory *record* for each event. When trying to recall an autobiographical memory, our central processes search the set of records with some information, which, following Norman and Bobrow (1979), I will call a *description*. So, if I ask you who you were with when you last went to a restaurant, you might search with the term 'restaurant'. It is commonplace that autobiographical memories are not always easy to recall and you may have to think about restaurants you know or friends you dine out with before you get the answer. One possible reason for this difficulty is that not all the information in a record is available for searching. That which is available we term the *heading* (Morton et al. 1985). Successful access to a memory record relies on some level of matching of the description with a heading. Following such a match, the record can be retrieved and processed. The relationship between heading and description is what underlies the context- and state-dependent memory phenomena described in the previous selection. Thus, I suppose that aspects of the context and the individual's internal state are routinely represented both in the headings and in the descriptions. So, the likelihood of a successful match to the target record would be increased when the external context and/or the internal state are the same.

On a computer, headings would correspond to extended file names. Searching file names is far quicker than searching for a word or phrase in a file, as long as the file names are well constructed.

Within this minimal framework, there are a number of ways in which apparent forgetting can occur.

1   No record laid down – this would happen if the processing was inter-rupted before the record could be stored. This can happen following a blow to the head, and may occur as a result of mental shock, such as being threatened with a weapon.
2   Poor encoding – if attention were elsewhere, particular information may not be registered: a record would be made of the relevant event but there could be significant gaps in it.
3   The information is lost through some process of physiological decay.
4   Retrieval is blocked:
   (a)   The normal operation of the retrieval system is such that success-ful access to a more recent memory record with a similar heading will block access to the target record. This is the principle behind the 'misinformation effect'. This is where subjects experience an event and later are presented with incorrect information about the event. This leads to erroneous recall about the event when the misinformation is retrieved instead of the event itself (Bekerian and Bowers 1983; Loftus et al. 1978).
   (b)   The description is appropriate, but there is executive censorship which inhibits the search process.
5   The description does not match the heading – a particular meal you are trying to recall may be classified under the name of the person you were with. If you are searching using the name of the restaurant, there would be no match and no retrieval.
6   The record is retrieved but conscious access is blocked. In this case, the material in the record can be processed in certain ways. For example, there might be an affective response. However, there will be other ways in which it cannot be processed, for example, explicit recall. We will say more about this in the following paragraph. This kind of apparent forgetting corresponds to repression, and contrasts with dissociation, wherein the material is not retrieved at all. Dissociation would arise where conditions 4b or 5 (above) were systematic.

In Figure 5.1, I have diagrammed a simplified version of the relevant aspects of our cognitive processes. The general layout is not controversial. At the centre is a buffer store. Effectively, this is where information which comes in from the environment is interpreted in the light of our previous knowledge. The processing in the buffer store is controlled by the executive. This is responsible for formulating the descriptions, the material used to search the record system, as well as deciding what the current priorities are so far as processing is concerned. In addition, the executive will decide which of the material in the buffer store is allowed into the monitor. Effectively, only

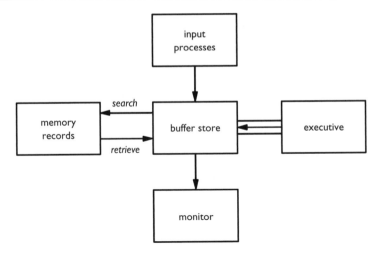

Figure 5.1 A minimum architecture for cognitive processing: the executive contains instructions for controlling the processing of information in the buffer store

material which is allowed into the monitor is available for conscious access. Thus, one of the properties of this system is that material can be retrieved from the memory records and processed in the buffer store without being available to consciousness. This would happen either because the monitor is occupied with other material which has precedence or because there are explicit prohibitions against particular material. Such a prohibition is given as an account for post-hypnotic amnesia. In one experiment, subjects are asked to produce free associations to a list of words. Then, under hypnosis, they are asked to forget about the task they have just performed, but then are given the task again. After this instruction, hypnotically susceptible subjects typically report no recollection of the first task, but nevertheless take much longer over their responses than would be expected if they had no knowledge whatsoever of the first task. In addition, they repeat the response they made the first time round far less than would be expected by chance. The conclusion is that their executive processes are trying to avoid producing the same response as before, an operation which takes time even when it is not consciously employed. Of course, they could not avoid the response unless they had retrieved it in the first place (Smith et al. 1999). This illustrates the phenomenon of repression, mentioned above. With dissociation, no material would reach the buffer store.

We are now in the position to make the bridge to DID. While discussing the effect of context, above, I mentioned the 'lumberjack' case of Schacter et al. (1982). These authors concluded that some notion of *self* could operate as a determinant in the retrieval of autobiographical information. We could generalise from this and suppose that all autobiographical memories contain some representation of our *self* in the headings. Equally, we can suppose that there is a default representation of *self* in all descriptions when we search for memory of actions. The advantage of this is that we will preferentially retrieve autobiographical information relevant to our own experience rather than events we have observed or heard about second- or third-hand. This would be especially useful in childhood, where it might be very inappropriate to act directly in a dangerous situation using methods learned from observing a parent or reading a comic book.

The next stage is to decide how to think about the phenomenon that a particular personality state is 'in control' at any time. While some of the phenomenology is impossible to handle at the moment (it is fair to say that the 'problem of consciousness' has resisted solution in information processing terms up to now) I find it convenient to imagine an analogy with a computer which has a number of users. Only one user can be logged in at any one time, and each user has privileged access to their own files and, occasionally, particular programs. There will, however, be programs and files which can be shared by all users. The personality state in control will, then, be able to report whatever is allowed into consciousness.

From this position it is natural to postulate that, in the case of DID, alternative personality states each have their own *self* markers. Such a marker would be present in the headings of all autobiographical memory records created while a particular personality state was in control. It would also be present in any *description*, the material used to search memory. Thus, at least, there would be a strong bias towards a particular personality state retrieving autobiographical memories which had been laid down while it had been in control. In the limit, it might mean that a personality state could only retrieve such memories and no others. In this case, we would say that there is a full dissociation.

Memory in DID

This, then, is the theory. What about the actual phenomena? Personality states in many patients claim that they experience only events that occur when they are in control and seem not to be able to recall what happened when other personality states were in control. The following dialogue between me (JM) and one of the personality states of KN illustrates the dilemma they find themselves in. Note that BN is one of the other personality states, and A is KN's daughter.

JM: So, tell me . . . what do you remember about today? . . . What was the first thing you remember doing?

KN: Looking around to see where BN was. To see if she was going to take A to school. She wasn't there, then I knew I had to do it.

JM: Sometimes she is there, is she?

KN: [puzzled pause] No. I've never seen her, but I said I'd help out with A and what she tends to do is just dump A and she's gone.

JM: And leaves her with you?

KN: Yeah. I said I'd help out because, because she found it a lot to take on.

Huntjens et al. (2003: 291) argue that 'the patients' denying knowledge of stimulus material learned by another identity should be taken not as objective evidence for an episodic memory impairment in DID but rather as a representation of the patients' subjective experience of amnesia'. Within the model presented above, it could be that the material presented to another personality state is not accessed, or that it is accessed but prevented from entering consciousness. We are interested in distinguishing between these two options. If the material is accessed and is present in the buffer, then it will be able to interfere with processing, even though the event it came from, springing from another personality state, is not acknowledged in consciousness. With the right experiment we can distinguish between these two. In order to control for the possibility of feigned amnesia, it is also important that any experiment include a control group of subjects instructed to pretend to have DID symptoms.

Ludwig et al. (1972) extensively studied one patient with DID symptoms. They found evidence that material learned in one personality state influenced its processing in other states, that is, there was a practice effect across states. They also found distinct differences between personality states in the way emotionally laden words were processed in memory, although emotionally neutral material was processed similarly across states.

Silberman et al. (1985) adopted the approach of assuming that interpersonality amnesia should facilitate 'compartmentalising' memories, and thereby facilitate correctly discriminating lists of words learned by different alters. Each of two alters first learned a list of words, and then both were subsequently tested after a two-hour interval. Although their overall recall and recognition performances were similar to controls, DID subjects did no better than controls in correctly assigning learned words to the personality that had learned them; their patients reported no awareness of hearing stimuli read to a different alter. Despite the subjective experience of separateness and amnesia reported by the DID subjects, there was no evidence of highly dissociated memory operations suggesting such memories had substantially 'leaked' between alters.

The most crucial experiment is that by Huntjens et al. (2003). In this study, one personality state was first of all presented with a list of twenty-four nouns and then asked to recall them. The same list was presented twice more to the same personality state, each time followed by free recall. This is List A. Following this, the second list, List B, was presented in a similar way to another personality state who claimed no knowledge of the first one. The second part of the experiment took place a week later without warning.

It involved the subject being presented with single words and saying whether or not they thought the words had occurred the previous week. The recognition list was made up of all the words from Lists A and B and an equal number of distractor words (new words from the same semantic categories), adding up to ninety-six words. We would expect normal subjects to recognise words from Lists A and B more or less to the same extent, with perhaps a small advantage for the List B, which had occurred more recently. By contrast, very few of the distractor words would be accepted.

Now, let us consider what might happen with DID patients. We have two personality states, X and Y. In the first part of the experiment, state X will be taught List A and state Y will be taught List B. For the second part of the experiment, Huntjens et al. (2003) ran the recognition test on state Y. If the state relationship is dissociative, the subject should recognise the B words as being old but should treat the A words as being new. In other words, there should be no differences seen in the responses to the A words and the distractor words.

Huntjens et al. (2003) ran the test on twenty patients with a diagnosis of DID, where at least one of the identities was reported being completely amnesic for the events experienced by the other participating identity during the experiment. In addition, the experiment was run on fifty normal participants. Half of these were a simple control group and the other half were asked to simulate dissociative amnesia.

For our purposes, the important part of the data is the recognition performance from the second week. In particular, we are interested in whether or not the List A words are rejected, as they should be if the DID patients are fully dissociative. In fact, on average, the DID group accepted 65 per cent of the B words and 50 per cent of the A words. This compares with a mere 14 per cent of the distractor words. For the simulators, the figures were 80 per cent, 69 per cent and 18 per cent respectively. For the controls the figures were 94 per cent, 91 per cent and 22 per cent respectively. For all groups the B words were accepted more often than the A words and there were no differences among the groups in this respect.

The important result is that the level of hits on the List A words for the DID group was well above the level for the distractor words. If there had been a strong dissociation between the personality states, then the A words and distractor words would have been at the same level. It was also the case that the mean values accurately represented the individual scores. There were no individual patients who behaved as one would expect from the dissociative assumption and treated the A words in the same way as the distractor words (Rafaële Huntjens, personal communication). Equally, there was no simulator who was able to achieve the equivalent goal. The differences between the groups in the overall level of performance need not concern us.

Huntjens et al. (2003) comment:

Our results contrast with the reasoning of Eich et al. (1997) and Peters et al. (1998), who claimed that amnesic barriers between identities do show up in explicit memory tests using neutral material. However, we wish to emphasize that the memory measures used in the studies by Eich et al. and Peters et al. should be taken primarily as a representation of the patients' subjective report of interidentity amnesia, whereas the measures used in this study index objective memory performance.

(Huntjens et al. 2003: 295)

Nevertheless, Huntjens et al. thought that the relative lack of compartmentalisation which they found may have been due to the fact that most of the stimuli were emotionally neutral.

I have produced an English version of the first of these experiments and initially ran it on control subjects, largely from the undergraduate population of University College London. There were two groups of subjects. One was instructed about DID and were otherwise treated in the same way as the simulators in Huntjens et al.'s experiment. The second group were given instructions after the initial free recall training on List A according to a directed forgetting protocol. This is to the effect that the material just learned is to be forgotten. Such instructions have proved effective in inducing apparent forgetting in a number of paradigms. In the event, neither group was able to distinguish between the two word lists. The simulator group responded to the words in List B 61 per cent of the time, with List A 48 per cent. The distractor words were accepted only 13 per cent of the time. For the directed forgetting group the respective figures were 59 per cent, 52 per cent and 14 per cent. As in the case of the Dutch subjects, there were no individuals who were capable of performing the task successfully.

This experiment was carried out with KN. To start with I had the cooperation of two of KN's personality states, PN and BN, who denied all direct knowledge of each other (they had exchanged emails). On the first day, PN learned List A and BN learned List B immediately afterwards. No mention was made of any recognition memory test. The following week, using the Huntjens et al. (2003) design, the recognition memory test was run with BN. The data were List B 71 per cent; List A 13 per cent; distractor words zero out of forty-eight. As can be seen, BN treated the List A words very differently from the List B words and almost in the same way as the distractor words. It should be noted that this result came as a great surprise. I had no reason to suppose that the Huntjens et al. (2003) result would not generalise. However, I had the opportunity to replicate the experiment on the same individual. To start with, the following week, again without warning, PN was given the recognition memory test. Recall that she had seen the List A words two weeks previously. In the test, she behaved as though she had never seen the B words (0/24), accepting the A words 63 per cent of the time. Two of the forty-eight distractor words were accepted.

Table 5.1 Probability of accepting a word as having been presented the previous week

	Huntjens		UCL controls		KN				Person with DID XY
	DID	Sim	Sim	DF	Run 1		Run 2		
					BN	PN	DN	JN	
Target words	0.65	0.80	0.61	0.59	0.71	0.63	0.88	0.83	0.46
Non-target	0.50	0.69	0.48	0.52	**0.13**	**0**	**0.04**	**0.13**	0.58
Distractor	0.14	0.18	0.13	0.14	0	0.04	0.13	0.21	0.04

The experiment was begun a second time a week later with two different personality states who also claimed no knowledge of each other. JN learned List A and DN learned List B. The following week, again, without prior warning, DN was presented with the recognition list. She accepted 21/24 (88 per cent) of the List B words, but only one of the List A words. She accepted 6/48 (13 per cent) of the distractor words. The Christmas break then intervened and it was six weeks later before JN could be given the recognition words. She scored 83 per cent with the A words, 13 per cent with the B words and 21 per cent with the distractor words. The larger score with the distractor words could probably be ascribed to the extra time between the learning and the recognition memory test. The complete experiment was run on one person with DID, XY, who scored 46 per cent on List B, 58 per cent with List A and 4 per cent on the distractor words. Like the Dutch patients and all the control subjects, she was unable to discriminate between the two lists.

The data from this experiment are summarised in Table 5.1. It is clear that only KN has been able to distinguish between the two lists. There are two possible explanations for this. The simplest is that her individual personality states have no access at all to material presented to other states. Thus, it is as if the words from the other list have not been presented. This is a full dissociation among the personality states which were tested. The alternative explanation is that KN has a most extraordinary memory which reveals itself in this design but not in straightforward tests of memory, where she is average. Let us consider the achievement. By the time JN was given the recognition memory test KN had seen both Lists A and B six times each in the course of the free recall learning. Then she had responded twice positively and once negatively to the B words and once positively and twice negatively to the A words. All this had happened between six and ten weeks previously. In contrast, no one else has been able to discriminate the two lists just one week after the initial presentations.

It is clear from these data that KN has a deeper inter-state amnesia than anyone else who has been tested using this technique. In terms of the model presented above, the simplest conclusion is that all the patients tested apart from KN are retrieving the memory of the list learned by the other personality state. This material is not allowed into the monitor, and so the individual reports that they have no knowledge of the learning event. However, since the material has been retrieved, and is in the buffer store, it interferes with the task. This is what I have called repression.

Kong et al. (2008) obtained similar results with a further seven DID patients. In this experiment the alter A heard a list of twenty-four neutral words. Shortly after, alter B heard a different list of twenty-four words. A few minutes later alter B saw both sets of words with distractor words in the same way as in the Huntjens experiment. The subjects all accepted a significant number of the A words as being familiar. Similar results were obtained using a physiological response by Allen and Movius (2000), who had alter A learn six words, then switched to alter B, who also learned six words. Then these twelve words and some others were presented to alter B while electrical activity in the brain (ERP) was measured. The ERP activity which followed presentation of the A words was consistent with them having been recognised, although alter B had no conscious recollection of having seen them. This last experiment differs from the Huntjens design in that the lists were very short and the time-scale was immediate, but the result is the same. In terms of the model, we would say that the A words were retrieved into the buffer store and so could exert an influence on the system, although information relevant to the event when these words were presented to alter A was not allowed into the monitor.

The words used by Kong et al. (2008) and by Allen and Movius (2000) were also neutral. Huntjens et al. (2003) speculated as to whether their failure to find dissociation in their experiment was because they had used neutral words. Huntjens and colleagues went on to explore what would happen when words with an emotional content were used in a similar experiment. These included negative words, including sexual ones, and positive words such as 'blossom'. As in the previous experiment, patients subjectively reported complete inter-identity amnesia for the material studied (Huntjens et al. 2007). As with neutral material, however, they found no objective evidence for inter-identity amnesia, treating the words presented to the other alter in the same way as the words they had learned themselves. These authors conclude that dissociators 'seem to be characterised by the *belief* of being unable to recall information instead of an actual retrieval inability' (Huntjens et al. 2007: 788, emphasis in original).

Conclusions

Personality states of DID patients appear to have no conscious recollection of words presented in a list to another alter. On the other hand, with one exception, they cannot distinguish between such words and words they had seen or heard themselves. It seems that we have to conclude, in the terms outlined in Figure 5.1, that, for stimuli of this type, the material is retrieved from the memory records and is processed in the buffer store. Why are they not conscious of the origin of such material? As mentioned in the previous paragraph, Huntjens et al. (2007) suppose this to be attributable to the patient's belief concerning their own memory. They would need to add that the belief itself is not necessarily conscious. For example, some alters regard the whole idea of DID to be ludicrous. To attribute memory loss to belief, then, is not as simple as it sounds. To consider the matter in terms of a cognitive model is less philosophically dangerous. In introducing the Headed Records model, I mentioned that the executive was responsible for controlling the initial access to material and then for controlling whether retrieved information is allowed into the monitor, and thence consciousness. Conditions for conscious recall could have been set up well in the past, and their current operation would not resemble what we would normally regard as a 'belief'. Nevertheless, for all except one of the people with DID who were tested with various versions of the word list experiment, the material was retrieved from memory and not allowed into consciousness. For this, the appropriate term seems to be *repression*. The exception is KN. Her alters did not seem to be at all affected by material presented to others. The conclusion in this case is that the material from other alters is not retrieved into the buffer store at all. In this case, then, we find *dissociation* between alters, even with word lists.

There are two final issues to be discussed. One of them has to do with possible differences between word lists and other material. The second has to do with the difference between KN and the other DID patients. Most of the experiments described here have involved lists of words. These are fairly primitive stimuli. Huntjens et al. (2007) attempted to complicate the material by including emotional words. However, the stimuli remain simple and it is not clear that we can generalise to other material such as events which engage the individual in interaction with others. It could be that such events, with some DID patients, are unretrievable except by the personality state who experienced them. That is to say it would not be surprising to find an individual with personality states who were repressive for some material and dissociative for other material. Indeed, it is possible that we would find a graduation of such material, with the most dissociative, as it were, being memory for abuse or other trauma.

Lastly, we should consider the status of KN, who is clearly rare, but unlikely to be unique. We have seen that she is dissociative between alters for the simplest material. We might speculate, then, what kind of difference there might be between her and the other people with DID who have been tested to date. Three broad possibilities would relate to the initial events leading to the dissociation, what has happened to her between then and now and her current circumstances. To go further would involve going outside the framework of this paper. It is clear, however, that DID is a complex phenomenon that will not be subject to any simple account.

References

Allen, J.B. and Movius, H.L. (2000) The objective assessment of amnesia in dissociative identity disorder using event-related potentials. *International Journal of Psychophysiology*, 38: 21–41.

American Psychiatric Association (APA) (1994) *Diagnostic and Statistical Manual of Mental Disorders*, 4th edn. Washington, DC: APA.

Baddeley, A. (1990) *Human Memory: Theory and Practice*. London: Lawrence Erlbaum.

Bekerian, D.A and Bowers, J.M. (1983) Eyewitness testimony: Were we misled? *Journal of Experimental Psychology: Learning, Memory and Cognition*, 9: 139–45.

Dorahy, M.J. (2001) Dissociative identity disorder and memory dysfunction: The current state of experimental research and its future directions. *Clinical Psychology Review*, 21 (5): 771–95.

Eich, E., Macaulay, D., Loewenstein, R.J. and Dihle, P.H. (1997) Memory, amnesia, and dissociative identity disorder. *Psychological Science*, 8: 417–22.

Eich, J.E. (1980) The cue-dependent nature of state-dependent retrieval. *Memory and Cognition*, 8 (2): 157–73.

Estes, W.K. (1972) An associative basis for coding and organisation. In A.W. Melton and E. Martin (eds) *Coding Processes in Human Memory*. Washington, DC: Winston.

Godden, D.R. and Baddeley, A.D. (1975) Context-dependent memory in two natural environments: On land and underwater. *British Journal of Psychology*, 66 (3): 325–31.

Goodwin, D.W., Powell, G., Bremer, D., Hoine, H. and Stern, J. (1969) Alcohol and recall: State dependent effects in man. *Science*, 163: 1358–60.

Huntjens, R.J.C., Postma, A. and Peters, M.L. (2003) Interidentity amnesia for neutral episodic information in dissociative identity disorder. *Journal of Abnormal Psychology*, 112: 290–7.

Huntjens, R.J.C., Peters, M.L., Woertman, L., Van der Hart, O. and Postma, A. (2007) Memory transfer for emotionally valenced words between identities in dissociative identity disorder. *Behaviour Research and Therapy*, 45 (4): 775–89.

Kong, L.L., Allen, J.J.B. and Glisky, E.L. (2008) Interidentity memory transfer in dissociative identity disorder. *Journal of Abnormal Psychology*, 117: 686–92.

Loftus, E.F., Miller, D.G. and Burns, H.J. (1978) Semantic integration of verbal information into a visual memory. *Journal of Experimental Psychology: Human Learning and Memory*, 4 (1): 19–31.

Ludwig, A.M., Brandsma, J.M., Wilbur, C.B., Bendfeldt, F. and Jameson, D.H. (1972) The objective study of a multiple personality: Or, are four heads better than one? *Archives of General Psychiatry*, 26 (4): 298–310.

Morton, J., Hammersley, R.H. and Bekerian, D.A. (1985) Headed records: A model for memory and its failures. *Cognition*, 20: 1–23.

Norman, D.A. and Bobrow, D.G. (1979) Descriptions: An intermediate stage in memory retrieval. *Cognitive Psychology*, 11: 107–23.

Peters, M.L., Uyterlinde, S.A., Consemulder, J. and Van der Hart, O. (1998) Apparent amnesia on experimental memory tests in dissociative identity order: An exploratory study. *Consciousness and Cognition*, 7: 27–41.

Schacter, D.L., Wang, P.L., Tulving, E. and Freedman, M. (1982) Functional retrograde amnesia: A quantitative case study. *Neuropsychologia*, 20 (5): 523–32.

Silberman, E.K., Putnam, F.W., Weingartner, H., Braun, B.G. and Post, R.M. (1985) Dissociative states in multiple personality disorder: A quantitative study. *Psychiatry Research*, 15: 253–60.

Smith, C., Morton, J. and Oakley, D.A. (1999) Hypnotic amnesia and the suggestibility of goal oriented recollection: Evidence for preconscious output inhibition? *Contemporary Hypnosis*, 16: 253–4.

Storm, T. and Caird, W.K. (1967) The effects of alcohol on serial verbal learning in chronic alcoholics. *Psychonomic Science*, 9: 43–4.

Teasdale, J.D. and Russell, M.L. (1983) Differential effects of induced mood on the recall of positive, negative and neutral words. *British Journal of Clinical Psychology*, 22: 163–71.

Tulving, E. (1983) *Elements of Episodic Memory*. Oxford: Oxford University Press.

Wilkinson, J. (1988) Context effects in children's event memory. In M.M. Gruneberg, P. Morris and R.N. Sykes (eds) *Practical Aspects of Memory: Current Research and Issues*. Chichester: Wiley.

do you know what I think   too that there are for Me, Us, definite
stages/phases that define dissociation/dissociating journey........................i am sure i
am just writing the obvious but it sort of amazes me as Jo, for me as
Jo.....................and I dictate very little as Jo, the parts dictate timing, exposure,
they re-write My life journey   how very strange is that?!   They begin to
build Me from the inside out......................and yet it is from the outside in too and
that equals agonies............sort of end of....................not sure i am making sense   to
you................i think i am trying to understand my journey...........

                                                                                    Jo

No-one else wants to understand, do they. They don't want to believe this could be going on under their noses. The cult leave people with mental health problems and so when they tell someone outside the cult people believe they are mad. So they carry on being in the cult because it is safer than escaping and no-one will help them get out. And so the cult gets their next generation because no-one believed the people who tried to escape. We don't want to be part of the cult and have carried on speaking out but only at our own expense. We have accepted the police will never arrest them because of our mental health history and how the police failed us. We are evidence that if you try to leave then no-one believes you and you end up going back because there is no other place to go.

David

Chapter 6

A clinical exploration of the origin and treatment of a dissociative defence

Margaret Wilkinson

Theoretical background and discussion

I wish to consider the origins of the dissociative response to new and challenging experience and the treatment of a young girl (who I shall call Rona), who experienced severe and very early relational trauma. Rona's experience seems to catch something of the development of the dissociative defence, in terms of the evolving symbolisations that may arise from it in the developing mind of an adolescent. As I have written this chapter I have found myself wondering how the dissociative defence would have manifested itself in Rona in adulthood if therapy had not been available to her in this crucial formative period.

Birth may be the first traumatic experience that a human being may encounter and that some babies enter the world in at best a surprised and at worst a severely shocked state of being. Of course we should not underestimate the prebirth trauma that some babies experience within the womb. Such trauma occurs when the baby to be has an inadequate intrauterine experience, whether caused by natural hormones that are produced when the mother becomes unduly stressed which then cross the placenta or street drugs shared by the mother with her developing child in the same way, or whether through physiological deficiencies. Antenatal care for mothers and their unborn children, such as the Solihull Approach (Douglas 2010), where the focus is on the relational from the very beginning, may go some way to prevent the trauma that my patient Rona and her mother experienced in the earliest phase of their relationship.

Each baby, whatever their earliest experience, enters the world in an unassociated state of being and through a meaningful relationship with its primary caregiver (usually, but not necessarily, the mother) gradually begins to make sense of his or her new world. The way the baby is able to achieve this is through the powerful affective engagement which occurs between mother and baby. As Schore reminds us, 'the mother's face is the most potent visual stimulus in the baby's world' (Schore 2002: 18), and as such becomes the most powerful affective stimulus for the baby's expectation of what relating to another will mean. Research demonstrates that the baby's right hemisphere is on line from birth and available for the affective engagement between mother and baby that gradually builds the baby's brain-mind, the mother's right orbital frontal cortex acting as a template for the development of the baby's right orbital frontal cortex that will become the emotional executive control centre for the new human being that baby will become (Schore 2003).

It becomes clear that the mother through the responsivity of her right hemisphere nurtures her baby with a responsive sensitivity and through this also develops its mind. In optimal circumstance a settled mother is able to allow her baby experiences of warmth, affection, love, joy, hope and delight through the medium of her right orbital frontal cortex as it is stimulated by the baby; that stimulation is revealed in her eyes, her facial expressions, her empathic ability to nurture, gradually repeated positive experiences over time between mother and baby builds the baby's capacity to experience a sense of self that is 'simultaneously fluid and robust' (Bromberg 2006: 32). Significantly the baby develops neural pathways that mirror the neural pathways that have been activated in the mother's right hemisphere. The mother's feeling states therefore directly determine the earliest feeling states of her infant, gradually building the patterns in the baby's developing mind that this new human being will use to determine how future relational experience will be, based on that earliest experience. In contrast a troubled mother will convey her sadness, anger, frustration, anxiety, fear or terror equally directly to her baby. Bucci describes these early experiences offered by the mother as 'repeated episodes with a common affective core, involving other persons in relation to the self' (Bucci 1997: 195). Sadly when such experiences with the mother are negative ones, they will become the precedents that will determine the child's future expectations from life and relationship, just as surely as precedent determines future decision-making in a court of law.

These patterns in the mind establish the nature of the attachment that builds between mother and baby and which in turn determines the nature of attachments that the child will expect to make with others. The baby may early learn to avoid the mother's eyes because what the baby experiences from his mother's fearful eyes is waves of anxiety and fear; such early learned anxiety may manifest in the consulting room later as a rather formless anxiety, a generalised dread that trouble is always around the corner. Another baby may deal with such anxiety by seeking to cling to its mother because it has been impossible to build a sufficient sense of safety and well-being to venture confidently into the world. The children who have become the most confused and shocked by what has been offered form what has become identified as a disorganised attachment to the mother. They cannot discern whether to avoid or to move closer to mother, to dread or to cling, their emotional world is filled with confusion, there is no clear path that they may follow that will take them confidently out into a world of successful relating. As Bromberg points out, 'unintegratable affect . . . threatens to disorganise the internal template on which one's experience of self-coherence, self-cohesiveness, and self-continuity' (Bromberg 2003: 689). For these children the first intimate relationship has been fundamentally flawed. Perry and his colleagues stress that such 'acute adaptive states, when they persist, can become maladaptive traits' (Perry et al. 1995: 271). Such babies are therefore seriously at risk of developing a dissociative response, not only to exceptionally painful experience but also to much new experience which feels too frightening or too confusing to be held in mind.

What I have tried to do so far is to locate the dissociative response to life challenges firmly in the relational, and arising from the earliest relation. Poor early experience is held in implicit memory, in the memory store of the right hemisphere, unavailable to conscious mind. It is to hippocampal function in the later developing left hemisphere that one must look for explicit or autobiographical memory that may be recalled at will. If earliest experience has provided sufficient security, there is some protection from the worst that life may hurl at the individual later. Fosha (2003: 228) points out that 'the roots of resilience are to be found in the sense of being understood by and having the sense of existing in the mind and heart of a loving, attuned and self-possessed other'. The avoidant, or clingy, or disorganised response of the insecure baby may lead the growing child to defend from further experience by a damping down, or more seriously a complete switching off of affect when opportunities for new intimacy arise. This child at school may seek to keep others at a distance, may look at another with fear in their eyes as if the new person in their world be it family, friend, professional carer or teacher were an ogre. Where the earliest foundations of the personality are flawed, then the challenges that life brings become likely to overwhelm the nascent self and to switch off becomes the preferred defensive manoeuvre that seems to work for the present crisis but which is damaging when it becomes fixed and inflexible. Such challenges to the developing self may arise through accident, illness or abuse. A child seriously hurt through an accident or overwhelmed by illness may experience the efforts of those who seek to help as attacks, and just as abuse whether physical, psychological or sexual leads to dissociative traits so these traumas may also evoke a dissociative response.

Bromberg (2008), concentrating on affect, notes that a coherent sense of self, of who one is and how one may go forth into the world is defined by who the parents perceive one to be and suggests that when the parents are unable to relate to the child as he or she actually is that constitutes a disconfirmation which 'because it is relatively non-negotiable, is traumatic by definition . . . and accounts for much of what we call developmental trauma' (Bromberg 2008: 424). Kradin (2007), turning his attention to cognitions, draws our attention to the effects of disinformation from the parents on the child's sense of being parented. He draws our attention to the 'crude parental imagos' that can develop when an early caregiver fails to provide good enough experience in this respect (Kradin 2007: 3).

Davies (1996) characterises such early traumatic experiences as

> dyadic experiences which are not yet assimilable [and suggests that metaphorically they roam] the mind in a hungry search for vulnerable moments, using their magnetic charge to disrupt the established order and to pull the patient into all forms of mystifying, inexplicable enactment.
>
> (Davies 1996: 563)

Nijenhuis and Van der Hart (1999) have outlined for us the effects of traumatic experience. They define dissociative defence mechanisms as primary if the individual is distanced from the experience which is available only in flashbacks, secondary if the different aspects of experience become dissociated from one another (affect from meaning for example) and tertiary if several dissociated identities with different schemas emerge during the therapy (Nijenhuis and Van der Hart 1999). A patient who suffers from the most severe structural dissociation, arising for instance from early experience of torture, suffers the complexities of severe dissociative identity disorder (DID) and manifests many vertical splits, with sub-personalities and lacks having a coherent inner core that would allow them to move seamlessly between the different aspects of personality which emerge in different contexts (Wilkinson 2006). Reinders et al. (2003) researched such inner splits in a small group of patients with the diagnosis of DID. They concluded that the emotional personality, who they describe as TPS, becomes stuck in the traumatic experience that persistently fails to become a narrative memory of the trauma, whereas coping, adaptive self within the person who they describe as the neutral personality (NPS), is characterised by avoidance of the traumatic memories, detachment, numbing, and partial or complete amnesia. They conclude that each displays a different psychobiological response to trauma memories, which includes a different sense of self. Nijenhuis and his colleagues, summarising research in this area, concluded that treatment must be geared to 'integration of feared mental contents in ways that are adapted to the current integrative capacity of the patient' (Nijenhuis et al. 2004: 2).

But what is the likelihood of a successful outcome to therapy with one hurt in such a fundamental way? Fosha (2003: 223) reminds us that 'through just one relationship with an understanding other, trauma can be transformed and its effects neutralized or counteracted'.

> Patterns in the mind become the essential key to our understanding of the processes underlying the change that occurs in therapy . . . their

change and development are triggered by experience such that new connections arise directly out of new experience. Thus the experience-dependent plasticity of the mind-brain-body becomes the key to understanding the possibility of changing minds and the learning that can take place in psychotherapy'.

(Wilkinson 2010a: 2)

Case vignette: Rona

In thinking about children who may be experienced by their mother as a catastrophe from the beginning, I was reminded of Rona (Wilkinson 2010b). When I encountered Rona she was 11 years old and was referred to me for counselling within a school setting. I saw her on a regular basis several times a week for her first three years of secondary school and then once a week for the last two years. Even before her birth Rona's mother experienced her as unknown, unwanted and feared. Rona was a first and very late child, whose birth difficulties were compounded by poor early experience. Her mother had not realised that she was pregnant but rather had assumed the cessation of her monthly periods indicated that, far from being pregnant, she was now past that stage of life. Recounting the arrival of her daughter it was clear that the notion had been so alien to her and so completely not wanted by her that it had seemed to her if she had not known what was happening to her until her waters broke and then she had waited several days before enlisting medical help. This neglect must have threatened the very existence of her daughter-to-be and seems to have represented an unconscious attempt to avoid the experience that was about to come and the arrival of her child. This may well indicate the mother's own tendency towards a dissociative defence in the face of trauma associated with the relational. She recounted her experience of giving birth as being catastrophic, she felt she had let herself down, that she had gone to pieces completely. She went on to describe their early days together in hospital as very difficult. She felt Rona's emotional difficulties in relating were caused by the formula milk that she had been given in hospital. I understand that symbolically to be a description of the difficulties they both experienced in that earliest phase of coming to know one another. Her mother, with unconscious cruelty, told her that she was the 'ugly duckling who was given the chance to become a swan'. Rona told me this as she sought to draw a picture of two swans which turned into a picture of two ducks; she commented, 'It's easier to do ducks isn't it?' She was deeply aware of not being what her mother and others wanted her to be.

Rona's difficult early experience was further complicated by a severe squint which must have made it difficult to 'see things as they really were' and painful surgery for this at 3 years old, a hospitalisation which seems to have recapitulated in a distressing way her poor early experience, reinforcing what one might think of as early trauma patterns in the mind leading to an expectation of that new experience would feel persecutory.

Rona was a lonely child who had spent most of her time with her ageing parents. She lacked the social skills which would have allowed her to engage effectively with other children; instead she had developed a pretend world peopled by constantly changing characters, interaction with whom occupied most of her waking moments. In the real world of school Rona was constantly bullied, despite considerable input from a skilled team of staff with very clear policies about bullying and strategies for dealing with it. Rona not only was persecuted outwardly by both boys and girls, but also felt attacked from within, especially by her changing experience of her body, and by the monthly onset of her period in particular. Both the bullying and the changing states of her body caused her acute distress: she would end up in tears which she then felt bad about and which caused further fragmentation of the self.

Rona's world was full of what superficially seemed like rapidly changing make-believe, but which I understood as manifestations of these alienated, dissociated aspects of her self, and her struggles to relate to others. It is difficult in a short space to convey the fragmented, dissociated, disorientated and disorientating quality of the inner world experience that Rona came to share with me. Indeed one of the hazards of writing such a clinical paper seems to be the danger of imposing an order on material so that the reader may comprehend something of the work at the expense of creating a sense of the utter fragmented inner chaos with which the patient presents at the beginning of therapy. However, Rona did remain able to distinguish between her inner world which she described as 'in pretend' and the real world. It may be that this capacity to distinguish between the two helped her to keep psychosis at bay. She found a good experience of relationship with an older female cousin who may have provided an accepting attachment which helped Rona to survive emotionally. She almost always began talking to me with the phrase 'in pretend' and then there would be an implicit invitation to venture together into a world that was far more real to her than what she knew to be the real world. In the outside world she had little idea how to manage, 'in pretend' she was sometimes persecuted but sometimes a star. At the beginning of our work together I felt that the real Rona was virtually inaccessible. It felt as if she was behind a wall of solid glass and that any attempts to interpret might shatter this and destroy her. In the first months of our work I felt that 'pretend' was a world where Rona moved freely but where I was left out, was confused and felt as if I was in a maze and unable to find my way. Only gradually did I come to realise how much Rona herself was a prisoner of her inner world and the cruelty that she encountered there.

Early in therapy Rona showed some awareness of the defensive nature of her pretend world: she explained that her special world had first come about when she was hiding behind the sofa watching an excerpt from *Dr Who*. She felt as if she heard Dr Who saying to her, 'If you are frightened come into my world and I will look after you'. Rona struggled with her sense of the utter reality of her special world and her knowledge that in fact it was hallucinatory, it only existed 'in pretend'. Dr Who was for her a powerful figure who protected her in her inner fragmented world.

As I reflect on my experience with Rona that came early in my career, I am reminded of Kalsched's (1996) later work concerning the way in which unbearable experience stimulates archetypal images and often contains a powerful protector/persecutor figure within the structure of the personality who actively seeks to guard the true self, from annihilation.

When I saw Rona much of the work from the world of trauma and neurobiology which currently informs our understanding of dissociated states had not yet been written. Jung's notion of inner persons in the psyche, indeed in his own psyche, informed my work and thus I learned to understand Rona's fantasies much as dreams, and to understand each figure from within as an aspect of the fragmented self. Now I would understand these figures as images emerging from the implicit, from earliest memory of relational experience, lodged in the right hemisphere, unavailable to conscious mind, or explicit hippocampal memory but emerging in the form of images which could be felt, thought about and talked about. Early communication between mother and child is an implicit, automatic process, occurring at levels beneath conscious awareness and which gives to all future expectations of how relationships with other people will go.

When we returned from the first holiday break of two weeks I found that Rona's pretend world had become peopled with a cruel mother and a little Rona whose legs were broken. At an unconscious level Rona often struggled with her mother's unconscious fantasies of wanting there to be no baby right from the very beginning and fantasies of damage done to her mother and of a damaged baby. Fonagy (1991) warns of the dire consequences for the child's robust development of mind if the child has to confront the parent's unconscious wish to harm the child. Rona was also aware that her mother had some difficulty with walking – the result of a childhood illness – and this was often reflected in the material that was brought.

Rona described the terrible time she had had 'in pretend' over the break: her mother 'in pretend' had not wanted her to be born, she had tried to have an abortion, she had broken Rona's legs giving birth, she had whipped her, stabbed her in the legs and left her unconscious and in a coma. However, in her fantasy the end of the story was rewritten: Rona was taken to hospital where she was adopted by a wonderful father, whose wife then died. She became his wife and helped to look after the children. Interpretation in terms of her distress at her loss of me brought relief and 'pretend' became more benign. At this stage her persecutory images reflected something of her own mother's feelings around her pregnancy and the birth of her child as well as containing oedipal fantasy. Inevitably there was almost always a bully in her inner world, one whose name was very similar to her own name, dominated and was a constant reflection of her experience of being bullied in the outer world and perhaps part of the reason why she so easily became the target for those bullies who reacted at an unconscious level to her inner vulnerability. As the therapy developed Rona's internal world became less persecutory, some of the cruel figures emerged less frequently; instead it seemed that one of the most exciting roles in pretend was to find herself cast as the principal boy in pantomime. It was clear that she had found a role where she could star, without having to struggle with becoming a woman, something she had learned to fear 'with her mother's milk'.

Slowly the work had become grounded in the relational, Rona explored the quality of our relationship in very concrete ways, for example she brought food and drink to her sessions, reflecting her uncertainty that I would give her a good feed and her long established self-care system reflecting an early giving-up of hope for something from the other. At first the drink she brought was frozen squash; she would suck at the ice, quite literally a chilling image of her notion of what I might have to offer her and a reflection of her earliest experiences of feeding which her mother had described as catastrophic. Her mother said that she felt she had a baby who never stopped crying, a baby who she rocked and rocked and yet who remained rigid in her arms. Later when she began to trust me and the possibility of good experience in the room, Rona began to bring a flask but as she poured herself a drink, she found it difficult to know when her cup was full and there was lots of exploration of spills and cleaning them up. Later it was as if she changed on to solids: she began to bring food, buns and biscuits that she would cram into her mouth at the moments when she was in greatest distress. Meanwhile in school the unremitting bullying continued, in spite of very considerable efforts from the staff to prevent it, but gradually she became more able to deal with it and both the bullying and its capacity to devastate her diminished somewhat.

At the beginning of the work the world of pretend had been incoherent, full of change, peopled with figures that persecuted as well as those who became friends, all changing with bewildering speed in the early days of our work together. Gradually 'pretend' became less fragmented and characters remained part of the narrative for longer periods of time. Towards the end of therapy, and after much interpretation of her feelings and fears about my anger, her anger with me and her fears that I might go away, there was a marked difference in the narrative that she brought in that both the bully and the cruel mother had ceased to feature as significant characters in her inner world. Gradually she seemed to reclaim aspects of herself. An important and enduring character emerged called Kemi, a very shy but very likeable girl; together we began to understand Kemi as the 'key to me' when crucially Rona began to be able to acknowledge her shyness and also her likeability.

When she was 16 it seemed important that she was given a chance to separate a little more from her parents and so she went to live with her cousin in another town for her college years and her work with me came to an end. As I write I find myself wondering whether there was also the meaning of 'keep me', hidden in the name, Kemi, which emerged as her therapy began to draw to an end; a hope that had not been possible in her earliest days when her mother's unconscious fantasies were of annihilation of an unwanted child. At the time I did not see it as the expression of the hidden hope that I might be able to hold her in mind, just as she might strive to internalise me. At the same time there were fantasies in which she had girlfriends with whom she could cope with the world; imaginary romantic attachments to young male figures from the world of entertainment also began to develop as she began to experience a more benign world among her peers and to begin the developmental journey into young adulthood.

Concluding discussion

Patterns in the mind arise from earliest experience and its processing by the early developing right hemisphere. Such 'imprinted patterns of neural excitation' (Bar-Yam 1993: 2) determine our ways of being and behaving throughout life. Rona's earliest experiences with her mother, the failure of bonding that resulted for both of them, her very lonely experience of growing up with insensitive and 'switched off' rather than deliberately cruel parents nevertheless led her to anticipate the worst, to retreat from hurt into her pretend world. This retreat from the relational in the real world often brought about just what she most feared as she experienced bullying and rejection at school.

Patients such as Rona have substantial difficulties with self-regulation, a deficit arising out of failure in the earliest attachment and the affect-regulating processes associated with it. I came to understand Rona's multiplicity of characters within as budding attempts of the mind to represent as yet inassimilable experiences, to transform emotion that had remained encapsulated in the emotional brain and in the body into feeling, its mental representation. Damasio (2003: 88) defines the essential content of a feeling as the mapping of a particular body state and explains that the substrate of a feeling is the set of neural patterns that map that particular body state from which a mental image can emerge. He observes: 'emotions play out in the theatre of the body. Feelings play out in the theatre of the mind' (Damasio 2003: 28). Rona struggled with undigested contents that spewed out over us again and again, much in the way she struggled with vomiting as a response to the inner pain that menstruation aroused in her.

Schutz (2005: 16) suggests that the 'most complex imagery of prediction and anticipation of what might come to be' may arise from right brain activity as it seeks to manage negative emotions such as threat, dread and fear. The meaning-making process in therapy may be understood as bringing about transformations by grasping the emotions underlying patients' narrations 'in such a way that they feel it is understood and shared' thus developing a sense of self in the world (Ferro 2005: 100). Over time Rona and I began to be able to understand together, albeit very slowly, the characters that emerged in her inner world as aspects of herself, and gradually it became clearer to her that her pretend world actually was her own inner landscape peopled with the fragmented aspects of herself.

With Rona I learned to think carefully about the patient's level of arousal towards the end of the session. Schore and Schore's (2008) work emphasises the need to help the patient to regulate affect in order to be able to work effectively. In particular I attend carefully to the last third of the session in order to help the patient's level of arousal to be appropriately regulated so that they may leave the session in a safe state of mind. Often Rona would find managing the beginning and end of the session difficult; she started her work with me with a very poor sense of time and she struggled with basic reality. By the time she finished therapy, this was no longer a difficulty. When I first saw her she spoke only in disjointed broken phrases; by the time she left she was speaking in sentences and had become successful academically in a way which had not been forecast by teachers or her educational psychologist. From her point of view when she began she could not manage relationships with her peers; they would always end in tears. When she came to finish she had begun to look on new relationships with a sense of hope rather than a certainty of hurt. I came to understand at a deep level that the secure affective therapeutic relationship with a reliable other over time enables the affect regulation that makes the establishing of stable relationships possible, along with the development of a coherent narrative, and a more coherent sense of self.

Shedler (2010), in his ground-breaking discussion of the efficacy of psychodynamic therapy, cites research (Castonguay et al. 1996) that indicates that the quality of the relationship established with the therapist, the working alliance, or therapeutic alliance, along with the capacity for experiencing, particularly the gaining of 'awareness of previously implicit feelings and meanings' (both of which he understands as distinctive features of psychodynamic technique), rather than interventions aimed at cognitive change, that are the best predictors of 'patient improvement on all outcome measures' (Shedler 2010: 104). Andrade (2005) suggests that the cognitive development that occurs both in early development and in therapy as 'spontaneously blossoming from the affective nucleus' (Andrade 2005: 677). Thus I conclude that progress in therapy will be through the affective encounter rather than merely our left-brained cognitive interpretations, especially with those patients, such as Rona, for whom early relational trauma has marred the earliest stages of affective development, Sinason (2006: 51) has also warned that in past psychoanalytic thinking and practice 'to cope with the privileged access to the mind of the client a split has been made that excludes the body'. Andrade (2005) argues that

> the affective relationship seems to have a real part to play in expanding neural circuits in the cognitive area, with an increase of its regulation of affects . . . [bringing about] a restructuring of what is properly termed psychic ego through body ego.
>
> (Andrade 2005: 692)

I would also emphasise the importance of an attuned engagement with the patient involving the whole therapist for successful work with pervasive early trauma. With McCluskey et al. I understand the attuned therapist to be one who is 'engrossed, modulates response, provides input, and facilitates exploration' (McCluskey et al. 1997: 1,268, emphasis in original). Earliest affective experiencing depends on the tone and musicality, the rhythm and lilt of the mother's voice, so affective experiencing of the therapist depends in part on the therapist's ability to speak in 'pastel not primary' colours (Williams 2004). This involves working in a 'right brained' empathic way; researchers now suggest that the discovery of mirror neurons has provided a potential neural mechanism that mediates how we understand other people's actions and intentions (Gallese 2007). It also requires a 'left brained' reflective approach, the mirroring of which enables the development of the reflective capacity within the patient. These insights are of crucial significance for our understanding of ways of working with patients such as Rona. I believe that the change in Rona came about not primarily through my developing her understanding of the difference between reality and pretend but rather through the quality of the relationship that was established between us, her freedom to explore and express feelings about her changing body, and the opportunity our time together offered for the process of the emergence of the implicit and the chance to reflect upon it together.

Note

The biographical case material presented here is composite and in what Gabbard (2000: 1073) has termed 'thick disguise' in order to preserve confidentiality.

References

Andrade, V.M. (2005) Affect and the therapeutic action of psychoanalysis. *International Journal of Psychoanalysis*, 86: 677–97.

Bar-Yam, Y. (1993) *Sleep as Temporary Brain Dissociation*. NECSI Research Report YB-0005. Available at http//necsi.org.

Bromberg, P.M. (2003) One need not be a house to be haunted: On enactment, dissociation, and the dread of 'not-me' – a case study. *Psychoanalytic Dialogues*, 13 (5): 689–709.

Bromberg, P.M. (2006) *Awakening the Dreamer: Clinical Journeys*. New York: Analytic Press.

Bromberg, P.M. (2008) MENTALIZE THIS! Dissociation, enactment, and clinical process. In E.L. Jurist, A. Slade and S. Burger (eds) *Mind to Mind: Infant Research, Neuroscience, and Psychoanalysis*. New York: Other Press.

Bucci, W. (1997) *Psychoanalysis and Cognitive Science: A Multiple Code Theory*. New York: Guilford.

Castonguay, L.G., Goldfried, M.R., Wiser, S.L., Raue, P.J. and Hayes, A.M. (1996) Predicting the effect of cognitive therapy for depression: A study of unique and common factors. *Journal of Consulting and Clinical Psychology*, 64: 497–504.

Damasio, A.R. (2003) *Looking for Spinoza: Joy, Sorrow, and the Feeling Brain*. London: Heinemann.

Davies, J.M. (1996) Linking the 'pre-analytic' with the postclassical: Integration, dissociation, and the multiplicity of unconscious process. *Contemporary Psychoanalysis*, 32 (4): 553–76.

Douglas, H. (2010) Our culture and the parent–child relationship: Supporting emotional health through the Solihull Approach. Paper given at the Solihull Approach in Kent Conference, Maidstone, 23 March.

Ferro, A. (2005) *Seeds of Illness, Seeds of Recovery: The Genesis of Suffering and the Role of Psychoanalysis*, trans. P. Slotkin. Hove: Brunner-Routledge.

Fonagy, P. (1991) Thinking about thinking: Some clinical and theoretical considerations in the treatment of a borderline patient. *International Journal of Psychoanalysis*, 76: 639–56.

Fosha, D. (2003) Dyadic regulation and experiential work with emotion and relatedness. In M.F. Solomon and D.J. Siegel (eds) *Healing Trauma, Attachment, Mind, Body, and Brain*. New York: Norton.

Gabbard, G.O. (2000) Disguise or consent. *International Journal of Psychoanalysis*, 81 (6): 1071–86.

Gallese, V. (2007) Before and below 'theory of mind': Embodied simulation and the neural correlates of social cognition. *Philosophical Transactions of the Royal Society: Biological Sciences*, 362: 659–69.

Kalsched, D. (1996) *The Inner World of Trauma: Archetypal Defenses of the Human Spirit*. London: Routledge.

Kradin, R.L. (2007) Minding the gaps: The role of informational encapsulation and mindful attention in the analysis of the transference. *Journal of Jungian Theory and Practice*, 9 (2): 1–13.

McCluskey, U., Roger, D. and Nash, P. (1997) A preliminary study of the role of attunement in adult psychotherapy. *Human Relations*, 50: 1261–73.

Nijenhuis, E.R.S. and Van der Hart, O. (1999) Forgetting and reexperiencing trauma. In J. Goodwin and R. Attias (eds) *Splintered Reflections: Images of the Body in Trauma*. New York: Basic Books.

Nijenhuis, E.R.S., Van der Hart, O. and Steele, K. (2004) Trauma-related structural dissociation of the personality. *Trauma Information Pages*. Available at www.trauma-pages.com/a/nijenhuis-2004.php.

Perry, B.D., Pollard, R.A., Blakley, T.L., Baker, E.W.L. and Vigilante, D. (1995) Childhood trauma, the neurobiology of adaptation, and 'use-dependent' development of the brain: How 'states' become 'traits'. *Infant Mental Health Journal*, 16 (4): 271–91.

Reinders, A.A.T.S., Nijenhuis, E.R.S., Paans, A.M.J., Korf, J., Willemsen, A.T.M. and Den Boor, J.A. (2003) One brain, two selves. *NeuroImage*, 20: 2119–25.

Schore, A.N. (2002) Dysregulation of the right brain: A fundamental mechanism of traumatic attachment and the psychopathogenesis of posttraumatic stress disorder. *Australian and New Zealand Journal of Psychiatry*, 36 (1): 9–30.

Schore, A.N. (2003) *Affect Regulation and the Repair of the Self*. New York: Norton.

Schore, J.R. and Schore, A.N. (2008) Modern attachment theory: The central role of affect-regulation in development and treatment. *Clinical Social Work Journal*, 36: 9–20.

Schutz, L.E. (2005) Broad-perspective perceptual disorder of the right hemisphere. *Neuropsychology Review*, 15 (1): 11–27.

Shedler, J. (2010) The efficacy of psychodynamic psychotherapy. *American Psychologist*, 65 (2): 98–109.

Sinason, V. (2006) No touch please: We're British psychodynamic practitioners. In G. Galton (ed.) *Touch Papers: Dialogues on Touch in the Psychoanalytic Space*. London: Karnac.

Wilkinson, M.A. (2006) *Coming into Mind: The Mind–Brain Relationship, a Jungian Clinical Perspective*. London: Routledge.

Wilkinson, M.A. (2010a) *Changing Minds in Therapy: Emotion, Attachment, Trauma and Neurobiology*. New York: Norton.

Wilkinson, M.A. (2010b) 'Working with Multiplicity. Jung, Trauma, Neurobiology and the Healing Process: A Clinical perspective', given as a joint presentation with Professor R. Lanius of the University of Western Ontario at the International Congress of the International Association for Analytical Psychology held in Montreal in August 2010.

Williams, G.P. (2004) Response to Dr Barry Proner's paper 'Bodily states of anxiety', given at the Scientific Meeting of the Society of Analytical Psychology, London, 4 October.

when one is forced to become two   eventually two forced to become
one   at some level .   is a skin meant to harbour such an aberration,
anomaly.................two fold process   two fold existences   one body
incongruant   but true.   how is it revealed?   how does it   unveil
itself.?...........itself being the incongruity.   outside with an inside   inside
with no outside   inside strives to be-come   outside   outside becomes inside   excruciation   X X zenithX X   yet   still one body
and can a miracle happen   if the outside has the guts to be-come inside
and if the inside has the courage to be-come outside   the experience of
being dissociative   (to be or not to be)

                                                                                        Jo

Scars remind us where we've been, they do not dictate where we are going.

Rainbow Crewe

Chapter 7

Towards a gnosology of body development

Susie Orbach

Framing the problem

We have little theory that discusses the development of a bodily sense of self.[1] Different schools of therapy have theorised the development of self from clinical evidence. We have Freud's original topology, then extended by Kleinian object relations, Fairbairn and Winnicott in the UK, Lacan in France and Woolf, Stolorow and Atwood and the Relational School in the United States. However, scant attention has been paid to the clinical evidence of the body *as a body* or, for that matter, *the body's psychical development*. The body is seen in three distinct ways. Following Freud, it has been characterised, first, as driven by developmental drives (oral, anal, genital) or physical urges such as hunger, excitement, anxiety; second, as a bearer of psychic distress in symptomatalogy (as in psychosomatic symptoms or hysterias), or third, described by Merleau-Ponty, phenomenologically.

The origins of psychoanalysis lay in Freud and Breuer's discussion of patients with physical symptoms that were without a discernible biological basis. From this they developed a new theory for hysteria and for the new discipline of psychoanalysis and since 1895, we have more or less accepted the formulation that bodies can act as psychic containers for unbearable emotional conflicts which then become reinscribed as bodily symptoms.

While this explanation undoubtedly accounts for certain bodily symptoms, it needs further elaboration as we understand more about bodies and minds in our time. There are two immediate theoretical shortcomings of this historical formulation. The first is that it idealises and neutralise the body in which the mind lives. It treats the body as though it were a tabula rasa to be written on by the mind, as a site almost purely available for the mind's endeavours. Second, the body in such a formulation is conceived of as a vessel for truth; it is charged with storing and remembering trauma and in so doing becomes the uber supremo, retaining precious and unfailing insights into memory and authenticity. These two contradictory conceptualisations – one which valorises the mind and the other which valorises the body – amount to a dismissal of the history and development of the body itself.

Observing the clinical body

Neither the disregard of the body nor its super elevation helps us much with three interlocking issues:

- understanding the development of the body
- the meaning of widespread body distress and disturbance we encounter in our patients today
- the sense of body discontinuity or unreliability felt by individuals as they go about their different activities – sports, love-making, child rearing, work and so on, which then fails to provide an ongoing experience of corporeal being.

We do not have a theory of body development which can approximate anything close to our theories of mind. We have clinical material which is explicit – '*I don't feel my body belongs to me*', '*I HATE my body*', '*I can't trust my body. It always lets me down*', '*I am not sure who I am going to be today*', '*My body has a mind of its own*' – in which patients demonstrate forms of alienation from the body, body detachment and objectification of the body self and although we can fit these to various existing mentalised conceptualisations – Winnicott's in particular – this is not a substitute for developing a theory of body.

Learning from multiple bodies

I start with people whose body issues hyper-illuminate what needs con-ceptualising. Psychoanalysis has always drawn its evidence and its theory from the in depth study of individuals in difficulty and it is in this spirit that I draw upon the experience of observing the different physicalities expressed by certain DID patients. From a video made by Valerie Sinason (John Bowlby Memorial Lecture in 2002) it is immediately apparent that a patient's multiple selves are not simply psychic constructs which inhabit her mind, but that these multiple selves are embodied too. Each dissociated self has its own particular body, its own idiosyncratic speech pattern, its own posture and its own way of relating.

Different physicalities encompassing stance, gait, facial expression including a sense of changed physiognomy, voice, clothing and physical engagement with others are immediately apparent when working with some people with dissociated self states. This does not occur with all DID patients but gross physical changes that occur in the consulting room (Orbach 2003), in which a woman appears alternately as a prim and proper 1970s style 'housewife'; a girlish, super prettified young adolescent; an energetic fitness instructor; or dressed for the part of principal boy, for instance, may alert the clinician to differently embodied self states that may indicate DID.

With some DID patients, the actual physical presentation via clothing, hairstyle and look may vary from session to session. For others, the shift of stance, appearance and physiognomy can be seen within the same session as the individual switches from one self state to another. This is evident in Sinason's video. The powerful clinical evidence which can be seen in the consulting room with those DID patients who do express with multiple bodies opens up a window to further understand the development of the body and a way to encounter in non-DID patients, the troubled bodies we see in the consulting room today.

Theory making

Freud's clinical study of the hysteric and the neurotic were what led him to develop an understanding of how we get a mind. Freud used the patient's story along with free association, slips of the tongue, dreams, inconsistencies and an examination of the transference–countertransference to build both developmental theory and to posit the ways in which defences structure the psyche. This has been the research method proposed and used from Freud onwards. Thus we can similarly draw on the in-depth clinical study of the dissociated, disturbed, disowned, somatised body, as we develop a theory of how we get a body and the various defences that structure the body.

The patient's body has an impact on the therapeutic field. It is there to be seen, observed and engaged with. It presents itself variously and forms part of the content of the sessions. Patients will talk about their bodies either purposefully or incidentally. Like an embodied form of free association, slips of the tongue and the movement of the body, the physical content of dreams, will be scrutinised by the therapist for both the manifest and latent content that pertains to the body. The therapist will also be reflecting on her or his subjective experience of the patient's body.

Just as we have come to see that the therapeutic encounter is an encounter between two subjectivities, so the therapeutic encounter (except when conducted by phone or email) is an encounter between *two physicalities, two bodies* (Aron et al. 1998). The patient's body and the therapist's body are both in the room. They impact on one another. The physical ambience that the therapist creates influences the emotional and physical feel of the therapy. Inescapably the therapeutic couple create a particular physical flavour between them which impacts on both bodies in a bidirectional manner (Orbach 2009).

In psychoanalysis we examine our subjective and countertransferential experiences for evidence of the patient's state(s) of mind and affect for what sense we can make of their internal and inter-personal world. We see how their mind affects and co-creates the mind we bring to our work with them (Mitchell, Aron 1999). Likewise, when we examine our embodied experiences, we will have evidence which can enable us to make sense of the patient's internal and interpersonal corporeality. Inevitably, the therapist will encounter with certain patients or at particular moments in the therapy and during assessment, strong bodily feelings. We have not been encouraged to specifically note these in any diagnostic sense as to what they indicate about bodies although we fold them into our understanding of the person we are working with, without much reflection: '*I felt myself drain away when I was with him*', '*I started to blush*', '*I found myself aware of her breasts*', '*His smell and toes offended me*'. Such comments may be automatically ascribed to psychic states: '*The patient lacked a sense of being*', '*I felt embarrassed by the patient*', '*I found the patient overtly sexual and wondered if this was the way they made a kind of contact that diverted one from her pain*', '*He was letting me know that he really could not take care of himself and needed to be looked after*', and so on. However, if we do take note of our bodily feelings and our response to patients' bodies in their own terms, we may discover interesting evidence or if not evidence, useful speculations about our patient's (and our own) bodily experience. Thus: '*I felt myself drain away when I was with him*' might translate as '*I wondered whether his body disappeared for him too*'. Just as '*I started to blush*' might translate as '*I felt ill at ease physically*' or '*I found myself aware of her breasts*' might translate as '*I felt her breasts to be disconnected from the rest of her and wondered about how physically integrated she felt*', and '*His smell and toes offended me*' might translate as '*Is this neglect of the body, a body dislike?*' These beginning speculations which add to rather than supplant the automatic psychic reflections made by a therapist begin the purposeful evaluation of body based material in an assessment.

I have detailed a range of countertransferential bodily experiences (Orbach 2002, 2009) which are unfamiliar or shifting including feeling physically overwhelmed or physically insignificant or physically at peace. In addition, I have written of specific physical sensations which have occurred in therapy sessions or when writing up notes such as sensing smells or feelings of revulsion. Experiences such as these can facilitate an understanding of body issues in their own terms and enable theory building about how we get a body. At present most psychoanalytic trainings do not draw attention to either the bodily states which a therapist routinely inhabits nor the ways in which her or his body is affected by and affects the bodies of those she or he works with. Thus we are a bit behind ourselves because experience of bodily perturbations in sessions or while reflecting on patients, has not had sufficient grounding or theory with which to be considered. In the section on Theories of Body (pp. 101–7), I shall offer some ways in which therapists may begin to situate their bodily based experiences. This will help both with the project of the psychotherapist understanding their bodily based experiences and will aid in the development of a set of constructs from which we can build an evidence base to theorise about body development.

The bodily sense of self

The DID patient can give us a particularly vivid view of the different bodies that reside in each self state. Each self or alter may have a personal body. Within each body there may be differing senses of bodily stability and instability. What looks at first glance to be fluid may be far more rigid and circumscribed. A teenage girl alter who is bulimic and continually stuffing and purging is not only in *a different* body but *a different body* psychology from the adolescent boy alter who feels more bodily stability. Not all body alters register the same level of disturbance. There may be contained within the person particular body states, some of which are unstable and others of which are stable.

My practice is not one in which I have seen or supervised primarily DID patients but the viewing of Valerie Sinason's tapes of DID patients has highlighted aspects of my own clinical experience in which I have been presented with many instances of dissociated self states (Bromberg 1998) in which different body personalities emerge in the therapy as well as dissociated body states. These patients are not the same as the explicitly DID patients of the Sinason tapes but there are continuities between dissociated body and self states and the more intense versions of dissociation.

Activated body countertransference is not always present when working with people but I keep an attentiveness to my own body. In much the same manner that I am aware of the presence of an erotic countertransference in the therapy and its hyper expression or absence, so I am aware of my body. For example, the lack of a troublesome countertransference erotic and the lack of a gaping void leads one to assume – unless the material speaks otherwise – of 'a good enough sexuality'.[2] We could extend this analogy to affects in general. Hyperarousal in the countertransference or an alexythaemic countertransference indicate to me difficulties at the level of reception to and digestion of affect. Usually this is parsed so that a particular analysand may demonstrate a capacity to express anger for instance but have difficulty with feelings of disappointment or loss or helplessness. This we know to be an indicator of how the defence structure is formed: anger comes to protect those split off aspects of feeling which have been disallowed. Often split off affects 'land' on the analyst but sometimes too, they are voided in the countertransference and retrievable or noticeable only by their absence. This is the bread and butter understanding of the role of affects in the countertransference and is a cornerstone of our work. By extension then, to experience myself as in either pole of body-less or indeed, intensely conscious of my body during or after a session alerts me to a body in the room that needs to be addressed or to aspects of split off and dissociated bodily experience.

Diagnostic categories

We regard personality organisation as ranging from stable to unstable in our gnosologies. Historically we have categorised those as either neurotic, schizoid, borderline or dissociated. More recently attachment theory categories have been used to group psychological disposition and I shall use these to suggest a gnosological schema to address the bodies we encounter clinically. I propose that:

- these diagnostic criteria rest on an understanding that bodies as much as minds are the outcome of relationship
- where body stability and a sense of body security has been achieved, this allows for flexibility, play, enjoyment and a sense of 'in-dwelling'
- where body instability is severe, this is a fixed category impelling that individual to engage with practices that involve the search for an elusive body stability and even an elusive body
- psychological practices such as cutting, eating and appetite disturbances, and body dysmorphias are symptoms of *body difficulties*
- forms of embodiment are *experienced* as immutable.

This conceptualisation supplements understandings from psychoanalysis which have privileged mental contents and seen the mind as acting on a body which has salience only for its developmental imperatives such as the oral, anal and genital stages. These proposals speak to a new calibration of the relationship between mind and body: one that is bidirectional.

The current interest in neuro-psychoanalysis, with its focus on the physical processes in the brain and the action of neuropeptides and synaptic movements, is not outside the scope of this argument about the importance of the body. It is not however the focus of this chapter. Certainly in broad terms, how we are raised, the literal physical handling of ourselves, the psychological feel of that handling, the role of the mirror neurone system in the formation and feel of body movement, the significance of benign touch in the development of oxytocin pathways and so on is crucial in the establishment of a bodily sense of self. The architecture of the post-womb brain/ body of the baby is shaped by the baby's experience. We have individual brains just as we have individual fingerprints and the individual brain is part of the body development story.

Theories of body

If we turn to the major theories of the self, we see that without considerable difficulty, these can be applied to the body. Clinical and diagnostic categories which apply to the theory of mind and mental processes can be extended to illuminate mental processes and bodily experiences that apply to the body. Historically we have seen unhealthy minds acting on bodies. Today we can see a variety of configurations. In many cases psychological and somatic development are parallel, whether the development is on the secure end of the continuum or the more unstable end. This does not, however, always occur. Instances in which these configurations are not always and inevitably in step mean that one can see a more securely attached female – to use the attachment schema – who has an insecurely or disorganised or preoccupied *body* attachment. The 'disorganised' or 'preoccupied' body then impacts on the secure self.

Substituting body for mind in the four attachment configurations established as part of the Theory of Mind, we can categorise bodies as falling into the following classifications: the secure body, the avoidant dismissive body, the preoccupied ambivalent body, the disorganised body, dissociated bodies states and merged bodies.

The secure body

Case vignette: Gemma

Gemma was a 50-year-old woman who was physically active, enjoyed sex and loved to dress experimentally when not in work mode. She enjoyed food, ate with gusto, occasionally fretted about ageing in a way that was culturally understandable, but for the most part felt alive and content in her body. The physical changes as she approached menopause both interested her and irritated her. She felt a diminishment in her energy level which she both accepted and felt sad about. She was interested to see whether the post-menopausal zest would occur for her. As a young teenager, Gemma had been sexually assaulted. The incident was shocking at the time but she had been able to tell her parents, who comforted and reassured her and enabled her to rebuild her own confidence around issues of safety. The event did not enter into her psyche in a body or psychically traumatic manner.

Case vignette: Janine

Janine was a new mother. She loved her 8 month old, was enjoying breast feeding and looking as much forward to weaning her baby as she was regretting the loss of that special time. Her own body was finding a post-partum equilibrium and she was looking forward to dressing it and getting back to her hobby, English folk dancing. Pregnancy and delivery had increased her sense of her body as generative and rich. She had always loved the smell of her parents' bodies, and that of her husband and now her baby.

These vignettes show bodies able to be alive to the self and available to connect with others. They exemplify bodies that experience a range, from fright, to yielding, to allowing other bodies to have an impact on them in relation to sex, to violence, to breast feeding, to exhaustion, to age etc. The body can be disturbed and also absorb new experience and thus exist for the individual in a meaningful manner.

The avoidant dismissive body

Case vignette: John

John was a hard-working manual labourer who drank a good deal and took recreational drugs over the weekend in a way that had him 'wrecked'. His wife would tackle him on looking after himself and try to get him to eat well and rest but he preferred to live hard, as he put it, using sleeping pills or whisky to come down and other drugs to enliven him. The physical strength he possessed was experienced as simply of use – the way he earned his living. It was not a source of pleasure or pride.

Case vignette: Sandra

Sandra dressed in an apparently nonchalant manner but this belied a form of body dislike and neglect which could never feel or look all right. In her job, Sandra was punctilious and diligent. She would stay late, correct the work of others and thought of herself as intellectually competent. She had little interest in sport, dancing or sexuality. Her eating was chaotic. She paid lip service to the idea that she should 'look after herself' but was disengaged from her body as an alternate to the despair she felt about how dissatisfied she felt.

In this category would be those whose bodies are either disregarded or treated disrespectfully. There is a sense of the body as somewhat separate, an object, a sense of non-ownership, of dismissal and a disinterest as though the body were not part of the individual except in a burdensome sense.

The preoccupied ambivalent bodies

Case vignette: George

George continually primped. He waxed his chest, surveyed himself in the mirror continually and went to the gym in a compulsive manner. When he sat in restaurants with a date, he would choose to face in if there was a mirror and he would constantly look at himself as though he were an 'other' that he was watching or admiring. When asked about this behaviour, of which he was unaware, he said he was making sure he looked good.

Case vignette: Maura

Maura was a dancer who spent hours exercising and preparing for performance. She never rested but became instead more and more focused on her physical routines and on dieting. She was driven to discipline her body and if ever she could not exercise she rapidly became depressed. Her body practice was a form of regulation giving her the means to achieve a body identity.

Such preoccupation suggests a body sense which is undeveloped and has gone unrecognised. It is constantly self-reverential or in need of disciplining because it has not, in developmental terms, been mirrored. It requires continual affirmation and a high degree of attention to confirm its existence and acceptability to the individual. This kind of relation to the body is reminiscent of the feature of narcissism (Kohut and Wolf 1978): a body needing to be related to constantly in order to be reassured of its existence.[3]

The disorganised body

Case vignette: Jennifer

Jennifer was always dieting or planning to be on a diet or thinking she should be dieting. Once a month or so she 'took a hold of herself', did drastic fasts or detoxes alongside intense aerobic exercise and weight training. Her body went up and down 15 pounds on a medium frame. She was never thin and never fat but to her she was unreasonably huge and felt her body and her appetites were unruly. She ate compulsively and blotted out her physicality to the level of somnolence. She craved thinness. When she lost her 15 pounds she was hyper-sexual and social. She felt no continuity between the two differing body states. Nor, in the 'narcotised' state, had she any awareness of the actual experience of the other state. When in the detox-diet phase she had no access to depression or a need to hide and self soothe. Her bodily experiences fluctuated wildly and there was no corporeal surety; only a body experienced as an object that needed taming or drugging. She said she was desperate to 'have a body'.

The disorganised body can be seen as akin to a borderline body,[4] in which there is a lack of coherence so that the body often fails to vivify and may only do so through the literalness of self harm, impulsivity and physical punishment. The disorganised body is unstable and unreliable. Sometimes it is a wonderful 'perfect' body, sometimes it is a despised 'abject' body. It is a body as object or body as signal or body as signifier of self. It is a body that is frequently 'taken in hand' and transformed through diet or exercise regimens or cosmetic surgery in the attempt to 'start anew'.

Dissociated bodies states

Case vignette: Sophie

Sophie was a large woman who was in considerable conflict about her size. She loved clothes and wanted to be slimmer but when she lost weight, she felt that she had disappeared and was hiding in the body of another. She could never stay slim long enough to inhabit that smaller body and see what it had to offer. Her maternal grandmother, who raised her in the West Indies, was a large woman whose body she cuddled up to every night. There was conflict between her grandmother and her mother, who was a working woman, not much available to her, physically or emotionally, and Sophie suffered considerable guilt that she was so much closer to her grandmother. This was heightened when her grandmother died and she went to her mother, who physically recoiled from her. Sophie had a split off internal bad object relation to her mother's body (Fairbairn 1953; Orbach 1986). She found it tantalising and rejecting. She perceived her own body to be the reason that her mother was distant and the thrust to transform her body to a slim body was an attempt to captivate her mother, believing somewhere that it was her plumpness and her attachment to her grandmother's plump body that had caused the rejection.

Case vignette: Hermione

Hermione inhabited several different body states. They were explicitly tied to different personalities or alters who carried aspects of the traumas she had lived through and they encompassed separate selves to deal with the different assaults. She had a violent boy who was a rugby player; a female artist who projected an earth-mother look; she had a young girl who was vulnerable and a strict teenage girl who was in charge.

Hermione and Sophie's body experiences match up with dissociated states. Dissociation is not an attachment category per se but I insert it here as it is of value when trying to understand dissociated self states. While Hermione is DID, Sophie's body experience more clearly parallels the Fairbairnian description of an endopsychic structure (Fairbairn 1952) in which there is a fracturing in the central body. Aspects of the body which have been adequately related to form the central body ego but where the body has been dismissed, disregarded or misperceived, there is a split and parts of the body, instead of being available in a robust form, are separated off from the central body ego. In the severed part there is a further splitting of the body into a 'good, tantalising' body and a 'bad, critical' body. Both these part body-objects are repressed providing the emotional compost for projection and dismissal from other bodies. The body as-it-is is not experienced or available for new experience. The split off body has become an internal body object which transforms external experience into the terms of the inner object world.

The dissociated body is an intensified calibration of the schizoid body. There is not just one major split in the endopsychic body but several splits which come to represent distinct self states with distinct body states which may encode different personalities with specific physical bodies which can cross age and gender. Multiple bodies exist within the same physical encasement although each body will look quite specific and personal.

Merged bodies

Case vignette: Janine

Janine had never felt secure in her body. She had had a breast enhancement as a teenager and rhinoplasty. She looked very like her mother, who had had both these procedures in her twenties. Mother and daughter dressed similarly despite a 25-year age difference and often dieted, went to health spas and yoga together. When Janine's mother got ill, their appearance diverged dramatically. Janine's body became psychosomatically symptomatic with similar pains to those of her mother. Although no organic reason could be found, Janine was unable to inhabit a well body. She felt she would be deserting the body of her mother. For her, their bodies were twinned.

A merged attachment is not within the conventional attachment gnosology but was posited by Luise Eichenbaum and me in discussing women's psychology and the development trajectory that can occur in the mother–daughter relationship (Eichenbaum and Orbach 1988). We looked at the struggle to form a separated attachment out of the glue of a merged attachment. If we now apply the category of merged attachment to bodies, we would describe these as bodies that are pre-differentiated. We do not mean merged in the Freudian sense or in the way in which Mahler, Bergman and Pines (1975) see the psychological birth of the human infant occurring with motor development. Merged attachments and hence merged bodies are bodies that appear not to have been related to as 'separate' but to have been so fully incorporated into the maternal body, perhaps because that body itself is an unseparated body requiring the body of another to stabilise it,[5] that it has not been seen or recognised as connected and yet differentiated.

In therapy, the individual may mimic body movements or the attire of the therapist. The patient may express disease unless she has close physical proximity to an other, a best friend, a lover, a mother. The troubled edge of this desire is that physically separated from the body of the other body, the individual experiences herself as without a body. In the therapy she may presume a physical bond with the therapist, move her chair closely in or create an atmosphere in which there is a sense of such physical frailty at a level that the therapist feels more than an ordinary level of protectiveness.

Reflections

This chapter attempts a new gnosology of body development. By extending conventional attachment categories to include the body and by linking these with two other diagnostic clusters – dissociation and merger – I have created six distinct categories with which to shape a discourse about the developmental issues involved in body difficulties. These categories can enable us to understand more specifically the intransigence of body based difficulties, to illuminate the intergenerational transmission of bodies, to alert psychotherapists to the significance of the body, to begin the effort to understand the various body countertransferences that can occur and to find a conceptual framework in which to begin to talk with patients about body difficulties more directly.

A disturbing aspect of paying attention to bodies in the clinical setting has been my observation that a body sense of self becomes fixed very early on in life. If a mother has a secure body attachment, she is likely to pass that on to her children in an uncomplicated fashion. The body will be taken for granted and 'lived from'. Her body will exist for her in almost all circumstances. She can yield, age, fight, connect, disengage, make love, play and so on, feel her appetites, her surrenders and her continuities. The secure body is a separate-attached body (in the schema proposed by Eichenbaum and Orbach 1988).

If she has an insecure body, however, which is to say either, an avoidant-dismissive, a preoccupied, a dissociated, a merged, or a split off body herself, such a body sense will form the basis of the child's body sense particularly if that child is a girl (Orbach 1986). Those bodies which are insecure then will show a certain malleability which might even look like flexibility and ease but which may come not from the presence of a supple secure body sense but out of a desperate search to find a secure body (Orbach 2006, 2009). These latter insecure bodies are the bodies we encounter in much of our work today and which rarely feel amenable to change and development without a change in therapeutic focus and technique. By assessing our patients' body sense and paying close attention to not only the content, feel, look and discussion of bodies but also body transference-countertransference material that arises within the therapy, we have the means to extend our therapeutic capacities and help our patients with insecure body attachments.

Notes

1 This is the subject of several papers and a recent book of mine (Orbach 2009).
2 I realise the irony of using Winnicott who was famously known for his pre-oedipal theorising here but what I am wanting to convey is an ordinarily enough contented sexual subjectivity.
3 In Kohut and Wolf's (1978) formulation, there are five subtypes of narcissistic personalities. The first, the mirror hungry personality, who seeks reflection to assuage feelings of worthlessness, chimes with the narcissistic body.
4 Otto Kernberg's work shows the main features of borderline personality organisation in which problematic affects are projected, ambivalence and complexity in relation to self and objects is unavailable.
5 See Eichenbaum and Orbach (1982) for this at a psychical level, and Orbach (1978, 1986) for this at a physical psychological level.

References

Aron, L. and Sommer Anderson, F. (1998) *Relational Perspectives on the Body*. Hillsdale, NJ: Analytic Press.

Bromberg, P.M. (1998) *Standing in the Spaces: Essays on Clinical Process, Trauma and Dissociation*. Hillsdale, NJ: Analytic Press.

Eichenbaum, L. and Orbach, S. (1982) *Outside In – Inside Out*. Harmondsworth: Penguin.

Eichenbaum, L. and Orbach, S. (1988) *Between Women: Love, Envy and Competition in Women's Friendships*. New York: Viking.

Fairbairn, W.R.D. (1952) *Psychoanalytic Studies of the Personality*. London: Routledge and Kegan Paul.

Kernberg, O. (1975) *Borderline Conditions and Pathological Narcissis*. New York: Jason Aronson.

Kohut, H. and Wolf, E.S. (1978) The Disorders of the Self and their Treatment: An Outline. *International Journal of Psycho-Analysis*, 59: 413–25.

Mahler, M., Bergman, A. and Pines, F. (1975) *The Psychological Birth of the Human Infant*. New York: Basic Books.

Mitchell, S.A. & Aron, L. (1999) *Relational Psychoanalysis*. Hillsdale, NJ: Analytic Press.

Orbach, S. (1978) *Fat is a Feminist Issue*. New York and London: Paddington Press.

Orbach, S. (1986) *Hunger Strike: The Anorectic's Struggle as a Metaphor for Our Time*. New York: Norton and London: Faber & Faber.

Orbach, S. (2002) *On Eating*. London: Penguin.

Orbach, S. (2003) There is no such thing as a body. John Bowlby Memorial Lecture: The Body in Clinical Practice, Part One. In K. White (ed.) (2004) *Touch: Attachment and the Body.* London: Karnac.

Orbach, S. (2006) How can we have a body? Desires and corporeality. *Studies in Gender and Sexuality*, 7 (1): 89–111.

Orbach, S. (2009) *Bodies.* London: Profile, and New York: Picador.

okay this day is fraught   i am without   she is within   i
am the outer layer   she is an inner layer   an inner shadow that fits my body
shape perfectly   the problem, tempest arising................i resist   for all My
life is worth   the irony is breath taking.............................no, the irony is mind
blowing

                                                                          Jo

Chapter 8

Consciousness and self-consciousness in dissociative disorders

Ellert R.S. Nijenhuis

Introduction

According to the *Diagnostic and Statistical Manual of Mental Disorders* (DSM-IV: American Psychiatric Association (APA) 1994), patients with dissociative identity disorder (DID) encompass 'distinct identities'. These identities have 'their own names and characteristics' (APA 1994: 484), and are marked by their 'own relatively enduring patterns of perceiving, relating to and thinking about the environment and self' (APA 1994: 487). Based on the understanding that dissociative identities constitute dynamic subsystems of a system as a whole, and that this overarching system involves the individual's singular personality, the term 'dissociative parts of the personality' seems more apt (Nijenhuis et al. 2002; Van der Hart et al. 2006).[1] Allport (1961) defined personality as 'the dynamic organization within the individual of those psychophysical systems that determine his characteristic behavior and thought'. However, this organization also comprises an individual's characteristic perceptions, sensations, and affects, and the intended psychophysical systems also mediate his or her interpersonal behavior. The definition can therefore be refined as follows: personality is the dynamic organization within the individual of those biopsychosocial systems that determine his or her characteristic mental and motor actions. Dissociative parts of the personality thus are insufficiently integrated dynamic subsystems of a biopsychosocial system as a whole that constitutes the individual's personality. In mental health, personality is a dynamic organization because it is open to change through experience and maturation. The dissociative personality as a whole system and the involved dissociative subsystems are, though still dynamic, unduly stable (Van der Hart et al. 2006). That is, the system as a whole and the dissociative subsystems are overly closed to adaptive change through new experiences, and new environmental and personal contexts (e.g., living in a different social context, maturation).

One way in which this maladaptive stability manifests in DID is the fixed belief of dissociative parts that they are or have their own self.

Case vignette: Jenny

As one of her dissociative parts, Jenny told her therapist: 'I am me, just me, Dorien. I want to be myself, and do not want the others around [i.e., Jenny's other dissociative parts]. They are the problem, not me. Please, send them away!' But most other dissociative parts that Jenny encompassed were as convinced of their subjective existence and were as strongly attached to their self as Dorien was. They were not in the least prepared to be 'sent away.' Dorien, Jenny, and all other dissociative parts also had their own ideas of the body, the world, and their place in the world. Thus, Dorien was convinced that she had her own body and that she was 14 years old, living with her parents, and physically, sexually, and emotionally abused on a daily basis.

Dorien and Jenny's other dissociative parts were not a whim, since they had been around for over two decades. Yet Dorien ceased to exist, for once and for all, within some ten minutes. This happened during a therapeutic session in which she had agreed to 'fuse' (i.e., completely integrate) with Anna, a different dissociative part of Jenny's. Anna, who had not been any less invested in herself than Dorien, also vanished from existence in this integrative action, in any case as Anna. Along with the fusion, a new dissociative part emerged that after some time would refer to herself as Eva, and that had her own idea of the body, the world, and her relation to this world.

These perplexing phenomena raise the primary questions of this chapter. What and who were Jenny, Dorien, Anna and Eva? What were their 'selves'? Where did these 'selves' originate from? Where did they go when they fused? How could these dissociative parts be so convinced of their personal existence and be so attached to their selves for such a long time, but forever disappear as two separate parts in a brief chunk of time? And how can a new self subsequently be generated in minutes? The quick dissolution of dissociative parts of the personality during fusion (that may only become possible after much preparatory work) and the appearance of a new dissociative part strongly suggest that dissociative 'selves' and their accompanying ideas of the body, the environment, and relations among self and world involve constructions. It thus seems worthwhile to examine the problem of dissociative selves in the light of an advanced constructivist theory of consciousness and self-consciousness (Metzinger 2003), and to use this theory as a heuristic for interpreting particular clinical observations and empirical research findings.

A closely related question that I wish to address is if dissociative parts of the personality are present only in DID? Or are, as Van der Hart et al. (2006)

contend, all dissociative parts of patients with dissociative disorders as recognized in DSM-IV (APA 1994) and ICD-10 (World Health Organization (WHO) 1992) endowed with at least a minimal degree of consciousness and self-consciousness? In other words, what are the natural boundaries of dissociative parts of the personality? Or, in case such natural boundaries do not exist, how can dissociative parts of the personality be usefully differentiated from other kinds of insufficiently integrated subsystems of the personality? For example, what would be the difference(s) between dissociative disorders, and ego-dystonic phobias or schizophrenia? Patients with ego-dystonic phobias know that their fear and avoidance regarding particular stimuli are unfounded, but this awareness all but inhibits their phobic reactions. Patients with schizophrenia commonly hear voices, and experience that particular emotions and motor actions are 'made' in them. Do such symptoms involve influences from a dissociative part of their personality, and, if so, would this imply that ego-dystonic phobias and schizophrenia are dissociative disorders?

A third question this chapter addresses pertains to consciousness more generally. Many contemporary clinicians and scientists believe that narrowing and lowering of consciousness belong to the domain of dissociative phenomena. This conceptualization does not follow Janet's original definition of dissociation (Janet 1907). He delimited dissociation to a lack of integration among two or more subsystems of the personality, and dissociative symptoms to manifestations of this structural division of personality. This stance has been revived by Van der Hart et al. (2004). Exploring what abnormal forms of consciousness are conceptually specific for patients with dissociative disorders, hence dissociative, I will use Metzinger's (2003) eleven constraints on consciousness, one of which involves a first-person perspective, and add a twelfth.

The mereological fallacy

A first issue that must be addressed in examining these kinds of questions is at what level of analysis dissociative 'selves' are studied best. It is a widespread philosophical assumption that goals and actions guided by explicit goal representations should be analyzed at the level of the whole system that constitutes a living human being (Metzinger 2003). For it is living human beings who have goals and execute actions, not their brains or other functional modules of them. The same argument seems applicable to personality as a whole dynamic, biopsychosocial system.

Ascribing psychological predicates to functional parts of a whole system involves a mereological fallacy (Bennett and Hacker 2003).[2] It is neither false nor true to ascribe psychological predicates to parts of a system such as the brain, but it makes no sense. As Wittgenstein (1953: entry 281) insisted: '[o]nly of a human being and what resembles (behaves like) a living human being can one say: it has sensations; it sees; hears; is deaf; is conscious or unconscious.'[3]

Cartesians engage in the mereological error by distinguishing between a body and a mind, and by ascribing thoughts, feelings, beliefs, fantasies and other psychological predicates to the mind rather than to a living human being or his or her personality as an embodied functional entity. But the mind is not a kind of thing that has such faculties. The mind rather is a term that denotes a range of human powers, the exercise of these powers, and a range of characteristic human character traits. Although many contemporary neuroscientists repudiate Descartes' body–mind dualism, they too assign features to parts of a whole that, in fact, are characteristics of the whole rather than of the parts. These scientists first exchange the body–mind divide for a separation of the body and brain, and subsequently ascribe psychological attributes to the brain. In their view, it is the brain or parts of the brain that perceive, experience, think, guess and decide rather than the individual as a whole system. But '[t]he brain is not a logically appropriate subject for psychological predicates' (Bennett and Hacker 2003: 72). These predicates are inherent features or functions of the whole biopsychosocial system that constitutes an individual.

Still, the idea that goals and actions mediated by these goals must be necessarily analyzed at the level of the whole system does not empirically hold in all cases (Metzinger 2003). The philosophical intuition that underlies the assumption is empirically incorrect, because the whole system can encompass two or more subsystems that each have goals and that each engage in explicit goal-directed behavior. Among other cases, this applies to mental disorders involving subsystems of the personality that are insufficiently integrated in a functional sense.[4] Considering the degree of relative autonomy and goal-directedness of many dissociative parts in DID, it is mereologically correct to maintain that a full understanding of this mental disorder must include an analysis of these functionally divided parts. This analysis encompasses an examination of the subjectively experienced 'selves' of these parts as well as their intentional relation to objects, situations and other subjects.[5] It makes sense to say that a dissociative part of a patient decides, thinks or feels something, provided it is realized that:

- this part is a subsystem of a higher-order system that constitutes the patient's personality
- this dissociative subsystem is not totally separated from other dissociative parts of his or her personality
- a full understanding of dissociative parts involves an analysis of their mutual relations
- a full understanding of the patient requires a structural and functional analysis of the whole system.

Metzinger's self-model theory of subjectivity[6]

The analysis of the construction of self-consciousness in dissociative parts of the personality can start with an exploration of Metzinger's theoretical reflection on the origin and nature of self in mentally healthy individuals. As integrated personalities, we believe we are or have a self, are strongly attached to it, and believe our self will be with us whenever we are awake or dream. However, Metzinger (2003) contends that there is no such thing as a self. In his view, self is not an independent entity or substance that could live by itself, not an unchanging center or invariant set of intrinsic properties, and not a unique and indivisible unity. The self rather is a mental model of ourself as a whole system that we continuously generate and adapt: nobody ever was or had a self. All that ever existed were conscious self-models that could not be recognized as models. The phenomenal self is not a thing but a process – and the subjective experience of being someone emerges if a conscious information processing system operates under a transparent self-model (Metzinger 2003: 1). The phenomenal self entails our conscious subjective experience of being someone, of being a bodily, emotional, cognitive, acting subject. What we often naively call our 'self' is this phenomenal self, i.e., the content of our self-consciousness as given in our phenomenal experience. A result of evolution, the phenomenal self is 'a wonderfully efficient two-way window that allows an organism to conceive of itself as a whole, and thereby to causally interact with its inner and outer environment in an entirely new, integrated, and intelligent manner' (Metzinger 2003: 1). Conscious awareness additionally encompasses a phenomenal world that appears to a phenomenal self.

In conscious experience, there is apart from a phenomenal self a phenomenal world that appears to a phenomenal self. The phenomenal self and its implied subjectivity emerge when a particular subsystem of us develops a theoretical and, as Metzinger (2003) suggests, empirical entity,[7] described as the phenomenal self-model (PSM) that represents our whole system for us, i.e., our whole organism. Our PSM becomes situated in and linked with a phenomenal world, when we (i.e., a subsystem of us as a whole biopsychosocial system) also develop a phenomenal model of the intentionality relation (PMIR). A PMIR concerns a model of how we and an object are linked during a certain episode (e.g., 'I am someone who is reading this book'; 'I am someone who understands the content of this sentence'). The essence of this consciously experienced mental model is the specific intentionality relation of the complete system as represented in a PSM ('I') and an object (in the examples, the book and the sentence). The 'object' of a PMIR can involve apart from objects existing in the environment, personal experiences (thoughts, feelings, behaviors, etc.) and other people and their mental and motor actions. There is an intimate relation of a PSM and a PMIR, because the content of consciousness never involves just an object, but a relation of a self-conscious system and an object. Thanks to PSMs and PMIRs, there is, phenomenologically, the experience of a self in the act of perceiving, knowing, feeling, thinking, doing, wanting and relating to other people (Metzinger 2006). In sum, conscious, phenomenal experience involves a phenomenal self, a phenomenal material and social world, and a connection between a phenomenal self and these phenomenal worlds. The ongoing interaction between the PSM and PMIR culminates in a lived, embodied first-person perspective.

Whatever we cannot integrate in a PSM, or appropriate under a PMIR, will escape our volitional control. For example, in alien hand syndrome (Marchetti and Della Sala 1998), a neurological condition, the patient is consciously aware of movements exerted by the non-dominant hand, that displays a will of its own. The patient neither experiences a desire to move this hand, nor experiences agency of the initiation and execution of the hand's goal-directed movements. In one case, the patient's non-dominant hand seized nearby objects, pulled and picked at her clothes, and even grasped at her throat as she was sleeping (Banks et al. 1989). In alien hand syndrome, the patient's hands movements are goal-directed, but beyond her volitional control. Neither the goal of the movement nor the agency are part of her PSM and PMIR. The alien hand seems to be driven by visual perceived objects in the immediate environment, i.e., by the affordances of the object (Gibson 1977, 1979). Affordances of the object involve the actions that individuals can in principle perform regarding the object. The automatic actions of the alien hand point to the function of our conscious first-person perspective: the stronger and more stable our conscious first-person perspective, the lesser the degree to which our actions are primarily driven by affordances.

Mental representation

Metzinger's theory is a representational theory of consciousness and self-consciousness.[8] Mental representation is a process by which some biosystems generate a functionally internal version of parts of reality. The object of representation or representandum can involve not only an external fact such as a source of food or an enemy, or an internal fact such as one's current sugar level, but also properties, relations (e.g., the distance to a goal) and classes (e.g., events that generate pain). For the current discussion on phenomenal self, it is important to notice that a part of particular biosystems can represent the system as a whole system, thus the individual's personality as a whole with all its internal, relational and public properties. There are four basic features of mental and phenomenal representation. First, mental representation is functional because it rests on a transient and continuous change in the functional properties of the system. Second, the representatum – i.e., the mental state or process that functions as the placeholder for the representandum – is a theoretical fiction. The fiction is that a representatum is not a kind of thing but a mental vehicle, a time slice of an ongoing representational process, or rather, action.[9] The representatum thus continuously changes as the representing proceeds. Insight into this fact should keep us from turning processes into things, from reifying the experiential content of a continuous representational action. Third, the representatum supervenes on internally realized functional, neurological properties, so that, in this sense, a theoretical distinction can be made between mental content (i.e., the representatum) and mental vehicle (i.e., the representational process or action).[10] In this view, phenomenal content is thus an abstract property of contemporaneous physiological processes (actions). And fourth, phenomenality is a property of a certain class of mental representata. This class encompasses the representata that the individual can become consciously aware of. Mental representata more generally include representata that the individual is not, or in principle cannot be consciously aware of.

The problem of presumed isomorphy

A major problem of many representational theories is the claim that there exists some kind of isomorphy between the representandum and the representatum (Braude 1979, 1997). Isomorphist theories assume a conservation of at least some structural similarity between the representandum and representatum. However, there need not be any such isomorphy between the two at all. It is important to realize that one thing or process must be made to represent another thing or process. For example, there is nothing isomorphic between the word 'angry' and the actual mood it represents, between my memory of a sunset and the actual sunset I remember, and between our representation of ourselves and ourselves as a whole system.

Metzinger (2003) recognizes the problem of isomorphist theories of representation, and seeks to resolve it by replacing a two-way relation between representatum (image) and representandum (object) for a three-way relation between the image, the object, and the representing system as a whole. In this configuration, there need not be any isomorphy of the representatum and representandum. What counts is how the representing system uses or defines the relation between the representatum and representandum. Anything can represent anything, if so used by the whole system in a certain context (Braude 1997). How the whole system represents the representandum will often depend on the history, goals and action tendencies of that whole system.

Representata as tools

Metzinger (2003) contends that representata exert a function for the whole system, that they are tools to achieve certain goals, for example, goals that have been or still are of importance in an evolutionary or social context. In this teleofunctional perspective,[11] the representational process is being optimized toward a functional optimatization of behavioral patterns of the whole system, that is of its viability, and not toward the perfectioning of a structure-preserving kind of representation.

One essential function of the representational action is to emulate objects, subjects, and relationships between them, so that the whole system can effectively work with them.[12] The emulation includes creating an illusion of the transtemporal identity of the representata, at least within episodic limits. We cannot transcend this illusion of constancy from a first-person perspective because the representational action hides its own temporality. That is, we cannot experience that this process requires time and that we, therefore, constantly and inescapably lag behind the reality we represent. From a theoretical third-person point of view, we may appreciate or believe that our representations involve a virtual domain, i.e., a domain of possible realities, but we cannot experience that we live at a principled distance from reality. This implies that our PSM and PMIR also involve possible rather than absolute realities, but that we nonetheless experience them as given. The illusory experience is due to the fact that we do not have phenomenal insight into the previous processing stages that generate these models of reality. They are absolutely transparent for us, we cannot 'see' that we engage in these mental actions, we 'look through' them.

We are commonly not consciously aware of (mis)taking a possible reality for an actual reality. This confusion, known as the reification of the phenomenal, is adaptive because it gives us a reference point. Metzinger refers to this reference point as the 'world zero'. The world zero allows us to take our present experience for real rather than for a simulation of reality. This evaluation, that from a third-person perspective is naive and mistaken, helps us to distinguish the actual and the possible (e.g., plans for the future; memories), reality and appearance, factuality and counterfactuality. The human brain is a system that is constantly engaged in simulating possible realities (Leopold and Logothetis 1999). Out of all simulated realities, we select one that subsequently becomes a reality for us. Representata, then, are those simulata whose function for the system consists in representing states of affairs in the real internal and external world with a sufficient degree of temporal precision: the representatum is the selected simulatum that constitutes for us, subjectively, the actual state of affairs in the real inner and outer world.

Mental simulation involves the representation of possible or counterfactual situations such as those that occur in dreams and hallucinations. Whereas mental simulations do not involve conscious awareness, phenomenal simulations are conscious. For example, we consciously explore possible worlds in planning and in predicting the probable future. Just as adaptive or viable mental simulation, phenomenal simulation serves survival interest.[13] It is of crucial importance for organisms to have a set of values that inform them what possible worlds are safe and attractive, or dangerous and aversive. Endowed with such values, they can compare future-oriented simulata ('what will happen if . . .' [possible worlds]) and representata that they regard as the actual reality, that constitute the world zero ('that which is Now'; 'the real world').

Another way in which phenomenal representation serves as a tool relates to introspection. Mental states we introspect are phenomenal states, i.e., the mental states we consciously experience. Introspection is the internal representation of active mental representata. Hence, introspection involves metarepresentation: in introspection, already active mental representations are represented for a second time. These metarepresentations are functionally internal states in the sense that their intentional mental content can be made globally available to us. More specifically, they can be made globally available for our attention, cognition and voluntary control of motor actions within a window of presence, within a phenomenal Now, discussed below, that we have realized.

The phenomenal self-model

The PSM includes three components: self-representation, self-simulation, and self-presentation.

Self-representation

A special phenomenal representatum emerges when a part of a whole system generates a representatum of that whole system. This representatum involves a phenomenal subject, a first-person perspective. Metzinger (2003) describes this representatum as the PSM that we create in an ongoing three-way representational action (representandum-representatum-representing subject). He asserts that a PSM is a representatum of the whole system, that a part of the whole system develops for the system as a whole. This part of the whole system represents the selection of properties of the system as a whole it can phenomenally access. As any representatum, this representatum is not a thing, but a mental action that, apart from occasional interruptions such as dreamless sleep and temporary complete loss of consciousness, goes on a lifetime.

According to Metzinger, we require a first-person perspective for the phenomenal experience of being someone, for the control of our actions, for becoming the object of our own attention, and for cognitive self-reference. This perspectivalness is also needed for creating a link between ourself as a phenomenal subject and our phenomenal world. When this link exists, we can appreciate that we are acting and experiencing subjects in a world. The phenomenal self-model and phenomenal world-model that we create are therefore intimately linked representations that allow us to experience how we exist in a world. We need the subjective experience of having a(n untranscendable) self, of having a consciously experienced first-person perspective, for living in a material world. We also need it for the experience of living in a world with other subjects, hence for our social existence.

Self-simulation

Self-representation involves a special case of self-simulation. Self-simulation as in fantasy and dreaming is opaque, because the system is consciously aware of creating possible worlds when it is engaged in actions such as fantasy, dreaming, and planning. In self-representation, the system also generates a possibility – a possible self. However, this self-modeling is transparent (see 7.1 and 7.2). That is, the system is not consciously aware of the fact that it confuses a possible self and a given self. This confusion is functionally adaptive in that the system can treat the current self-representation as a reference point. It helps the system to distinguish between the current self-model (phenomenally experienced as immediately given in the mode of naive realism) and possible self-models (as in memory and in planning).

Self-presentation

Like Damasio (1999), Metzinger proposes that a primitive, pre-reflective form of phenomenal self-consciousness constitutes the origin of our first-person perspective. Pertaining to the feeling of being in contact with ourselves, it is a 'subjectively immediate and fundamental form of non-conceptual self-knowledge preceding any higher forms of cognitive self-consciousness' (Metzinger 2003: 158). Because this awareness of the presence and current state of the body is immediate and noncognitive, it does not involve a self-representatum but a self-presentatum. Self-presentations are seldom available for categorical perception, concept formation, and autobiographical memory because they are noncognitive. However, self-presentations are available for inward-directed attention, so that they serve as an excellent reference base. Bodily self-consciousness is, in fact, the most important source of invariance for human beings, both phenomenologically and functionally. It entails nonconceptual knowledge about the presence and current state of one's own body. Self-presentation also provides centered-ness, an inner world and an inward perspective. Commonly centered in bodily self-consciousness, self-presentation creates a consciously available divide between self and world.

Having a subjective, centralized point of view, i.e., a phenomenal self entertaining a perspective – we generally experience ourselves as the center of our world – is intimately tied to embodiment because our sensory and motor systems are 'physically integrated within the body of a single organism' (Metzinger 2003: 161). This embodied perspectivalness is crucially linked to internally generated, elementary bioregulatory processes, such as the beating of the heart, and breathing. Together with the sensory and motor systems, these processes create a global region of maximal stability and invariance because in standard cases, the body is always more or less present, and can therefore serve as a much needed stable point of reference.

At higher levels of mental action, the representational space centered by a phenomenal self can enable the attribution of psychological properties to the system itself. That is, at these levels, we can attribute psychological properties to ourselves. These higher level mental actions require a meta-representational ability that is a precursor to our reflective subjectivity and social cognition.

The PSM thus encompasses integrated self-presentational, self-representational, and self-simulational phenomenal actions and the contents these actions generate: our subjectively experienced bodily and emotional feelings, thoughts and fantasies, autobiographical memories, and plan for the future. These different components of the PSM are integrated by the mental action of personification (Van der Hart et al. 2006). Personification is the ability of a part of the whole system that we are to make experience our own, which stimulates us (i.e., the whole system that we are) to take responsibility for engaging in particular mental or behavioral actions. For example, when we personify our current bodily and emotional feelings, we might express that we are tired and want to take a rest or that we made a mistake and wish to correct it. Personification generates such motivations. It also generates the property of mineness. Mineness exists in kinds and degrees. For example, the sense of agency ('I did it') differs from the sense of ownership ('It happened to me').

In sum, the basic function of a PSM is to make system-related information globally available for the system as a whole. Generating a PSM, the self-modeling subsystem simulates the observable output of the whole system, and emulates abstract properties of its own internal functioning, i.e., of its own mental actions. Following the background assumption of teleofunctionalism, it engages in this simulation and emulation for itself as a whole system.

In the ongoing representational action, the PSM regards the target system as subject and object at the same time. The degree to which the PSM is conscious depends on the degree to which it satisfies the constraints for conscious content, discussed below.

Consciousness and multiple PSM and PMIR in DID

We can now examine to what extent dissociative parts of the personality in patients with DID include their own PSM and PMIRs. Considering that self-consciousness is a special type of consciousness, an analysis of self-consciousness and consciousness in mentally healthy individuals and in dissociative parts in DID must be embedded in an analysis of consciousness.

Consciousness, hence phenomenal experience, exists in many different forms, intensities, and degrees of internal complexity. These differences can be expressed in terms of Metzinger's preliminary catalogue of constraints on consciousness. The degree to which these constraints are fulfilled indicates if a certain representational mental state may also be a conscious, phenomenal state. The catalogue is intended to serve as a set of provisional but workable tools. The primary level of description is the first-person perspective, but Metzinger has extended this level with several other levels of description such as the functional, computational and neurobiological level. The focus in this chapter will be on the first-person perspective, although without specification, sometimes a few other levels of description are briefly considered as well. Each of the constraints will be discussed first. Next, they will be applied to dissociative parts of the personality in patients with dissociative disorders, but far from exhaustively.

1.1 Global availability

From a phenomenological perspective, global availability means that the contents of states of consciousness never stand alone but are found and integrated in a single world. This world commonly is a highly integrated representation of the actual world. It consists of many connected but differentiated components that are unified in a whole model. A world, in this sense, involves a highest-order situational context in which the phenomenal contents of more or less distinctive conscious states are embedded.

All systems operating with globally available information are systems which experience themselves as living in a world, provided a number of other constraints on consciousness, discussed below, are met as well. Metzinger contends that global availability is one of the few necessary conditions in ascribing phenomenality to information currently operating within a whole system.

The contents of states of consciousness can be globally available in a variety of ways. A somewhat crude classification is that they can be globally available for guided attention, cognitive reference, and control of behavioral action. For example, we can deliberately attend to the content of our consciousness, say, focus on an object, on its color or shape, or on a subject and his or her behavior. In at least some cases, we can form thoughts about these contents, say, think about a subject, form a concept about a certain class of subjects, or talk about these features and concepts. We may also be able to use these contents, say the shape of an object, to control our behavior, e.g., to sit down on the thing, or to sort a variety of things into coherent groups. Global availability of mental contents is thus an adaptive tool. Because the intentional content of phenomenal representata is globally available for further processing such as attention, memory, concept formation, planning and motor simulations, phenomenal states increase the flexibility of the behavioral profile of the system as a whole. The more information is phenomenal, the higher are the flexibility and context sensitivity with which the system can react to environmental challenges. From a teleological perspective, the features of global availability are of particular importance for goal-directed actions in which adaptation does not exclusively depend on speed – as in defensive reflexes – but also depends on volitional control, planning, and cognitive processing.

Some phenomenal contents do not involve representata, but presentata.[14] As indicated before, presentata are simple stimulus-correlated internal system states that are globally available for our guided attention and behavioral action control, but not for cognition. That is, we cannot further subjectively differentiate or penetrate presentata by representational processing. Presentata include, for example, sounds, smells, pleasant sensations or pain, and perceiving fine shades of colors. We can attend to these phenomenal states, and use them to guide our behaviors, but we cannot cognitively categorize or cognitively integrate them in the form of a perceptual memory. For example, we can attend to and distinguish delicate shades of red from each other, but we cannot conceptualize these subtly different shades when we do not actually perceive them. The same would apply to minor nuances of sounds, smells and temperature. Presentational content is unable to stand by itself: it always is integrated in some relation, in a higher-order whole. For example, as a presentatum, pain is always experienced as localized in some body part. Phylogenetically, presentational content is probably one of the most ancient forms of conscious content. It is functionally most reliable. Being an ultrafast process, we cannot trace how we process the stimuli that activate the presentation. In this sense, presentational content is fully transparent: we have no introspective access to the perceptual process. An important function of presentational content is to 'flag the present'. As subjectively instant sensory experience, this phenomenal content helps us to prevent confusion between what (we assume that) actually exists and what we simulate.

1.2 Global availability in dissociative parts of the personality

No matter how simple and limited a dissociative part's content of conciousness can be at times, it is commonly an inherent component of this part's world-model.

Case vignette: Ingrid

Ingrid, a dissociative parts patient with DID, felt extremely threatened when a picture of a man with an angry facial expression was moved in the direction of her face in the context of experimental research. At this point, she had the experience of leaving her body and floating above it. Despite her out-of-body experience, Ingrid integrated these diverse experiences in a quite limited world-model: she saw her body below, and saw how it was threatened by the 'man'. She also bound but differentiated a number of other components of her experience, such as her fear and her perception of the picture of the man. For example, she appreciated that her body and the picture were two different things. However, subjectively floating above her body, bodily feelings and control over her behavioral actions were not globally available to her. With her eyes averted from the threat cues, staring into nothingness, she was physically completely passive, just as she had reacted as this part when she was sexually and physically abused. Ingrid later reported that her body had been paralyzed during the exposure to the picture and the first minutes after this experimental test. It also appeared that she was unable to recall what had happened when the picture had been within 70 centimeter from her face. It seems that her level of consciousness had been so low at this time that she had not formed a memory of the event.

Disintegration of the focal content of consciousness may also happen, which implies the loss of the single, coherent world-model. For example, some dissociative parts report their world (and their feeling of being someone; see 6.1 and 6.2) disintegrated into many disconnected bits and pieces when they had been extremely threatened and abused.

This happened to a 6-year-old girl when a close relative raped her with a gun, and told her how eager he was to fire the weapon. As a dissociative part of her told the therapist many decades later, she (her PSM) and her world (her PMIRs regarding the abuser and several objects) had shattered during the most horrible moments of the abuse. She also conveyed that the loss of a coherent perception of the world and phenomenal self had been exceptionally frightening.

Dissociative parts sometimes experience presentata where they actually would, for adaptive reasons, better experience representata. This happens, for example, when they reexperience traumatizing events. Dissociative parts that are fixated on these events do not remember them as autobiographical, narrative memories, i.e., as representata, but as so-called traumatic memories that impress more as presentata. Traumatic memories are involuntary, mostly nonverbal sensorimotor and highly affectively charged experiences that are insufficiently condensed in time (Janet 1928; Van der Kolk and Van der Hart 1989; Van der Hart et al. 1989). For example, dissociative parts may feel pain in some body parts, smell particular body odors, feel that someone touches or hits them. These presentata subjectively 'flag the present' for them. For such parts, the dread happens again, here and now. As phenomenal presentata, traumatic experiences are globally available for the patient's attention, and, within narrow limits, for the control of some behavioral actions, particularly defensive actions. For example, a patient who reexperiences a traumatizing event she was exposed to in her childhood, may hide behind a couch as she did when the event happened.

To the degree that traumatic memories involve presentata, they are commonly unavailable for cognitive control. Dissociative parts who contain such memories have therefore very little cognitive control over them. When patients as one or more of their dissociative parts manage to transform traumatic memories into autobiographical memories (e.g., in treatment), these phenomenal presentata become phenomenal representata. With this significant shift, trauma survivors gain the ability to attend to these memories deliberately, think about them, comprehend and categorize them, assign them their place in the history of their life, and use them for behavioral action control in a far more flexible way (e.g., they can now refrain from acting out the memory), which obviously enhances the patient's capacity for adaptation.

2.1 A phenomenal Now

Information in the nervous system is never completely actual information because of the fact that information determination,[15] conduction and processing take time. This implies that our phenomenal Now is a specious present (James 1890) or remembered present (Edelman and Tononi 2000). It entails a 'window of simultaneity' or 'window of presence' in which we commonly integrate different but physiologically not completely synchronous mental actions such as our sensations, perceptions, emotions and memories (cf. Janet 1935; Van der Hart et al. 2006). To create the phenomenal Now at the level of mental content, the representing system must exclude representations of the time frames of the actual different mental vehicles that are involved in the mental content. For example, the different processing times for mental actions of generating sensations, emotions and memories should not become a part of our phenomenal content, or else our phenomenal Now would dissolve. Considering that from a third-person perspective there is no now, past or future, the phenomenal experience of time is a simulation. Phenomenal mental content is thus a simulation existing in a world – it is globally available – and in a phenomenal Now.

2.2 Window of presence in dissociative parts of the personality

Clinical observations suggest that all dissociative parts of the personality experience that they live in a present, and that all naively believe that their sense of the present – their phenomenal Now – equals the actual Now. As these parts, patients with dissociative disorders can be confused in a double sense. First, they do not experience that their phenomenal Now is a simulation, as goes for all humans. I already discussed that this simulation is adaptive. But, second, the phenomenal Now of dissociative parts can be confused in a pathological sense. For example, the phenomenal Now of some dissociative parts may, in fact, involve a remote past. They may believe it is 1970 or any other past time. Sometimes their phenomenal Now shifts, say, from 1968 to 1972, and from that year to 1981. Other dissociative parts may not be able to state the year in which they subjectively live, and refer to their experienced present in the context of sentences such as 'I must go to class in a minute.' Dissociative parts who exert functions in daily life (e.g., those who take care of children, who explore the environment, or who engage in a sport) are commonly far better oriented to the actual present than dissociative parts who are fixed in traumatic memories. Some dissociative parts may at times have a weak phenomenal Now (Van der Hart et al. 2006). For example, they may just drowse on a coach for hours with hardly any sense of time.

3.1 Situatedness and global coherence

Global availability (see 1.1) is a functional reading of a more general constraint, which holds that we subjectively always live in a world, that we are phenomenally situated beings. In other words, phenomenal experience involves situated actions, it is a being-in-the-world. We are situated because we preconsciously bind our individual phenomenal experiences into a global situational context, into the context of a single world that is presented in the mode of naive realism. Naive realism entails that we (or a part of us) confuse the representations of the world that we generate and reality as such.

Although the phenomenal world-model we entertain is highly differentiated, it is also coherent at any given moment. It constitutes a whole, not a sum of parts. We thus integrate our phenomenal content into a highest-order representational structure that can be described as our world-model. To continuously embed new phenomenal contents in the global world-model, the system that we are requires the integrative ability to bind and differentiate figure and ground, as well as many different modalities (e.g., what we hear, see, feel, do) on many different levels of granularity.[16]

3.2 Situatedness and global coherence in dissociative parts of the personality

Just like mentally healthy individuals, dissociative parts of the personality commonly experience that they exist in certain situations and that they live in a single world. Although their models of the world may be quite curtailed, incomplete, anachronistic, and more or less hallucinatory, they constitute in most cases a highest-order coherent whole for that part, that constitutes the context for lower-order phenomenal contents. Consistent with Metzinger's theory, dissociative parts usually integrate their present experiences into their model of the world. However, dissociative parts may temporarily lose their sense of situatedness and the coherence of their world-model. As discussed in 1.2, this can happen when they are extremely anxious or when they are excessively absent-minded. Loss of situatedness and global coherence does not imply that these parts lose consciousness in every regard. A dissociative part who experiences the world in loose bits and pieces is still conscious of these fragments, and a part who loses the feeling that her experiences are tied to a particular situation (e.g., a part who experiences 'I do not know where I am and what really happens'), is still consciously aware of some unbound or undifferentiated perceptions. More generally, patients with dissociative disorders lack global coherence in the sense that each of their dissociative parts entertains his or her own world. Their phenomenal perception of a particular situation can be quite dissimilar, and they embed their different perceptions in their different phenomenal worlds. For example, a patient can feel as one dissociative part that the environment is safe, whereas she believes as another part that she is in danger. These different phenomenal worlds may alternate with the successive reactivation of these different parts, or may coexist in a parallel fashion (Van der Hart et al. 2006). Just as for mentally healthy individuals, for dissociative parts their perceived world – their world zero – is the world. To the degree that different parts communicate with each other, they can be, and often are in conflict with each other over how the world really is. They may disagree how the world currently is, how it has been, and how it will be. If only because their different world-models are transparent, different dissociative parts commonly find it hard to understand that different parts have dissimilar world-models. They do not easily grasp these disparate world-models of other dissociative parts, if at all. This fact strongly contributes to the maintenance of the structural dissociation of the personality.

4.1 Convolved holism

Different phenomenal wholes do not tend to coexist as isolated entities, but commonly appear as flexible, convolved or nested patterns or multilayered experiential gestalts, organized in mereological hierarchies. These hierarchies consist in lower-order wholes that constitute a higher-order whole. Phenomenal wholes include phenomena such as perceived objects (e.g., a synthesis of perceived form, color and texture), sensory wholes (e.g., a synthesis of what we see, feel, hear and smell), complex scenes and situations (e.g., a synthesis of two successive events) and a phenomenal self in-the-act-of-knowing (cf. Damasio 1999). Thanks to the convolved holistic nature of consciousness, we can bind but differentiate such different phenomenal wholes into higher-order structures.

To constitute a presence, phenomenal wholes have to be integrated within a phenomenal Now. As noted before, we do not have the faintest idea how we continuously and automatically integrate phenomenal parts into phenomenal wholes, because the involved integrative mental actions occur at a preattentive and preconceptual level of information processing. These actions are transparent: we engage in them, but we do not have phenomenal access to them (see 7.1 and 7.2). However, we can access our conscious thoughts: they are opaque for us. This implies that 'to experience a world is different than to think a world' (Metzinger 2003: 145).

Whereas conscious experience constitutes a whole, it is not an undifferentiated mass. For example, we live in brief moments of time through a wide range of different conscious states. A major advantage of convolved holism, i.e., of well-differentiated but nested mental and phenomenal contents, is that the contents of individual representata can be recurrently updated in a fast, flexible and context-sensitive manner. But what guides these integrative actions? I already remarked that mental and phenomenal simulation serve survival interests, and that adaptive functioning requires values that define what is safe and attractive, or dangerous and adverse. These values guide what we tend to perceive, feel, think and do, and they strongly influence what meaning we assign to external and internal stimuli. As Hurley (1998; see also Gibbs 2005) contends, perception, cognition and motor actions are not 'vertically' distinct general modules of mind, as the classical view on how the brain is organized would have it. This classical perspective constitutes a linear input-output model suggesting that we first perceive a stimulus or situation, then develop thoughts and plans, and finally engage in motor actions. However, this sequential model will not work because adaptive functioning requires recurrent feedback loops among perception, affect, thought and motor action, and because general modules do not provide the specific values needed to guide our functioning. Hurley (1998) alternatively asserts that perception, affect, cognition and motor action are organized in integrative 'horizontal' modules, in which these different mental and motor actions are tightly interconnected in recurrent feedback and feedforward loops. As has become clear in artificial intelligence and psychobiology, these modules must include values, or else they do not work.

Values do not exist in a psychobiological void. They rather constitute an essential component of action systems like attachment, play, exploration, reproduction and mammalian defense with subsystems such as flight, freeze, flight and total submission. Action systems have also been described as motivational (Lang et al. 1998) or emotional operating systems (Panksepp 1998). They are evolutionary derived psychophysiological tools for approaching attractive cues or for avoiding aversive stimuli (see also Fanselow and Lester 1988; Timberlake and Lucas 1989). For example, the action system of attachment tells us to connect to certain individuals, and the action system of mammalian defense informs us what objects and individuals we would better avoid. Horizontal modules within action systems provide specific action-organizing values. Thus, the action system or constellation of action systems and the implied horizontal modules activated at a given moment strongly influence what an individual likely perceives, feels in a bodily and emotionally sense, thinks, wants, fantasizes and does, and how these various mental and motor actions get integrated.[17] Recent research suggests that personality can be understood as a certain constellation of action systems (Nijenhuis and Den Boer 2009). In mental health, the various action systems for functioning in daily life (approaching attractive cues) and functioning under threat and attack (avoiding and escaping from aversive cues) are integrated into a whole that constitutes the individual's personality. This integration allows for links and flexible shifts among various action systems or modules within action systems.

In sum, values organize action systems as well as horizontal modules within action systems, and the mentally healthy personality as a whole system integrates a set of different action systems. This integration allows for flexible, adaptive functioning in a changeable internal and external milieu. Values, action systems and personality as an integration of multiple action systems strongly support the capacity for convolved holism of the individual as a whole system.

4.2 Convolved holism in dissociative parts of the personality

Like integrated individuals, dissociative parts of the personality generally do not experience isolated objects, subjects or scenes, but integrated, nested wholes. However, the experiential domains of dissociative parts – i.e., the range of their integrated mental and physical states – tend to be more limited, and sometimes far more limited in scope, restricting their degree of convolved holism. The consequence of this restriction is that dissociative parts, and the dissociative patient as a whole cannot embed non-integrated mental contents in a quick, flexible and context-sensitive manner in the whole of their other experiences.

By the theory of structural dissociation of the personality (Nijenhuis et al. 2002; Van der Hart et al. 2006), dissociative parts are primarily mediated by one or more but limited set of action systems and their implied values. The action system or limited constellation of action systems activated at a given moment strongly influence what a dissociative part likely perceives, feels in a bodily and emotionally sense, thinks, wants, fantasises and does. In this light, the range of objects, subjects and scenes that these parts of the personality emulate, and the wider whole or wholes in which they embed these mental contents – hence their capacity for convolved holism – are limited by the action systems or constellation of action systems that mediate them.

From a philosophical point of view, the personality can become divided in an endless number of ways in the context of traumatization. A related issue is that the particular way in which a personality has become divided does not necessarily say anything about the way in which the previously integrated personality was organized (assuming it was integrated in the first place). Believing otherwise would be succumbing to the mistaken premise of compositional reversibility, also described as the 'Humpty Dumpty Fallacy' (Braude 1995). This principle erroneously holds that the structure of the pre-existing personality can be inferred from the organization of the subsequent dissociative personality: 'just because something is now in pieces, it does not follow that those pieces correspond to permanent or previously existing natural elements or divisions of that thing' (Braude 1995: 139). According to the theory of structural dissociation, some kind of divisions of the personality in traumatization are nonetheless more probable than other divisions. The basic prototype of structural dissociation of the personality involves a division between two types of dissociative parts. One 'large' part (i.e., a part that encompasses a wide range of manifest and latent mental states) is foremost mediated by action systems for approaching attractive cues.

These action systems are for functioning in daily life, and for survival of the species, and include energy management, reproduction, bonding, care taking, play and exploration. Another, far 'smaller' dissociative part is principally guided by the mammalian defensive system. This complex action system mediates reactions to aversive stimuli that threaten the survival of the individual. The stimuli include separation from caretakers, as well as reactions to threat to life and physical attack. The defense system includes subsystems such as attachment cry, hypervigilance, freeze, flight, fight and total submission. Following Myers (1940), Van der Hart and colleagues metaphorically describe the first type of dissociative part as the apparently normal part of the personality (ANP),[18] and the second type as the emotional part of the personality (EP). They also distinguish more complex prototypes of structural dissociation (which involves a spectrum of severity). In DID, there is more than one ANP and more than one EP. Dissociative parts and their limited mental and phenomenal contents constitute efforts to survive a traumatizing environment given insufficient capacity to integrate the traumatic experiences.

Limited degrees of convolved holism can manifest as psychoform and somatoform dissociative symptoms (Nijenhuis 2004). Dissociative symptoms, which flow from a structural dissociation of the personality (Van der Hart et al. 2004), relate to a limited degree of convolved holism because they reflect a lack of integration of particular presentata and representata into the personality at large. For example, amnesia is a psychoform dissociative symptom when the patient does not recall something as one part, say ANP, but does recall it as another part, say EP. Along the same lines of reasoning, analgesia is a somatoform dissociative symptom when one dissociative part does not feel pain in a particular part of the body, whereas another dissociative part has this pain.

5.1 Dynamicity

Phenomenal states hardly ever involve static or highly stable mental contents, but rather generally include elements such as (flow of) time, duration, change and agency. Hence these states are in ongoing motion. They are dynamic: 'Our conscious life emerges from integrated psychological moments, which, however, are themselves integrated into the flow of subjective time' (Metzinger 2003: 151). This dynamicity is not given but results from a physically acting individual who is an attentional, cognitive and volitional agent. From a teleological point of view, phenomenal dynamicity makes dynamical properties of our behavioral space or ecological niche available for a multitude of processing systems at the same time. It provides us with temporal information that helps us to adapt to a changeable inner and outer world. Our experiences of duration and change are superimposed on our phenomenal Now, on the present as we experience it. This superposition involves the mental action that Janet (1928, 1935), many years ago, referred to as presentification. It is the action of integrating our present, past and future, while realizing that the past and the future are linked to the present, and that the present is the most real. Assigning the highest degree of reality to the phenomenal Now is adaptive because we can only act in the present.

Whereas a PSM is in constant flux, most individuals experience that they remain the same person despite the ongoing shifts. According to Metzinger, it is the invariance of bodily self-awareness through proprioceptive and kinesthetic feedback, of agency, and of autobiographical memory which constitutes the conscious experience of an enduring self that is stable across time and changing situations.

5.2 Dynamicity in dissociative parts of the personality

Dynamicity is deficient in patients with dissociative disorders. The lack manifests in compromised autobiographical memory, planning, ideals, meaning making and integration among action systems. For example, dissociative parts may fail to phenomenally represent change, or represent change only in a limited sense. It may occur to them that every hour and every day are the same, and when hypoaroused, they can experience that hours pass by in a void. Some dissociative parts lack all sense of time, and have to be educated in treatment about the characteristics of time.

The phenomenology of dissociative patients confirms Metzinger's hypothesis that dynamicity is not a necessary feature of consciousness. The limited dynamicity that many dissociative patients display does not imply a complete loss of consciousness but an attenuation thereof. The degree of dynamicity can be particularly limited in EPs. Fixated on a traumatic past that they experience as the present, these parts' mental contents are abnormally and maladaptively invariant. Their lack of dynamicity also affects their subjective sense of age and time. One child EP of a patient with DDNOS told her therapist: 'You have grown older this week, because you have been around for many hours, but not me. I have not been around much, thus I hardly grow older.' Dynamicity is also limited in most ANPs, albeit less severely in most cases (Van der Hart et al. 2006).

Whereas many dissociative parts integrate at least some significant experiences across time and situations, none integrates them all: adaptive dynamicity and presentification are major problems for all dissociative parts. For example, ANPs typically do not integrate one or more traumatic memories, and EPs commonly do not integrate a host of autobiographical memories, the actual present, and adaptive simulations of the future. The PSM of many EPs involves a child-like identity, which shows that these dissociative parts do not integrate the ageing body and large parts of the patient's life history. ANPs may also lack autobiographical memories that do not pertain to traumatic experiences, and some only simulate a future in a very limited sense. Most ANPs thus also develop a limited degree of dynamicity. Most dissociative parts experience that they remain the same 'person' across time, also when they in fact change to a degree. However, they may feel that they change with major increases of their PSM. They feel their body more with the lifting of dissociative kinesthetic or emotional anesthesia, they develop a stronger sense of agency or mineness when they engage in the mental action of personification more (Van der Hart et al. 2006), and they can extend their autobiographical memory, as happens when they integrate traumatic memories. For example, an ANP who was focused on work believed that she did not have a child, whereas another dissociative part of the patient recalled the rapes of her stepfather, the pregnancy, the birth of the child, and twenty years of caretaking of the daughter all too well. The ANP experienced a profound subjective and objective change when she integrated this other part's traumatic memories of giving birth to a daughter from her stepfather when she was 15 years old. This integration happened in a psychotherapeutic session more than twenty years after the actual event. It instantly and immensely affected her interactions with her daughter.

6.1 Perspectivalness

I have already detailed how according to Metzinger (2003), the PSM offers a first-person perspective, i.e., the phenomenal experience of being someone, and how this PSM encompasses self-presentata, self-representata and self-simulata.

6.2 Perspectivalness in dissociative parts of the personality

Self-presentata

Dissociative parts with a first-person perspective are the phenomenal center of their phenomenal world when they minimally experience some basic bodily feelings. In this case, they experience a phenomenal self. Many dissociative parts have strong, explicit bodily feelings. They own these sensations – so that they are self-presentata – and experience in close relationship with the personified bodily feelings that they are the phenomenal center of their phenomenal world. Some dissociative parts, however, have (a degree of) bodily anesthesia or analgesia regarding the whole body or particular body parts. As one part with severe somatoform and emotional anesthesia wondered: 'Do I really exist? Am I a dream?' The fact that this particular dissociative part referred to herself as 'I' suggests that she had a PSM, however faint. She generated a PSM, but lacked a centralised point of view as she felt that she was floating 'everywhere'. With this degree of bodily anesthesia and similar somatoform dissociative symptoms (Nijenhuis 2004), sensing the body as a stable point of reference is severely weakened, and together with it, the PSM. These clinical observations are consistent with Metzinger's hypothesis that self-consciousness primarily entails bodily awareness, thus in a synthesis of bodily feelings in a PSM. Therefore, we can say: few or no body sensations, little or no phenomenal self.

Self-representata

The PSM of a dissociative part is very limited in some cases, but can be far richer in other cases. For some ANPs, it can even be highly differentiated and coherent. But the PSM of the dissociative parts of a patient is less complete and complex than the PSM of the patient when fully integrated.

Self-simulata

As goes for the PSM of mentally healthy individuals, the PSMs of dissociative parts denotes a possible reality that they subjectively experience as the reality. And as applies to the mentally healthy, this confusion is adaptive because the dissociative part can use the current PSM as a point of reference. This reference base is needed for the ability to distinguish between the current self-model (phenomenally experienced as immediately given in the mode of naive realism) and other possible self-models (that the patient generates when remembering an experience, making plans, or fantasizing).

7.1 Transparency

Phenomenal transparency implies that 'whatever is transparently represented for the system as a whole is experienced as real and as undoubtedly existing by this system' (Metzinger 2003: 167). That is, transparency entails functioning in the mode of naive realism. Functioning in the mode of naive realism is most useful, because it allows us a phenomenal distinction between reality and appearance. It allows us to engage in actions such as planning and fantasy, because we can distinguish between phenomenal facts, perceived in the mode of naive realism (e.g., 'I see my friend', which means: 'There is no doubt in my mind that what I see is my friend; he and my perception of him are real') and generated possible worlds ('I will see my friend tomorrow').

Metzinger (2003) suggests that for any phenomenal state, the degree of phenomenal transparency is inversely proportional to the introspective degree of attentional availability of earlier processing stages. There are, thus, degrees of transparency and opacity. For example, we can sometimes, perhaps with considerable mental effort, experience that we engage in a projection as a psychological defense, rather than in an objective assessment of someone's actions or intentions. More generally, our conscious thoughts are more or less opaque.

7.2 Transparency in dissociative parts of the personality

Transparency is present in all dissociative parts, who, as provisionally suggested above, have a degree of consciousness and who entertain a phenomenal self-model, however minimal. This clinical observation fits the self-model theory of subjectivity, which proposes that transparency is one of three minimal constraints on consciousness. The other minimal constraints are global availability of mental contents within a phenomenal Now. Although some dissociative parts find it subjectively difficult to tell facts from fantasies, many parts do not doubt the reality of most of their phenomenal representations. Because the representations can be quite different, there are frequent conflicts among dissociative parts regarding the question what is real, as well as conflicts of this nature between these parts and individuals (e.g., spouses, therapists) who challenge their phenomenal world-model and self-model. The representational character of these models becomes particularly evident when they are at odds with the facts, when two or more dissociative parts fuse into a new, now larger subsystem of the patient's personality, or when all dissociative parts blend into one whole system. For example, the representational nature of a part's self-model is clear when an EP of a man who is 40 years old, who lives on his own and who is not abused any more, believes that 'she' is a girl of 7 years old who is living with her parents, and who is about to be abused again. The representational character of PSMs of dissociative parts is also demonstrated by the sudden disappearance of these models and the sudden appearance of a new PSM when two or more dissociative parts have fused. However, it may take a lot of integrative therapeutic work before this fusion can take place. This work includes making opaque the transparent aspects of the PSM of dissociative parts that can be made opaque. For example, the therapist helped Robert realize that the 7-year-old part believed she was a girl and that she was seen as a girl by himself as ANP because 'girls get raped, not boys'. By holding on to this belief, Robert could believe as ANP that he had not been sexually abused.

The loss of homogenous presentata and representata (see 10.1) may involve a limitation of transparency in dissociative parts. This loss happened to the patient who was introduced in 1.2. She experienced that her world and herself shattered into many bits and pieces when she was exposed to extreme sexual abuse that included a threat to her life. In these cases, dissociative patients may experience that components of presentata and representata become disconnected. This phenomenon could reflect a certain degree of opacity regarding mental actions that are normally transparent.

8.1 Offline activation

Functioning in the mode of naive realism strongly depends on embodiment, sensorimotor action and a phenomenal Now. These features define the phenomenal present for us as a whole system: we sense and move in the experienced reality of the here and now.

Non-intended phenomenal simulations (e.g., spontaneous dreams and fantasies) and intended phenomenal simulations (e.g., our deliberate planning of actions) are less dependent on actual sensorimotor input. They involve representations of the past or the imagined future, that can include a degree of sensorimotor imagination (Weber et al. 2006). By means of our offline simulations of the past, that are usually more opaque than transparent, our historicity becomes cognitively available. Autobiographical memory appears: 'I now remember what happened to me. I know that what I currently experience is a memory.' In intended simulations, we represent ourselves as agents, who generate phenomenologically opaque mental representations. For example, in planning we develop an opaque representation of a possible world and a possible self: 'I imagine (think, picture, believe) that I can do it in this manner.' This kind of simulation of a possibility allows us to reflect on ourselves, so that we can regard ourselves as historical persons.

Offline simulations thus enable self-simulations (e.g., 'How will I act best?'), as well as simulations of other agents (e.g., 'What would he do?'), which support social cognition. To the extent that these predictions are at target, they obviously greatly enhance adaptive behavior. They promote adaptive behavioral actions in the short run – as in sensorimotor loops – and in the long run – as in long-term planning – and in simulations of the behavior patterns of other people (Gallese 2007). Generally speaking, beings that can engage in offline simulation are intelligent systems.

8.2 Offline activation in dissociative parts of the personality

Dissociative patients often confuse online and offline simulations. For example, they take traumatic memories, that are offline simulations pertaining to the past, for online, present experiences. Normative autobiographical memories are largely opaque, offline representations of the past that go along with a capacity for self-reflection ('I remember that I wrote the letter, and I am consciously aware that I remember that I wrote the letter'). In contrast, traumatic memories are subjectively experienced as if they were online presentata and representata ('It hurts, he is dangerous, I run'), and usually do not include self-reflective actions. In other words, what should, for adaptive purposes, be an offline representation of the past, is experienced by the survivor as if it were an online current event.

Patients with DID sometimes remember emotionally charged non-traumatizing events with significant somatosensory components as well (Van der Hart et al. 2005), hence as a mixture of presentata and representata. Furthermore, these patients may believe that offline simulations of the future (e.g., 'I imagine how I hit him') have, so to speak, online consequences (e.g., 'I am bad because I would like him to be dead; I deserve punishment'). The failure to distinguish offline simulations and online presentata and representata seriously limits the individual's capacity for adaptive action.

9.1 Intensity

Presentations, such as pain, the perception of shades of a color or of temperature, vary along a dimension of intensity. From a teleofunctional, evolutionary perspective, it is clearly adaptive to experience the intensity of stimuli. For example, we would better feel how painful a particular stimulus is. Presentation of intensity is functional in that it generates a motivation to act ('This is really hurting, I must see a doctor').

9.2 Intensity in dissociative parts of the personality

Some dissociative parts experience a loss of intensity of interoceptive or exteroceptive stimuli, and consequently underreact to these stimuli. For example, analgesia and bodily and emotional anesthesia are distinctive somatoform and psychoform symptoms in dissociative disorders to the extent that these phenomena appear in some dissociative parts but not in other parts (Nijenhuis 2004). When the intensity of presentata and representata is low, it may seem to the patient that their phenomenal contents are not very real, or not at all real, so that they do not act where they should. For example, one dissociative part completely neglected serious physical wounds. Depersonalization symptoms in dissociative parts also relate to a lack of experienced intensity of interoceptive stimuli, and dissociative parts may only vaguely appreciate that their own or other dissociative part's autobiographical memories pertain to real historical events. Dissociative parts with symptoms of derealization do not sufficiently assess the reality of external events. In a word, some stimuli are not real enough for them (Van der Hart et al. 2006). Dissociative patients can also experience that presentata and representata are exceptionally intense. One type of mental state (or series of mental states) in which this intensity evidences is reexperiencing traumatizing events. These experiences are too real for them (Van der Hart et al. 2006).

There is a subtle difference between the intensity of stimuli and the assignment of the degree of reality of presentata and representata. Phenomenal simulations can be intense, but this does not necessarily imply that they are also experienced as real (Janet 1919/1925, 1928, 1932), and stimuli that are not particularly intense such as a murmuring internal voice can become very real for some dissociative part when the voice whispers: 'I will kill you if you talk about this.' We will therefore add a constraint regarding the assessment of the degree of reality of experiences to Metzinger's list (see 12.1 and 12.2).

10.1 Homogeneity or ultra-smoothness of simple content

Homogeneity also only pertains to presentations. It denotes the internal, structureless density of, say, the color of an object. We do not perceive bits and pieces of color, no 'perceptual grains', but objects that are colored in a homogenous way. The fundamental features of our sensory perceptions of the world and of ourselves are ultra-smooth, grainless and simple. Without these features, we could penetrate earlier processing stages, which would dissolve our phenomenal model of the world and of ourselves.

10.2 Homogeneity in dissociative parts of the personality

Clinical observations suggest that dissociative parts generally experience phenomenal presentata in a homogenous way. However, the holistic character of presentations and with it their homogeneity may be lost to a degree for these parts in extreme situations. For example, previously simple and smooth presentata can become complex and fragmented for an exceptionally frightened dissociative part.

11.1 Adaptivity

Conscious experience, a phenomenal self and a first-person perspective have been acquired in millions of years of psychobiological evolution. As first persons, we can experience our evolutionary background in terms of our phenomenal emotional states. Our experienced emotions are about 'the logic of survival' (Damasio 1999: 54), because they involve a phenomenal 'affective tone' that informs us about the adaptive value of a certain situation, action or person. Phenomenal emotions represent the biological or social value of a state of affairs for the organism as a whole, and they make this information globally available for the flexible control of behavioral action, for cognition, for memory and for attention. Emotions involve embodied goal representations. However, emotions are more than representations. As they developed in evolution, Metzinger (2003) suggests, emotional conscious states must actually have possessed functional survival value.

Consciousness can more generally be seen as a virtual organ for the generation of adaptive behavior. It is a device for motor control and sensorimotor integration. As answers to evolutionary challenges, presentata and representata can also be seen as transient virtual organs. They are 'good' presentata and representata if and only if they successfully and reliably meet those challenges.

11.2 Adaptivity in dissociative parts of the personality

As discussed before, action system are major organizers of attention, cognition and behavioral action. They guide what is to be integrated and ignored, and what is to be pursued. From this perspective, dissociative parts are subsystems of the personality, and their mental and phenomenal contents are best seen as an organism's efforts at adaptation under conditions of limited integrative capacity (Nijenhuis et al. 2002; Van der Hart et al. 2006). Many authors regard dissociation as a mental defense, but there is nothing defensive about positive dissociative symptoms. For example, hearing voices and reexperiencing traumatic memories are very disturbing experiences. Negative dissociative symptoms may support adaption, however, when the individual's integrative capacity is low. Thus chronically abused and neglected children may be able to cope better with daily life when they develop one or more ANPs. As ANP, they will be less aware of traumatic memories and associated emotions and sensations. But the high price they pay is that it will be fixated on these memories as EP to the day that they integrate these memories as ANP. Reactivated by conditioned inner or outer stimuli, the traumatic memories of EPs can intrude the phenomenal domain of ANPs. When ANPs do not integrate EPs' memories (that is, EPs' mental actions), that is, do not nest them in the totality of their (ANPs') autobiographical memories, EPs will remain fixated in these sensorimotor and highly emotionally charged actions. Consequently, these traumatic memories will intrude the domain of the ANPs time and again. The patient as a whole will thus remain stuck in a lack of flexible, fast and context-dependent control regarding non-integrated mental actions, particularly but not exclusively traumatic memories, when ANPs and EPs remain structurally dissociated. Put in other words, given a sufficient capacity to integrate previously dissociated mental contents/actions, ongoing structural dissociation with its implied lack of convolved holism, personification and presentification constitutes a major adaptive problem. The deficient convolved holism strongly restricts the patient's control over traumatic memories, and leaves classically conditioned trauma-related reactions that may not fit the patient's present life unaltered. And, worse, the patient's control regarding functions such as attention, emotion, cognition, and motor action will eventually become deficient in a much broader sense. In this sense, structural dissociation is all but a mental defense.

12.1 Degrees of reality

The world zero and transparency are tools to understand how we do not recognize phenomenal representations as simulations, and how we generate a reference base for what we regard as our present, past and future and we feel is real. According to Janet (1919/1925, 1928, 1932; see also Van der Hart et al. 2006), who proposed a hierarchy of degrees of reality, to adapt we must experience that the present is more real than the recent past and immediate future, and that the recent past and immediate future are more real than the distant past and future. Our 'ideal self' – our phenomenal simulation of our phenomenal future self – should be quite real, but not as real as the present self to motivate us to go ahead, and it should not be too distant, or else we would be without hope that we can realize the ideal. Dreams, vague ideas and thoughts should be even less real than the distant past and future. Janet's hierarchy is a useful, though perhaps overly fixed set of principles that may in reality be more flexible (Van der Hart et al. 2006). For example, how real something should be for us is also context-dependent. Sometimes it is more adaptive to focus more on the probable consequences of our actions or that of others, than on the reality of the present.

12.2 Degrees of reality in dissociative parts of the personality

Many dissociative parts of the personality misjudge the degree of reality of their presentations and representations. As EP, they experience representations of the past as too real, and the real present as unreal, if not as nonexistent. As an EP who totally submits to actual or perceived danger and who is very absent minded and anesthetic, dissociative patients tend to experience reality as a dream. As a depersonalized ANP, they may not experience the present as very real. When depressed, ANPs may not see any near or distant future for them and they may lack ideals. ANPs who function quite well commonly assess the reality of the present and the future quite accurately, but for them, the past, and in particular the traumatic past may not seem to be real. Non-realization is a core symptom in patients with dissociative disorders (Van der Hart et al. 2006).

Minimal constraints on consciousness, and overview of constraints on consciousness

According to Metzinger (2003), our mental contents are also phenomenal contents when they are:

- globally available for our guided attention, cognition and/or behavioral control (there is a world)
- appear in a window presence (that world is Now)
- in a transparent fashion (there is no introspection into the ongoing presentational and representational processes that generate this world and this Now).

When the constraint of convolved holism is added, we can segment scenes and experience complex situations.

Dynamicity adds the dimensions of duration and change, so that our phenomenal contents can become organized in a framework of the present, the past and the future. With the introduction of the sixth constraint of perspectivalness, our phenomenal content involves a point of view. When we start to represent ourselves, we develop a first-person perspective that is integrated into our phenomenal state. Memory, planning and self-representation as a special, phenomenally inward directed (bodily feelings, emotions, thoughts) case of phenomenal representation emerge with constraint eight that concerns offline activation.

Minimal constraints for consciousness and DID

According to the theory of structural dissociation, dissociative parts in DID involve dynamic subsystems of an overarching dynamic system that is the patient's personality. In the light of Metzinger's analysis of consciousness, I submit that these subsystems are phenomenal subsystems of the personality because, with some exceptions such as loss of consciousness in dissociative convulsions (WHO 1992) aside, they fulfil the three minimal constraints of consciousness. They involve transparent PMIRs in the context of a global and usually coherent model of the world – however limited this model may be – and they embed these PMIRs in a phenomenal Now.

As illustrated with some case examples, dissociative parts in DID can have problems regarding any of the other constraints on consciousness. They may not have or temporarily lose one or more of these qualities. However, what always characterizes awake or dreaming dissociative parts is their own PSM, their own first-person perspective. With few exceptions, these parts are convinced that they exist. They experience that they are someone, that they a subject. But the more these parts start to share experiences, sensations, emotions, cognitions, memories, skills and other motor actions, the more their PSM (and PMIRs) become similar. When two or more dissociative parts fuse, i.e., fully integrate, they lose their different and separate PSMs and PMIRs. Metzinger's theory suggests that this implies their disappearance of the former PSMs, and the quick and transparent appearance of a new PSM with associated PMIRs. Clinical observations are consistent with this hypothesis. After a while, newly created dissociative parts or the patient's fully fused personality find it commonly quite difficult to recall how their previous subjective existence has been. Their actual PSM seems far more real to them than the PSMs of the dissociative parts out of which they have evolved. The new constructions encompass many elements of the older versions, but often many new elements as well. Theoretically, these new elements appear because a fusion of nonlinear dynamic systems that dissociative parts are in a third-person perspective (Van der Hart et al. 2006), generates more than the sum of the properties of the previously dissociated parts of the personality.

Metzinger contends that the PSM is a theoretical as well as an empirical entity. Reinders et al. (2003, 2006) found supportive evidence for this hypothesis. They invited women with DID to listen to a description of a traumatic experience that they experienced as a personal experience as EP but not as ANP. EP and ANP were associated with very different sensori-motor, emotional, and physiological reactions (heart rate, heart rate variability and blood pressure), and patterns of neural activity. Sar et al. (2007) documented different patterns of neural activation for mentally healthy women and ANPs in women with DID. This finding is consistent with the idea that ANPs are 'apparently normal'. In future research, my colleagues and I intend to examine if the neural activation of ANP and EP also differs when they focus on non-shared neutral or positive memories, listen to a description of their PSMs and PMIRs, and listen to their own recorded voices, the voice of one or more different dissociative parts, and the voice of an acquaintance.

Multiple PSMs and PMIRs in other dissociative disorders

According to the theory of structural dissociation (Nijenhuis et al. 2002; Van der Hart et al. 2006), the existence of two or more dissociative sub-systems of the personality that are aware of themselves and their Umwelt,[19] however rudimentary these subsystems and their PSM and PMIRs may be, constitutes an essential property of all dissociative disorders. A possible exception in most cases of depersonalization disorder, because these patients do not encompass dissociative parts. However, the category does include post-traumatic stress disorder (APA 1994; Van der Hart et al. 2006) and dissociative disorders of movement and sensation (WHO 1992) that in DSM-IV are classified as conversion disorders. Clinical observations suggest that even rudimentary dissociative parts in simple dissociative disorders have their own first-person perspective and Umwelt.

Case vignette: Hanne

Hanne, a young woman with recurrent nightmares, encompassed an ANP exerting functions in daily life and an EP who only contained the brief episode during which the patient was involved in a motor vehicle accident and lost consciousness when she was 3 years old. The very limited phenomenal content of this part was: 'I am 3 years old, I play with a ball, I fall, a car is approaching, runs over me, I feel a blow against my head, everything turns black.' The 3 year old was immersed in a phenomenal Now, and integrated the accident – that she recurrently relived as a presentation in nightmares – in a coherent model of the world, however limited this model was: a joyful word that invited her to play. As ANP, Hanne's PSM and PMIRs were highly differentiated and largely coherent. These models encompassed two decades, a wide range of bodily feelings and perceptions, countless emotions that related to many different action systems, a broad behavioral repertoire, as well as plans for the future and a will to realize them. But as ANP she did not understand anything about her nightmares, and she could not control them. All she knew about them as ANP was that they included intense fear of something and that she found herself back in the living room or garden of her house without any notion as to how or why she had gone to these places. The nightmares instantly disappeared once the ANP had integrated the traumatic experience and the EP in therapy. The new PSM and PMIRs that evolved included more than the phenomenal content and actions that were previously constituting the phenomenal domain of the ANP and the EP. For example, Hanne became more aware of bodily and emotional feelings and personified these more than she had done as ANP. She also became far more lively socially.

Mental contents become phenomenal contents for a dissociative part when they are included into the part's PSM and PMIR. Dissociative parts can attend to particular mental contents, think about them, and use them for volitional behavioral action control when these mental contents are phenomenal contents. Thus, the more limited a dissociative part's PSM and PMIR are, the less attentional, cognitive and volitional control the part will have, and the more it will be directed by affordances and conditioned stimuli. The part's actions may then be impulsive and reflex-like. Elaboration of the PSMs and PMIRs of the different dissociative parts is therefore an explicit and major treatment goal. To this end, therapists found their treatment on an analysis of the functioning of the different ANPs and EPs, of these part regarding each other, and of the system as a whole.

The cardinal feature of patients with dissociative disorders is that they involve multiple first-person perspectives. They encompass at least two dissociative parts, each of which generates a PSM and a set of associated PMIRs, however simple these dissociative PSM and PMIRs may be. This definition implies that ego-dystonic phobias and the like do not involve dissociative parts of the personality when the patient includes only one PSM. Although the subsystem of the personality that causes an ego-dystonic phobia is not fully integrated into the personality at large, it does not encompass its own PSM. Such patients still will say that they are afraid (I [the patient's singular PSM] fear and avoid heights, although I know my phobia is silly).

A different view is that dissociative parts of the personality do not necessarily involve consciousness and self-consciousness (Brown 2006; Holmes et al. 2005). Phrased in Metzinger's terminology, they would not encompass their own PSM and PMIR. Dissociation, by Brown and Holmes' perspective, involves a compartmentalization of higher-order and lower-order information processing systems. All dissociative symptoms would result from a loss of normal high-level attentional, conscious control over low-level processing systems that do not necessarily involve conscious awareness and self-awareness. Brown and Holmes' view is problematic because it does not define the minimal constraints on the concept of dissociative parts of the personality. Human individuals include many low-level processing systems (molecules, neurons, neural organs, neural groups, etc.) that may not operate in fully integrative ways. In other words, Brown and Holmes do not clarify what compartmentalized processing systems are of a dissociative nature and what compartmentalized systems are of a different kind. For example, they should provide a criterion that can be used to say why subsystems mediating ego-dystonic phobias and complex tics as in the syndrome of Gilles de la Tourette would or would not be dissociative parts of the personality.

Multiple perspectivalness, i.e., the existence of two or more different PSMs, can serve as a useful criterion for delimiting the category of dissociative parts of the personality, and thereby the category of dissociative disorders. Acknowledging that all categorizations are human-made, hence artificial (Wittgenstein 1953), we emphasize that non-integrated subsystems of the personality with and without a first-person perspective involve different properties that are of theoretical, scientific and clinical interest. For example, it is of clinical importance to realize that it is even possible to communicate with rudimentary dissociative parts because they have a PSM and PMIRs. A thorough understanding of the PSMs and PMIRs of dissociative parts of the personality helps the clinician to empathize, accept, understand and influence the different parts, and to assist them to become more empathic, accepting, understanding each other: all pivotal ingredients to attain cooperation among the dissociative parts, as well as their eventual fusion.

Alterations of consciousness in dissociative disorders, other mental disorders and mental health

Global availability, a phenomenal Now and transparency aside, individuals who do not have a dissociative disorder or any other mental or neurological disorder can fail to meet one or more constraints on consciousness. For example, any one of us may sometimes experience that our phenomenal contents are not very real, appear less intense than they normally do, or do not fit our world-model so well. We can also experience shifts in the flow of time (time may seem to speed up or slow down), we may have difficulty remembering certain experiences, and we can feel less centered or present at times. Many phenomena that have been described in literature as dissociative in fact entail common alterations of consciousness rather than the specific phenomena that flow from a structural dissociation of the personality (Van der Hart et al. 2004). These common alterations of consciousness include changes with respect to situatedness and global coherence, convolved holism, dynamicity, intensity, adaptivity and degree of reality of mental contents. In statistical terms, they are sensitive but not specific for dissociative disorders. It, therefore, seems odd to conceptualize common alterations of consciousness as dissociative symptoms.

What does not exist in psychiatric patients who do not have a dissociative disorder and in mentally healthy individuals are multiple PSMs and associated PMIRs. Thus, it is structural dissociation of the personality, i.e., existence of more than one PSM and the associated different PMIRs, and the symptomatic manifestations of this organization of personality that are specific for dissociative disorders. Exceptions to this rule are individuals who develop multiple perspectivalness in response to hypnotic suggestions, and particular mediums. Table 8.1 offers some examples of normal and pathological alterations of consciousness and shows that only multiple perspectivalness is specific for dissociative disorders.

Summary and discussion

Based on the theory of structural dissociation and the self-model theory of subjectivity, we can say that dissociative parts are dynamic subsystems of the personality, each of which generates its own PSM and its own set of PMIRs. Dissociative part of this kind have evolved most strongly in patients with DID, but exist in all dissociative disorders. However, EPs may be rudimentary in that they may encompass only a few mental actions and implied mental contents. Structural dissociation of the personality manifests in various dissociative symptoms. These symptoms must be distinguished from other alterations of consciousness, i.e., from those that are sensitive but not specific for dissociative disorders. The latter symptoms are also ubiquitous in mentally healthy individuals, in patients with other mental disorders, and in patients with a neurological disorder. In the context of traumatization, dissociation thus entails a division of personality – i.e., of the dynamic, biopsychosocial system as a whole that determines an individual's characteristic mental and motor actions – into two or more dynamic but unduly stable subsystems. Each of these subsystems generates its own, at least rudimentary phenomenal models of self, world, and relation of self and world. Phenomenologically, such lack of integration of personality manifests in dissociative symptoms that can be categorized as negative (functional losses such as amnesia and paralysis) or positive

Table 8.1 Different alterations of consciousness in mental health, dissociative
disorders and other mental disorders

Mental health	Dissociative disorders	Other mental disorders
1 Global world Intact, but availability for attention, cognition and motor control can decrease, as happens in absorption, and restriction of the field of consciousness.	Intact, but availability for attention, cognition and motor control is often limited, and can be exceptionally restricted for EPs.	Intact, but availability for attention, cognition and motor control can be pathologically limited.
2 Phenomenal Now Intact.	Intact, but EPs often confuse the actual and the perceived phenomenal Now.	Vague sense of the present in major depression.
3 Situatedness Intact.	Dissociative parts may not always be aware of the complex situation in which they are.	Severely depressed or psychotic patients may hardly be aware of the situation in which they are.
4 Convolved holism Intact, but the field of consciousness changes constantly.	Commonly intact in the sense that the experiences of dissociative parts are embedded in a model of the situation in which they are. However, the field of consciousness of dissociative parts is not only changeable, but also permanently unduly restricted.	Commonly intact, but the field of consciousness may be unduly restricted.
5 Dynamicity The sense of duration and change shifts, but the phenomenal Now is always linked with a sense of duration and change, i.e., with the past and the future.	Presentification is deficient: EPs live in the past that is experienced as the present; ANPs have insufficiently integrated the past; EPs and often ANPs as well, do not generate an adequate idea of the future.	Lack of an (adaptive) idea of the future in major depression; strong maladaptive negative anticipations in anxiety disorders.
6 Perspectivalness Singular.	Multiple.	Singular.
7 Transparency (regarding PSM) Intact.	Intact, possibly some exceptions in extreme fear.	Intact.

continues

Table 8.1 (*continued*)

Mental health	Dissociative disorders	Other mental disorders
8 Offline activation Commonly, online and offline activation are distinguished from each other.	Sometimes confusion of offline and online activation.	Confusion of offline and online activation in psychosis.
9 Intensity Changeable.	Changeable. Can be too strong or too weak.	Changeable. Can be too strong as in anxiety disorders or too weak, as in major depression.
10 Homogeneity Intact.	Disintegration of homogeneity may occur in EPs.	Fragmentation possible with extreme anxiety.
11 Adaptivity Adaptive.	Adaptive given insufficient integrative capacity; non-adaptive when integration would be attainable.	Maladaptive.
12 Degree of reality Commonly intact.	Usually better assessment of reality in ANPs than in EPs, but limitations in all dissociative parts.	Limited in acute anxiety, depersonalization, psychosis and major depression.

(intrusions such as flashbacks or voices), and psychoform (symptoms such as amnesia, hearing voices) or somatoform (symptoms such as anesthesia or tics) (Nijenhuis and Van der Hart 2011). Many clinical implications can be derived from the combined theories. For example, only when mental contents become phenomenal contents, dissociative parts can attend to them, think about them, and use them for the conscious control of their actions. In Metzinger's view, this control of attention, cognition and motor action are exerted by fractions of the system as a whole that the individual that generate the PSMs and PMIRs. The PSMs and PMIRs of the different dissociative parts are not mutually exclusive, because there is usually mental and phenomenal overlap among their models of self, world and self-in-the-world. This implies that the different dissociative parts have at least some epistemic access to each other. When this phenomenal access exists, patients will know as one dissociative part that they are dissociated from another dissociative part. The mental and phenomenal overlap among the dissociative parts will ever increase during successful treatment. Their mental and phenomenal differences will eventually disappear altogether. This is when they fuse.

We can also deduct empirically testable hypotheses from both theories. For example, using neuroimaging techniques, the hypothesis can be tested that the neural activity for ANP will be different when this ANP listens to audiotape that contains (1) this part's own self-spoken self-description, (2) an EP's self-spoken self-description, or (3) an acquaintance's self-spoken self-description (Nijenhuis, Weder and Schlumpf, in preparation). Such differences would also exist when EP listens to his or her own self-description, ANP's self-description and an acquaintance's self-description. However these different reactions of ANP compared with EP would not exist for controls who are instructed to imitate ANP and EP to the best of their abilities.

The study of neurological disorders has provided major insights into the neural functioning of healthy individuals. The psychobiological study of consciousness and self-consciousness in dissociative disorders can similarly greatly enhance the understanding of normal consciousness and self-consciousness. If only for this reason, it is remarkable that so very little effort has been invested in the psychobiology of dissociative disorders to date.

Metzinger's theory has met positive and critical reactions from other philosophers (see in particular *Psyche*, 11 (5) 2005 and *Psyche*, 12 (4) 2006, with powerful rebuttals from Metzinger). It is beyond the scope of this chapter to discuss these epistemological, ontological and anthropological critiques. However, some frequent misunderstandings regarding the theory should be corrected. One misunderstanding is that Metzinger would think that the self is an illusion. This is not what he has in mind. The illusion, he says, is that the self is a thing or substance, rather than a recurrent presentational and representational process. Another mistaken belief regarding the theory is that the PSM and PMIRs are senseless because they are simulations. The critique is that distinguishing between reality and appearance is impossible if all that exists are appearances. I have described in this chapter how according to Metzinger individuals are able to take particular simulations for reality, and how some simulations work better than others. To reiterate, chronically abused and neglected children may be unable to integrate their exceptionally difficult life into one coherent PSM and model of the world. It can be adaptive in these circumstances to generate one or more ANPs and one or more EPs. The truth of this statement can, among others, be derived from clinical experiences with adult patients with a dissociative disorder who were severely abused as children. Attempts to expose them as ANP to the self (PSM) and world (the characteristic set of PMIRs) of one or more EPs while their integrative capacity is still too low commonly to result in serious decompensations (suicide attempts, self-mutilation, panic reactions and so on). The rationale of phase-oriented treatment of trauma and dissociation is to gradually increase the patient's integrative capacity (Van der Hart et al. 2006), so that the dissociation of the personality can eventually be overcome. This development generates simulations of self, world and self-in-the-world that are more viable and liveable than the simulations of the previously dissociated parts of the personality, provided a sufficient integrative capacity and an Umwelt that has changed for the better.

Metzinger's theory is a representational theory and there is philosophical critique regarding representational theories (e.g., Bursen 1978). Further analysis will be needed to examine if the critique is resolved when the traditional two-way relation between representandum and representatum is substituted for a three-way relation with the representing system as the third player. In closing, one last remark. Metzinger claims that the PSM supervenes on functional, neurological properties and that it can therefore be empirically found. But how can we assess that a particular pattern of neural activity involves an individual's PSM of that moment? Does this assessment not always require a combination of a first-person perspective (here: the subjective experience of being someone) and third-person perspective (here: a pattern of biochemical brain activity)?

Notes

1 Patients with a dissociative disorder have only parts of the personality that are dissociated from each other. Therefore, a term such as the 'normal part of the personality' is incoherent.
2 Mereology is the logic of part–whole relations.
3 The issue that Wittgenstein (1953) addresses is applicable not only to 'human beings, and what resembles (behaves like) human beings', but also to all living systems include mental features. Jonas (1966: 1) contends that there is a strong continuity of the mental and the biological, of mind and life: 'the organic even in its lowest forms prefigures mind, and . . . the mind, even on its highest reaches remains part of the organic.' This continuity may start with the cell that can be regarded as the most basic autonomous dynamic system (Thompson 2007).
4 Although these disorders are basically functional disorders, they may also involve structural brain abnormalities. For example, DID is associated with small hippocampal and parahippocampal volume (Ehling et al. 2007; Vermetten et al. 2006).
5 Intentionality is a philosophical term that is often simplistically summarized as 'aboutness' or the relationship between mental acts and the external world. Every mental act has a content, and is therefore intentional: it is directed at an object (the intentional object). Thus every perception, belief, desire, etc. has an object that it is about: the perceived, the believed, the wanted. (see_http://en.wikipedia.org/wiki/Intentionality_(http://en.wikipedia.org/wiki/Intentionality)). As Thompson (2007) holds, in phenomenology, consciousness is intentional in the sense that it 'aims toward' something beyond itself. The term 'intentionality' stems from the Latin *intendere*, which once referred to drawing a bow and aiming at a target.
6 Metzinger (2003) hardly refers to his inspirational sources. Some of the concepts he proposes or discusses can also be found in the work of predecessors, for

example in that of the phenomenologists Husserl, Heidegger and Merleau-Ponty. It is also grounded in neuroscience.

7 Empirical entities are entities that can be found. According to Metzinger (2003), the PSM would be found in terms of particular neural correlates.

8 Representational and information processing theories have met philosophical criticisms. One criticism is discussed in the present section and some others are addressed later. However, it is beyond the scope of the chapter to discuss all of them.

9 Metzinger (2003) uses the impersonal term 'processes' to denote mental vehicles, and regards representation as a physiological process. However, it can be doubted that mental vehicles are best understood as physiological processes – suggesting that the mental can be completely reduced to the physiological – rather than as psychobiological actions that individuals engage in, consciously or unconsciously. Thus, Van der Hart et al. (2006) describe mental vehicles as mental actions. For example, in their view, perception involves an intentional action.

10 More generally, mental content and mental vehicle cannot be separated. Mental content and mental vehicle are two strongly interrelated aspects of one and the same phenomenon. They constitute two sides of a coin: each mental vehicle has mental content, and each mental content requires a mental vehicle.

11 *Telos* is Greek for goal, end, purpose.

12 To emulate means to strive to equal or excel, particularly but not necessarily by means of imitation by an emulator. In computer science, an emulator is hardware or software that permits programs written for one computer to be run on another computer (Merriam-Webster). The use of the term 'emulation' in this chapter does not imply that human beings would operate as computers.

13 The term 'adaptation' masks that healthy organisms not only adapt themselves to their environment, but also shape or create their environment. Thompson (2007) therefore proposes to exchange the term 'adaptation' for the term 'viability'. In this chapter, I use the term adaptation in the sense of (promoting) viability, but I also use the term viability at times.

14 Metzinger proposes that the concept of phenomenal presentation – involving the most simple forms of phenomenal content – replaces what used to be called qualia (see Metzinger 2003: 63–86).

15 I use term information determination to emphasize that there is no information that is independent from the perceiving agent (Merleau-Ponty 1945/1962). As Thompson (2007: 51–2) contends: 'information is context-dependent and agent-relative; it belongs to the coupling of a system and its environment. What counts as information, is determined by the history, structure, and needs of the system acting in its environment.' Information determination thus involves meaning making. This essential issue is often overlooked or ignored in information processing theories.

16 Granularity can be defined as a measure of the size of the components, or descriptions of components, that make up a system (www.en.wikipedia.org).

17 Action systems can be understood as dynamic, nonlinear systems with emergent properties (see Hurley and Noë 2003; Thompson 2007). Values can be seen as attractors that organize these dynamic systems.

18 These labels do not imply at all that the ANP would lack emotions. On the contrary, all action system encompass values, hence include emotions. As Panksepp (1998) says, they are emotional operating systems. Mediated by action systems of daily life and survival of the species, ANP thus also includes emotions.

19 The concept of Umwelt stems from Von Uexküll (Agamben 2004). It entails the environment as perceived by an organism given its build, maturation, and development. We can say that the totality of someone's PMIRs constitutes his or her Umwelt.

References

Agamben, G. (2004) *The Open: Man and Animal.* Stanford, CA: Stanford University Press.

Allport, G.W. (1961) *Pattern and Growth in Personality.* New York: Holt, Rinehart & Winston.

American Psychiatric Association (APA) (1994) *Diagnostic and Statistical Manual of Mental Disorders,* 4th edn. Washington, DC: APA.

Banks, G., Short, P., Martinez, A.J., Latchaw, R., Ratcliff, G. and Boller, F. (1989) The alien hand syndrome: Clinical and post mortem findings. *Archives of Neurology,* 46: 456–9.

Bennett, M.R. and Hacker, P.M.S. (2003) *Philosophical Foundations of Neuroscience.* Oxford: Blackwell.

Braude, S.E. (1979) *ESP and Psychokinesis: A Philosophical Examination.* Philadelphia, PA: Temple University Press.

Braude, S.E. (1995) *First Person Plural: Multiple Personality and the Philosophy of Mind.* Lanham, MD: Rowman & Littlefield.

Braude, S.E. (1997) *The Limits of Influence: Psychokinesis and the Philosophy of Science.* Lanham, MD: University Press of America.

Brown, R.J. (2006) Different types of 'dissociation' have different psychological mechanisms. *Journal of Trauma and Dissociation,* 7 (4): 7–28.

Bursen, H.A. (1978) *Dismantling the Memory Machine: A Philosophical Investigation of Machine Theories of Memory.* Dordrecht: Reidel.

Damasio, A.R. (1999) *The Feeling of What Happens: Body and Emotion in the Making of Consciousness.* New York: Harcourt Brace.

Edelman, G.M. and Tononi, G. (2000) *A Universe of Consciousness: How Matter Becomes Imagination.* New York: Basic Books.

Ehling, T., Nijenhuis, E.R.S. and Krikke, A.P. (2007) Volume of discrete brain structures in complex dissociative disorders: Preliminary findings. *Progress in Brain Research,* 167: 307–10.

Fanselow, M.S. and Lester, L.S. (1988) A functional behavioristic approach to aversively motivated behavior: Predatory imminence as a determinant of the topography of defensive behavior. In R.C. Bolles and M.D. Beecher (eds) *Evolution and Learning.* Hillsdale, NJ: Lawrence Erlbaum.

Frith, C. (2007) *Making Up the Mind: How the Brain Creates our Mental World.* Malden, MA: Blackwell.

Gallese, V. (2007) Before and below 'theory of mind': Embodied simulation and the neural correlates of social cognition. *Philosophical Transactions of the Royal Society of London: Biological Sciences,* 362: 659–69.

Gibbs, R.W. (2005) *Embodiment and Cognitive Science.* New York: Cambridge University Press.

Gibson, J.J. (1977) The theory of affordances. In R. Shaw and J. Bransford (eds) *Perceiving, Acting and Knowing.* Hillsdale, NJ: Lawrence Erlbaum.

Gibson, J.J. (1979) *The Ecological Approach to Visual Perception*. New York: Houghton Mifflin.

Holmes, E.A., Brown, R.J., Mansell, W., Fearon, R.P., Hunter, E.C.M., Frasquilho, F. and Oakley, D.A. (2005) Are there two qualitatively distinct forms of dissociation? A review and some clinical implications. *Clinical Psychology Review*, 25: 1–23.

Hurley, S.L. (1998) *Consciousness in Action*. Cambridge, MA: Harvard University Press.

Hurley, S.L. and Noë, A. (2003) Neural plasticity and consciousness. *Biology and Philosophy*, 18: 131–68.

James, W. (1890) *Principles of Psychology*. New York: Holt. Also available at http://psychclassics.yorku.ca/James/Principles/index.htm.

Janet, P. (1907) *The Major Symptoms of Hysteria*. New York: Macmillan.

Janet, P. (1925) *Psychological Healing*. New York: Macmillan. Previously published 1919 as *Les Méditations psychologiques*. Paris: Félix Alcan.

Janet, P. (1928) *L'Evolution de la mémoire et de la notion du temps*. Paris: A. Chahine.

Janet, P. (1929) *L'Evolution psychologique de la personnalité*. Paris: A. Chahine.

Janet, P. (1932) On memories which are too real. In C. Macfie Campbell (Ed.), *Problems of Personality* (pp. 141–50). New York: Harcourt, Brace and Company.

Janet, P. (1935) Réalisation et interprétation. *Annales Médico-Psychologiques*, 93: 329–66.

Jonas, H. (1966) *The Phenomenon of Life: Towards a Philosophical Biology*. New York: Harper & Row.

Lang, P.J., Bradley, M.M. and Cuthbert, B.N. (1998) Emotion, motivation, and anxiety: Brain mechanisms and psychophysiology. *Biological Psychiatry*, 44: 1248–63.

Leopold, D.A. and Logothetis, N.K. (1999) Multistable phenomena: Changing views in perception. *Trends in Cognitive Sciences*, 3: 254–64.

Marchetti, C. and Della Sala, S. (1998) Disentangling the alien and the anarchic hand. *Cognitive Neuropsychiatry*, 3: 191–207.

Merleau-Ponty, M. (1945/1962) *Phenomenology of Perception*. London: Routledge & Kegan. Previously published as *Phénomenologie de la perception*. Paris: Gallimard.

Metzinger, T. (2003) *Being No One: The Self-Model Theory of Subjectivity*. Cambridge, MA: MIT Press.

Metzinger, T. (2006) Conscious volition and mental representation: Towards a more fine-grained analysis. In N. Sebanz and W. Prinz (eds) *Disorders of Volition*. Cambridge, MA: MIT Press.

Myers, C.S. (1940) *Shell Shock in France 1914–1918*. Cambridge: Cambridge University Press.

Nijenhuis, E.R.S. (2004) *Somatoform Dissociation: Phenomena, Measurement, and Theoretical Issues*. New York: Norton.

Nijenhuis, E.R.S. and Den Boer, J.A. (2009) Psychobiology of traumatization and trauma-related structural dissociation of the personality. In P.F. Dell and J.A. O'Neil (eds) *Dissociation and the Dissociative Disorders: DSM-V and Beyond*. Abingdon: Routledge.

Nijenhuis, E.R.S. and Van der Hart, O. (2011) Dissociation in trauma: A new definition and comparison with previous formulations. *Journal of Trauma and Dissociation*.

Nijenhuis, E.R.S., Van der Hart, O. and Steele, K. (2002) The emerging psychobiology of trauma-related dissociation and dissociative disorders. In H. D'Haenen, J.A. Den Boer and P. Willner (eds) *Biological Psychiatry*. London: Wiley.

Nijenhuis, E.R.S., Weder, and Schlumpf (in preparation)

Panksepp, J. (1998) *Affective Neuroscience: The Foundations of Human and Animal Emotions*. New York: Oxford University Press.

Reinders, A.A.T.S., Nijenhuis, E.R.S., Paans, A.M.J., Korf, J., Willemsen, A.T.M. and Den Boer, J.A. (2003) One brain, two selves. *NeuroImage*, 20: 2119–25.

Reinders, A.A.T.S., Nijenhuis, E.R.S., Quak, J., Korf, J., Paans, A.M.J., Haaksma, J., Willemsen, A.T.M. and Den Boer, J. (2006) Psychobiological characteristics of dissociative identity disorder: A symptom provocation study. *Biological Psychiatry*, 60: 730–40.

Sar, V., Unal, S.N. and Ozturk, E. (2007) Frontal and occipital perfusion changes in dissociative identity disorder. *Psychiatry Research*, 156 (3): 217–23.

Thompson, E. (2007) *Mind in Life: Biology, Phenomenology, and the Sciences of Mind*. Cambridge, MA: Harvard University Press.

Timberlake, W. and Lucas, G.A. (1989) Behavior systems and learning: From misbehavior to general principles. In S.B. Klein and R.R. Mowrer (eds) *Contemporary Learning Theories*. Hillsdale, NJ: Lawrence Erlbaum.

Van der Hart, O., Nijenhuis, E.R.S., Steele, K. and Brown, D. (2004) Trauma-related dissociation: Conceptual clarity lost and found. *Australian and New Zealand Journal of Psychiatry*, 38: 906–14.

Van der Hart, O., Bolt, H. and van der Kolk, B.A. (2005) Memory fragmentation in dissociative identity disorder (www.onnovdhart.nl/articles/memoryfrag.pdf). *Journal of Trauma and Dissociation*, 6 (1): 55–70.

Van der Hart, O., Nijenhuis, E.R.S. and Steele, K. (2006) *The Haunted Self: Structural Dissociation and the Treatment of Chronic Traumatization*. New York: Norton.

van der Kolk, B.A. and Van der Hart, O. (1989) Pierre Janet and the breakdown of adaptation in psychological trauma. *American Journal of Psychiatry*, 146: 1530–40.

Vermetten, E., Schmahl, C., Lindner, S., Loewenstein, R.J. and Bremner, J.D. (2006) Hippocampal and amygdalar volumes in dissociative identity disorder. *American Journal of Psychiatry*, 163: 630–6.

Weber, C., Wermter, S. and Elshaw, M. (2006) A hybrid generative and predictive model of the motor cortex. *Neural Networks*, 19: 339–53.

Wittgenstein, L. (1953) *Philosophical Investigations*. New York: Macmillan.

World Health Organization (WHO) (1992) *ICD-10: The ICD-10 Classification of Mental and Behavioural Disorders. Clinical Descriptions and Diagnostic Guidelines*. Geneva: WHO.

Yes thank you for bearing witness and for your words now, I glimpse the beginnings of what is being asked of Me, Jo. I thought I would have to stand in her shoes . . agony . . now I see it is two way, two selves, two separate pairs of shoes . . both full of identity, experiences, and unfamiliar familiarities. Delaying, she emerges like a desolate, untouchable living thing, lost to the now, knowing only herself her name her barbaric history her lifetime now one of the biggest problems she faces is ME and I her . . DID and living

Jo

Chapter 9

Talking with 'Me' and 'Not-Me'

A dialogue

Richard A. Chefetz and Philip M. Bromberg

What follows is a revised transcript of what was originally an oral presentation. The event was prepared as a dialogue, with each of our offerings serving both as a means to present our own point of view and a response to what the other had just presented about his. The material appears in the order in which it was originally presented. In 'Speaking for Myself', we each outline our own clinical perspective on our common theme, 'Talking with "Me" and "Not-Me,"', a phrase we chose to indicate the central importance of working with dissociative processes as a routine aspect of every treatment. Next comes clinical material selected by Chefetz from his own work – a verbatim record, transcribed from an audiotape (originally played aloud to the audience) of a therapy session. The dialogue concludes with Bromberg's commentary on Chefetz's clinical material, followed by Chefetz's reflections on Bromberg's commentary. Chefetz's final response also includes his own later reactions to his work.

Structuring this material as a dialogue came naturally. The two of us became acquainted by the accidental discovery (through a patient of one of us, who had heard the other speak at a conference and brought in the tape of the talk) that our sensibilities were remarkably similar to one another – so similar, in fact, that it took a little while for us to recognize that the languages we each used were not the same. The words come from different conceptual systems – Bromberg's primarily from psychoanalysis, Chefetz's more often from the field of trauma. Even when we recognized these differences, they gradually faded into a single larger and more meaningful context. That is, even though we were raised in different 'families', there is a unique commonality in the way we think about patients, about the mind, about human relatedness, and about what we do as therapists. The rising of that commonality out of what might otherwise appear to be difference is what we hoped to demonstrate by structuring the original presentation as a dialogue. The fields of trauma and psychoanalysis are inextricably linked

Note: From *Contemporary Psychoanalysis*, Volume 40, 3, July 2004, pp. 409–64.

through the concept and clinical process of dissociation, and the time is ripe for both fields to recognize this. This presentation was just such a recognition, underlined by the fact that the meeting was jointly sponsored by the William Alanson White Institute and the International Society for the Study of Dissociation (ISSD). As far as we know, this event marked the first time the White Institute has shared sponsorship with a 'not-me' organization – a society of nonpsychoanalyst clinicians and researchers committed to a theoretical and clinical perspective with its own roots, its own frame of reference, and its own rightful claim to center stage.

SPEAKING FOR MYSELF: PHILIP BROMBERG

The therapeutic action of 'safe surprises'

How is it that I, as a psychoanalyst, am so involved with something as traditionally 'unpsychoanalytic' as dissociation, and have been for more than twenty years. The obvious reason is not the only one – that I was analytically trained at the White Institute and influenced by the work of Harry Stack Sullivan (1940, 1953, 1954). It is true that I was, but my work has always been more shaped by what I encountered in my office than by what I read, and the fact that dissociative phenomena existed in every treatment captured my attention pretty much from the beginning, even though early in my career I didn't know what I was seeing. Even back then I recognized that changes in self-experience don't take place simply through talking *about* things, but depend on the linkages that become possible between here-and-now states of consciousness otherwise kept isolated from one another. My problem was how to make use of this recognition in a way that would enrich what I was doing as an analyst rather than replace it.

Sullivan's theory of therapy was based on two interlocking dimensions – inquiry into the unmentioned details of experiences reported by the patient, while simultaneously trying to maintain the patient's emotional security when this 'detailed inquiry' was taking place. Sullivan believed that in order to modulate the patient's level of affective safety (keeping it at the low end of what he referred to as an 'anxiety gradient'), it was necessary for the therapist to stay out of the transference-countertransference field as far as possible. His approach rested on what Leston Havens (1976) astutely labeled 'counterprojection'. Sullivan believed that if you become caught up in the patient's projections, you have made an error. Because Sullivan was working primarily with a population of hospitalized patients, most of whom were at that time diagnosed as schizophrenic, his 'counterprojective' technique was based on a principle that was very useful, at least in the initial phase of the treatment. He was able to help maintain the patient's dread of autonomic affective hyperarousal at a level sufficiently low that he could conduct a detailed inquiry without the patient either affectively destabilizing or dissociating to *prevent* destabilizing. In other words, Sullivan was functioning as a therapist in a way that wasn't dissimilar to what traumatologists do in what they call 'trauma work'. He established a context of affective safety by preventing himself from being drawn into the patient's enactment of unprocessed trauma, and helped access and process these experiences from outside of it. By so doing, he helped the patient process experiences that could not be thought about, but could only be felt, and were always threatening to erupt and destabilize his mind. My interest became captured by the fact that although there were certain patients for whom staying out of the field was absolutely necessary at least for a period of time, the most powerful source of growth for most patients came about through working *in* the field, as long as the patient's level of affective safety could be sustained well enough to permit it. For the deepest growth to take place, patients needed to allow themselves to be a 'mess' *within* our relationship, and in order for me to truly know them, I had to become a part of the mess in a way that I could experience internally. During certain periods, Sullivan's stance was indeed therapeutic, but over the long haul it did not lead to what seemed most central to a patient feeling recognized. Patients seemed to need attention focused on their state of mind *itself*, as a part of what went on between themselves and others. They needed something that approached what Sullivan advocated as an exquisite attention to detail, but where the details were experiential rather than objective events. These patients, at these times, did not need to be understood; they needed to be 'known', to be 'recognized'. And most to the point, each self-state needed to be known and recognized in its own terms. My expression 'standing in the spaces' eventually emerged as my shorthand way of formulating what many contemporary clinicians are, in their own metaphors, coming to frame as the essence of therapeutic action in any given treatment – a physical as well as psychological developmental process that helps bridge psyche and soma, affect and thought, and self-states that have been isolated through dissociation (Bromberg 1998, 2003b).

'Me and Not-Me' in everyday life

Thinking about therapeutic action as a facilitation of the patient's capacity to stand in the spaces between 'me' and 'not-me' states of consciousness speaks to an aspect of the therapeutic relationship that powerfully echoes Sullivan's (1954) method of 'detailed inquiry' in its effort to reconstruct reported events so precisely that 'forgotten' interpersonal details of the patient's story will emerge, bringing with them a reexperiencing of the affectively distressing self-experience that often will have been dissociated. The difference is that Sullivan's attention was focused on the interpersonal field between the patient and some external other, whereas my own approach requires that this be contained within an *overarching* attunement to the ever-shifting intersubjective field between himself and his patient – their respective 'Me and Not-Me' activity. The goal is a dyadic, here-and-now reconstruction of this activity in such subjective detail that the patient's dissociated self-states, being affectively *enacted* as 'not-me' elements in their relationship, become symbolically processed as part of 'me'. The way I work with dreams is an example. Most analysts know that in order for an 'interpretation' of a dream to have more than cosmetic value, there has to be at least some self-state link between patient and 'dreamer' – referring here to the affective reality that was the patient's self while asleep. In other words, 'associations' to a dream are valuable only to the degree they are affectively alive. It is from this vantage point that I look at the 'reported' dream as a living event that can be potentially *reentered* during a session, rather than as a story told *about* an experience that happened when asleep. In this regard, I treat it in the same way that Sullivan's traditional detailed inquiry enters waking life events by helping to reconstruct them in such experiential detail that the dissociated affect will be reexperienced in the here and now. The moments when such experiential linking of patient and dreamer become possible can't be planned, but they can be encouraged. This way of working with dreams makes use of natural hypnoid processes, processes that are the foundation of dissociative mental structure (both in dreams and as a response to trauma). I don't attempt, as a rule, to do an explicit hypnotic induction, because I feel it important that my way of working with dreams is not inconsistent with the way I work in general with a given patient. If done with careful attention to the patient's experience of what it feels like *while* we are engaged in dreamwork, the patient is often able to bring 'the dreamer' into waking consciousness and into the room with relative safety.[1] By 'bringing in the dreamer' (Bromberg 2000) – a self-state different than that of the patient who 'reports' the dream – the dream can be reentered by the 'dreamer' as it is being told by the 'patient.' Because the 'dreamer' self-state is experientially very close to the way the dreamer existed while asleep, it facilitates the patient's ability to stand in the spaces between self-states that include even those *normally* isolated dissociatively as part of the natural process through which waking consciousness is kept separate from dreaming consciousness. I want to now share a story with you – a story I recently heard from a patient – that I think will serve well in bringing to life the phenomenon of 'Me and Not-Me' as it exists in all of us.

Case vignette: Julian

My patient was about to get remarried in a few weeks and was driving his fiancée, a somewhat difficult lady who was in an even more anxious state than usual, to pick up her wedding dress. He entered an intersection just as the light was changing from yellow to red, and made one of those judgment calls. Bad move. A cop pulled him over and told him he went through a red light. He, naturally, said to the cop, 'No I didn't. It wasn't red yet. Also,' he said, 'we're just about to get married. If you can give me a break, I'd really appreciate it.' At that moment, his fiancée took over. 'How can you say that? Of course the light was red! You know you went through a red light. How can you lie like that? How can you lie to a policeman?' As she went on and on, he was getting more and more enraged, but didn't say anything. When she paused for breath, the cop, who was listening to all this, leaned over to him and said, 'I'm not going to give you a ticket. . . . if you're marrying *her*, you already have enough trouble.' As they drove off he said, still furious, 'How could you have done that? How could you have been so mean to me?' 'You didn't get a ticket, did you?' she replied. He, in a state of total consternation, could barely get his words out: 'You . . . you . . . you mean you did that on purpose?' 'Well . . . I'm not sure . . . Sort of,' she mumbled. 'Sort of.' If I had been a fly on the wall, my guess is she would have been looking into space as she said 'sort of.' And though I don't know what *he* looked like at that moment, I could easily imagine his eyeballs spinning. Eventually, when she was back to 'herself,' she acknowledged that she was terribly sorry and ashamed at what she had done, and that she hadn't done it on purpose. She also revealed that since childhood she has always been terrified of cops and 'wasn't herself' whenever she was around one.

For our purposes, the most interesting question is this: at the moment she was berating my patient in front of the cop, did her behavior come from what was felt as 'me' as opposed to 'sort of?' I think so! Once the threat of the cop was gone and she was saying to her irate husband-to-be, 'You didn't get a ticket, did you?' the vituperous 'me' of a few moments earlier became 'not-me' in this new state of mind. Clearly, she experienced no conflict at either point – a hallmark of dissociation. At each point, she experienced what she did as 'right' but in different ways. The one place she might have felt conflict was when he asked her if she did it on purpose. Her mind, however, couldn't contain the complexity of trying to bring the two self-states together long enough to reflect on their disjunction, so again she dissociated to avoid what was too much for her mind, this time to avoid the mental confusion created by a question that required her to reflect on the possibility that *both* were 'me'. In response to 'You mean you did it on *purpose?*' all she could do was offer a non-reflective, 'sort of.' I'm sharing this story to put it on record early that I see dissociation as a normal function of the human mind and ubiquitous in every human relationship.[2] Stimulated by Putnam's (1988, 1992) research findings, much of which supported my own clinical experience, I proposed (Bromberg 1993) that self-experience originates in relatively unlinked self-states, each coherent in its own right, and the experience of being a unitary self is an acquired, developmentally adaptive illusion. It is when this illusion of unity is traumatically threatened with unavoidable, precipitous disruption that it becomes in itself a liability, because it is in jeopardy of being overwhelmed by input it cannot process symbolically and deal with as a state of conflict (Bromberg 1993: 182).

In such situations of trauma, the mind, if able, will enlist its ability for normal dissociation as a protective solution to assure self-continuity. It suspends linkages between cohesive self-states, preventing certain aspects of self (along with their respective constellations of affects, memories, values and cognitive capacities) from achieving access to the personality within the same state of consciousness. Here's another story, arguably less dramatic but, in another way, more powerful because the subject is *me*. While writing the preceding vignette, I recalled a moment that took place in my late teens with a girlfriend I was seeing at the time. She would frequently complain that I never told her I loved her, my response to which was to find myself hundreds of miles away and speechless. One day, in the midst of our having a particularly great time together, she looked at me and said, 'Tell me you love me. *Lie* a little.' At that moment, something totally unexpected happened. I *felt* love, and I told her so. It was as if I was released from a dissociative paralysis created by a 'not-me' state whose function was to wave a danger flag to keep me from being trapped by something I might not see until it was too late. This time it was different. I'm sure it was because when she said, with humor, 'Lie a little,' this 'protector' part of me felt validated – as if she spoke to me with the part that felt *entitled* to have serious reservations in mind. I remember this incident because it not only improved my relationship with that girl, but also helped me in all the relationships that followed. Right! It didn't lead to our getting married and living happily ever after.

The mind, the brain, and the self

To best understand how these stories are relevant to the topic of this conference – talking with 'Me and Not-Me' in clinical practice – it might be helpful for me to make a few observations about the development of human communication and the relational context that facilitates its more-or-less normal outcome. Let me start with a brief overview of what seems to take place at the brain level in relation to a person's subjective experience of 'self' and 'other.' Research by cognitive science and neuroscience points more and more convincingly toward the fact that there are parallel, but functionally dissimilar, information processing modes in the brain that have implications for understanding the complexity of subjective self-experience. For example, LeDoux (2002), in neurobiological terms, suggests that the enigma underlying multiple selfhood reflects a parallel enigma in comprehending brain processes. He states, 'different components of the self reflect the operation of different brain systems, which can be but are not always in sync . . . allowing for many aspects of the self to coexist' (LeDoux 2002: 31). The first processing system, mediated by the brainstem and the limbic system, primarily the amygdala and hippocampus, is responsible for nonverbal encoding of emotion. The second, mediated by the neocortex, is in charge of verbal and representational symbolization of experience. How to get the two systems to collaborate when they don't want to is the neuroscience version of the clinical question: how do we, as clinicans, talk with 'Me and Not-Me' so as to enable them to increasingly talk with each other as an internal process? LeDoux (1996) describes what takes place in the brain, more or less as follows: the amygdala assesses the emotional significance of incoming information, which it then passes on to areas in the brainstem that regulate the autonomic and hormonal systems. It then transmits this to the hippocampus, the function of which is to integrate this information with previously existing information and with cortical input. Under ordinary conditions of amygdalic arousal, the event is then processed by the hippocampus, which transforms the experience into a thinkable event by first 'filing' it (Van der Kolk 1987) within cognitive schemas to which it is linked. If all goes well, increased *cortical symbolization* increases, and a traumatic situation can more easily be distinguished perceptually from one that may contain certain similarities, but is otherwise relatively benign. As we know, however, all does *not* always go well. One reason is that the cortical symbolization of experience is divided between a more sensory-based right-brain function, and a linguistically based left-brain function. To the degree this is accurate, then right-brain encoding, more mediated by the amygdala, tends to function most dramatically when the person is in an emotionally overwhelming state. When emotional life is calmer, the hippocampus is better able to get the information it needs, to associate it to a storehouse of knowledge in the left frontal lobes and other neocortical locations, and to assist in the creation of spoken narrative. Schore (2003: 43) notes that 'right brain attachment mechanisms are expressed within the regulating and dysregulating emotional communications of any dyad, including transference-countertransference interactions that lie at the core of the therapeutic alliance.' He goes on to say that 'any successful treatment must optimally access not "the trauma" but the immature biological systems that inefficiently regulate stress, *especially the right brain survival mechanism, dissociation, that is characterologically accessed to cope with dysregulating affective states*' (Schore 2003: 42, emphasis added). Along with many psychoanalytic clinicians, Schore then cites the mechanism of projective identification (a core element in the process of enactment) as a major 'subsymbolic' channel of communication that, neurobiologically, represents right-hemisphere-to-right-hemisphere communication between child and parent, as well as between patient and therapist. He writes, more or less endorsing my *own* position, that this form of subsymbolic communication 'may be the only way that *infants* or severely traumatized persons can communicate their stories of distress' (Schore 2003: 43). Developmentally, the course of events seems to go something like this (though this is an admittedly oversimplified account). Before the onset of speech, parent-child communication takes place through affectively regulated patterns of relational interchange – familiar, repetitive patterns of interpersonal experience that become known and remembered through what has come to be called 'procedural memory'. These early interpersonal modes of relating form the child's affective core of personal identity – a highly concrete, attachment-based foundation of self-experience on which more flexible self-development will be built. As Lichtenberg (2003: 498) succinctly notes, 'significant communication begins before an infant has the language for either an inner monologue or outward speech.' The enduring power of this preverbal phase of self-development, he writes, cannot be overemphasized, because 'failure to communicate the recognition of a baby's humanness (subjectivity) and essential uniqueness will impair the development of that baby's attachment . . . and his or her sense of self' (Lichtenberg 2003: 499). With the onset of verbal language, words become a new medium through which communication takes place, but until about age 3, the use of words is itself highly concrete and does not immediately develop into the use of language symbolically. For a while, words are really just a new form of affective communication and serve primarily as carriers of personal feeling – a new medium for the child to express what he feels and what he needs. So, even though he now uses words, the child is still communicating subsymbolically (Bucci 1997, 2003) through the relational experience – not through the content of the words, but through the emotional impact on the mental state of the parent that the child makes *while* he is speaking the words. If the parent is emotionally accessible to the child's communication, his or her meaning is not as much 'understood' as it is affectively 'recognized', though not yet symbolized by words. Through the parent's reciprocal affective aliveness to the child's vocal and gestural efforts to communicate his or her emerging sense of self, while simultaneously offering verbal language that is in sync with the shared affective context, a give and take develops that comes to include exchanges of verbalized symbolic meaning tied to the child's sense of core identity. Some parents, however, because they do not wish (or are unable) deal with the child's subjectivity if it is not in sync with their own, are *not* emotionally accessible and dissociate their child's here-and-now impact, if it reflects a self-state in the child that they experience as too destabilizing to their own sense of self. In other words, the parents react to their child as if his or her state of mind at that moment had *no meaning* – leading to a weakening of the child's ability to hold and express certain of its own self-states as a communicable 'I'. When this happens as a steady diet, there's trouble ahead. It leads to the birth of 'not-me' aspects of self: dissociated self-states (or selves) in the child that persist into adulthood and come to our attention as therapists if we are open to their presence through repetitious enactments into which we are drawn – a not unfamiliar experience for most therapists. Around age 3, words normally become more than carriers of affect; they become building blocks in the construction of personal meaning through shared symbols. Developmentally, words are no longer only an emotional expression of what you feel, but can now be used symbolically. They can now convey who you *are* as part of conveying what you feel and what you need. The earlier, affectively organized modes of self-experience, however, do not die when symbolic speech is born. Subsymbolic affective communication continues to participate in meaning construction throughout life. This is why we best understand what someone *means* by what he is 'saying' when we're affectively engaged while he is saying it. We have greater access to the affective communication taking place as the words are spoken. This is why in my first vignette I imagined that if I had been a fly on the wall, I would have seen my patient's girlfriend looking into space as she said 'sort of'. My sense was that she dissociated from the highly charged here-and-now confrontation with her boyfriend and that her words 'sort of' were empty of meaning, other than to convey she had 'disappeared'. For the relational construction of self-representation to take place securely, as part of the process of being socialized through language, the child must be validated as who he is in the moment and through his transitions between his self-states. If this fails to happen, then words are felt as untrustworthy and empty – both the child's own words and those of others. Developmentally, the main reason seems to be the failure to carry symbolized self-experience through state-change transitions. If a child is confirmed as existing to a parent only in certain states, then the natural continuity of 'me' from one state to another is rendered impossible, or at least is seriously disrupted.

Dissociation as adaptation, creativity and protection

I've described the self as a multiplicity of 'self-states' that during the course of normal development attain a feeling of coherence that overrides the awareness of their discontinuity. I've argued that the human capacity for creative living is based on the intrinsic multiplicity of the self and the 'ability to feel like one self while being many'. As an analyst, I find it delightful whenever I find this supported by people whose lives are dedicated to creativity, and I thought it might be interesting to present an excerpt from a book written by a rather well known performing artist and drama teacher, Kristin Linklater (1997). No matter how often I read this, it still has a powerful impact on me.

There is a . . . style of teaching that . . . says 'you become a character and for a brief moment on stage you escape from yourself.' The notion of losing myself in a character implies that the character is bigger, more estimable, more exciting than *I* am, while the idea of *finding the character in myself* suggests that I am multi-faceted and illimitable, and that each character I play finds the roots of its truth in the fact that *I am All as well as One; that from my wholeness I can create multiplicity*; that I have the capacity to understand the natures of all people and can become any of them *by expanding the seed of my understanding until it dislodges and rearranges the ingredients of my personality and a different part of me dominates.* This temporarily dominant characteristic proceeds to rearrange my physical and vocal behavior as I develop a character that is rooted in truthful experience because it is rooted in me, and . . . is unrecognizable to my familiar self.

> (Linklater 1997: 6, emphases added)

OK . . . where do these other selves 'go' when we're not noticing them? Right; you already know the answer. They don't 'go' anywhere. They are just kept from interfering with what is going on at the moment and this is a normal part of everyday mental functioning – like being free from thinking about a difficult meeting with your boss tomorrow while you are playing with your kids. They are watching and always 'on call', if needed. They are dissociated, but only temporarily, and not fundamentally as a defense against trauma. It is, however, dissociation as a defense against trauma that *is* of most interest to working clinicians.

The mind employs dissociation both as a mental *process* (a defense against destabilizing affective flooding it cannot regulate or escape) and as a mental *structure* (a proactive 'early warning system' against the recurrence of an experience that exists mainly as an affective memory held by the body, that the mind is never quite sure what really happened in the first place). It is this latter use of dissociation as a mental structure to which Sullivan was referring, in his own way, when he formulated the 'me' and 'not-me' distinction. Listen to Sullivan's (1953) wonderful comment on the issue of where do the 'not-me' parts of you go?

Dissociation can easily be mistaken for a really quite magical business in which you fling something of you into outer darkness, where it reposes for years quite peacefully. This is a fantastic oversimplification. Dissociation works very suavely indeed as long as it works *but it isn't a matter of keeping a sleeping dog under an anaesthetic.* It works by a constant alertness or vigilance of awareness, with *certain supplementary processes* which prevent one's ever discovering the usually quite clear evidences that part of one's living is done without any awareness.

> (Sullivan 1953: 318, emphases added)

Sullivan is speaking of supplementary processes that allow a person both awareness and vigilance, without being aware of the awareness – that is, without 'me' knowing about 'not-me'. It is the primary nature of traumatic experience to 'elude' our knowledge, except physically and affectively, because of the formation of psychic structure into 'me' and 'not-me' – a dissociative gap, by virtue of which the mental experience of what was unbearable is relegated to a part of the self that is unlinked from what is preserved as a relatively intact 'me'. The thing is, this describes *many* people who end up in our offices, not only those diagnosed with dissociative disorders per se, but also people with personality disorders, including borderline personality, schizoid disorder, obsessive-compulsive disorder, bipolar disorder, narcissistic disorder, paranoid personality, hysteric personality disorder, even schizoaffective disorder. It's my view that the one overarching clinical issue that embraces the differences in character diagnoses is that we, as clinicans, must find ways to talk with all dissociated parts of the self, so as to enable them to increasingly talk with each other as an internal process – to enable the parts to slowly collaborate, even though the person has spent a lifetime protecting his or her safety by making sure they don't. As we know all too well, it is never simply a matter of getting a patient to 'confront' dissociated self-experience, especially 'memories'. Even when the effort may seem to have been successful, the emergent awareness of something from the past does not necessarily lead to a thinkable experience of what has been confronted, much less an experience available to self-reflection. What keeps unsymbolized experience so rigidly unyielding to cognitive understanding and reflection is that it is organized around elements more powerful than the evidence of reason – what the Boston Change Process Study Group refers to as 'implicit relational knowing' (Lyons-Ruth et al. 2001). They offer the view, increasingly supported by other researchers and clinicians, that it is the relational *process* of communication in a therapy session, rather than the *content* of the session, that is the foundation of a patients growth in therapy psychoanalysis included. In other words, contrary to the long-held axiom of classical analytic theory about making the unconscious conscious as a necessary condition for change, evidence is accumulating that 'process leads content, so that no particular content needs to be pursued; rather the enlarging of the domain and fluency of the dialogue is primary and will lead to increasingly integrated and complex content' (Lyons-Ruth et al. 2001: 16). This does *not* mean that content is unimportant; rather, it is in the relational process of exploring content that the change takes place – not in the discovery of new content per se. The 'content' that is traumatic, is embedded in relational experience that is itself part of the content, and this unsymbolized relational experience is relived by being enacted repeatedly between patient and therapist as an intrinsic part of their relationship. As Susan Sands (1994: 150) has put it, when one seems to be doing primarily 'memory work', the memories are often in the service of the transference rather than vice versa; that is, the recovery of memories may allow the patient to get closer to or more distant from the therapist, may 'test' the therapist's ability to understand and respond to various need states . . . or may pose any number of other 'questions' regarding the relationship. What makes it possible, through a relationship, to link two functionally dissimilar information processing modes in the brain? My answer is a 'safe enough' interpersonal environment to permit an enacted replaying and symbolization of early traumatic experience, without blindly reproducing the original outcome. It is through this process that I believe the dissociated ghosts of 'not-me' are best persuaded, little-by-little, to cease their haunting (Bromberg 2003b) and participate more and more actively and openly as an affectively regulatable self-expression of 'me'. What analysts call the 'unconscious communication process of enactment' is, from this vantage point, the patient's effort to negotiate unfinished business in those areas of selfhood where, because of one degree or another of traumatic experience, affect regulation was not successful enough to allow further self-development at the level of symbolic processing by thought and language. In this light, a core dimension of the therapeutic process is to increase competency in regulating affective states without pointlessly triggering the dread of retraumatization. Speaking *about* a part of the patient's self to another part is an inherent aspect of the work, but it inevitably leads to an enactment with the part of the patient's self we are speaking about – and we are never in command of our ability to anticpate it. Of necessity, we are always most alive to the part of the patient's self with which we are relationally engaged at the moment, until the enactment begins. There's little doubt that enactments happen long before they reach the threshold of our awareness. I think it is safe to assume they begin at whatever point the part of the patient's self we are speaking *about* begins to feel ignored relationally because we are not affectively alive enough to it. When we speak of a self that is listening – a 'hidden observer' (cf. Hilgard 1977) – what we mean by 'listening' is a part of the self that is affectively reacting to the session in a manner that is not being processed through the patient-therapist relationship as the session is taking place, and therefore cannot directly be engaged until it 'comes out', as many therapists working with DID patients call it. Not-me selves always come out, however, in ways that are discernible, even when they are not organized in the form of alter personalities as in DID. They come out as a subsymbolic affective experience that is received affectively by the therapist who sooner or later notices something peculiar going on – most often in himself. The dissociated part of the patient's self holding the unsymbolized experience is not in relationship with the therapist, and until the therapist feels its impact as an experience linked to a part of *himself* that has been dissociated, it stays *lost* and its existence remains enacted. Only when the therapist (often against his will) feels the enacted voices of his patient's dissociated self-states as alive in himself, is there hope of those parts being found. Through being recognized by another mind that is affectively alive to it and affectively engaging it, the patient's wordless experience of being hopelessly trapped in an internal prison begins to be raised to the level of thought.

Safe surprises

At the 2002 Division 39 conference in New York City, I shared a panel with a cognitive researcher (Wilma Bucci) and a neuroscientist (Joseph LeDoux). The concepts of dissociation and the multiplicity of self, and the implications of these ideas for psychoanalytic theory and practice, were explored at length. Bucci, at this meeting, discussed the clinical ramifications of her research findings (Bucci 2002), which led her to the conclusion that Freud's repression-based conception of the therapeutic action of psychoanalysis was in need of serious reconsideration. Bucci writes that 'the goal of psychoanalytic treatment is integration of dissociated schemas' and 'it follows that concepts such as regression and resistance need to be revised as well' (Bucci 2002: 766, 788). Bucci offered the view that the goal of psychoanalytic treatment depends on the connection of components of emotion schemas that have been *dissociated*, and this requires activation of subsymbolic bodily experience in the session itself in relation to *present interpersonal experience* and memories of the past. Resulting from this panel, Bucci and I have published papers (Bromberg 2003a; Bucci 2003) focusing from different vantage points on the clinical fact that in order for what is dissociated to *become* symbolized and available to participate with other self-states in internal conflict resolution, a link must be made in the here-and-now between the mental representation of an event that resides in short-term or working memory and a mental representation of the self as the agent or experiencer.

In therapy, the more intense the fear of triggering unprocessed traumatic affect, the more powerful are the dissociative forces, and the harder it is for episodic or 'working' memory to cognitively represent the here-and-now event that (in the therapy itself) is 'triggering' the affect, or to access long-term memories associated with it. Even in routine analytic work, telling 'about' oneself leads surprisingly frequently to a dissociated reliving of frozen self-experience that was too much for the mind to contain, and remained unprocessed as affective or somatic memory. To use this therapeutically requires sufficient relational safety to free working memory while the activation of painful dissociated experience is taking place. The issue of a patient's affective 'safety' is a complicated one, and a source of much debate and discussion in the trauma literature. I've proposed that safety and growth are part of the ongoing negotiation of the analytic relationship itself, and that the basic principle involves what a given patient and analyst do in an unanticipated way that is *safe but not too safe* – an analytic approach that works at the interface of stability and change, through a replaying of the relational failures of a patient's past as *safe surprises*. 'Not-me' is engaged when the experience reaches the threshhold of our awareness. But, for a while it is *dis*-engaged – dissociated by us – to keep it from becoming disruptive to the 'work'. Ironically, our patient helps us dissociate her 'not-me' voice. She hates that part of herself more than *we* come to hate it when we access our own 'not-me' feelings, but we hope we eventually stay long enough with those feelings to recognize that they are private, but that does not make them our 'private property'. Our own 'not-me' feelings are at the heart of the work providing we allow them to be, but using them relationally is neither easy nor neat. Rather, it is a process of typically messy, nonlinear spurts, closer to 'lurching ahead' than to the more euphemistic term 'growth'. During this process, the source of therapeutic action is in the therapist's ability to relate fully to whatever aspect of self the patient is experiencing and presenting as 'the real me', while not forgetting to let the other, more dissociated parts know he is aware that they too exist and are listening. The challenge for the analyst is to make what is enacted useful analytic material, and as this happens, both analyst and patient derive more and more of their knowledge from verbal and nonverbal sources simultaneously. As words are found and negotiated between them, the traumas of the past become 'safe surprises' in the present, and facilitate the patient's growing ability to symbolize and express in language what she has had no voice to say. The goal is for the patient to move, slowly and safely, from a mental structure in which self-narratives are organized primarily dissociatively, to one in which she is able to cognitively and emotionally stand in the spaces between self-states, experience them conflictually, and find new and more flexible ways of being simply human.

SPEAKING FOR MYSELF: RICHARD CHEFETZ

'Diss-ing' the Self

We are going to talk a lot about Diss-ing today, though not the kind that New Yorkers usually think about. And we also talk about Self. Actually, few people in psychoanalysis seem to be able to agree on a definition of Self. There is a lot of heat, but not a lot of light about the overarching concept of Self. That probably has some meaning, but it may be more a reflection on psychoanalytic theory than on Self. Whether or not we can agree on technical definitions, we must still figure out how to talk to our patients about their Selfhood, Self. Our patients are people who are not so tortured as we are about the definition of what everyday people would call

Obvious: 'My Self. You know, Me, the Person I am.' The *Oxford Dictionary* says 'Self: a person's own individuality or essence.' My very own essence. My Self.

A fundamental belief regarding me and my essence is that I will do anything I need to do, consciously or unconsciously, to protect and maintain the safety of my essence. Would you do any differently? Of course, my thoughts are of those things I would consciously do to protect myself; or should I say 'my Self?' I wonder what I would have done to protect my Self before I knew I had a Self and before I knew I was an 'I?' How would I know what my essence was before I knew how to spell 'essence', or before I knew that there was a thing called 'spelling'? Just like the 2 or 3 year old who learns for the first time to say 'No', we may get more mileage in considering Self if we allow ourselves both the convenience of not fully understanding what my Self is, and at the same time assert with conviction what Self isn't. That's not who I am. That's not me. Not-Me! I am not jealous, envious, sarcastic, hurt, intimidated, controlled, humiliated, disrupted, annihilated. . . . Not-Me! Not-I! Then who am I? I don't know, but I know that is 'Not-Me!' I disavow and disown. I deny and dismiss. I ignore and avoid. I even pretend and distract. Sometimes I do these things without realizing I do. And when the chips are down, and these other things fail to keep my Self safe, then I diss-ociate; I depersonalize, derealize, and forget, or I confuse, and alter my identity to such an extent that I (or should I say, Me, My Self, and I?) become unrecognizable to Me. I become Not-Me! And it is a real loss to then lose track of Me, but at least my Self is safe, wherever or however or whoever I (should I say 'It,' in the depersonal sense?), my essence may be.

When I am Diss-ed via Dissociation, then 'I' am safe in my lostness, my safe numb protected-ness. And this is true until I grow much older and there is not so much need for lostness and nothingness of being. Then I may find myself in pain over my numbness, and long to be alive, fully alive, essence-ially speaking, that is. And so, when our patients come to us with their problems for us to shrink, to make their problems smaller and more manageable, we must learn to talk to each Me who comes for a visit, and to attend to all the Not-Me aspects of those Selves who crowd the room, dissociatively and disavowedly, and push the conversation to and fro (should we call this 'transference'?). We hope, between those Me's and Not-Me's 'I' bring to the session (should we call this 'countertransference'?), and those Me's and Not-Me's of my patient, there will be room for all of Us. Having gone without defining 'self', can we afford to avoid defining 'state'? But what are we talking about, state? It seems like we are talking about a state of mind, 'state', for short. Siegel (1999) writes:

> A state of mind can be proposed to be a pattern of activation of recruited systems within the brain responsible for (1) perceptual bias,

(2) emotional tone and regulation, (3) memory processes, (4) mental models, and (5) behavioral response patterns.

(Siegel 1999: 211)

Beyond the need of a definition of a state of mind is the need to move from the neurological perceptual level to that of the personal and interpersonal. What Siegel calls 'specialized selves' is the closest I have come to finding a theoretician who writes about what a relational psychoanalyst or traumatologist would call a self-state:

> The proposal here is that *basic states of mind are clustered into special-ized selves, which are enduring states of mind that have a repeating pattern of activity across time. . . .* Each person has many such interdependent and yet distinct processes, which exist over time with a sense of continuity that creates the experience of mind.
>
> (Siegel 1999: 231, emphasis in original)

If Siegel had gone just a little bit further, he might even have written, 'that creates the experience of Mind, or Self.' I think, however, he was too wise to do that. Wise or not, we are stuck with the clinical observations that arise when we become sensitized to the presence of unintegrated Not-Me thoughts and feelings in our patients. These Not-Me self-states contain essences like unspeakable terror from physical abuse, unknowable crushing humiliation from chronic emotional dismissals, and unthinkable thoughts from murderous rage or jealousy. We can see the trajectory of these presences streak across our field of vision in cloud chambers with names like eating disorders, substance abuse, sexual addiction, sadomasochism, and many others. These action filled lives are conducted as if there were often no 'driver' in the body of the person sitting with us and telling their story. Disavowal, denial, confusion, amnesias, despair, shame, and humili-ation slowly and relentlessly beat the fragile, nearly nonexistent self-esteem of these patients within an inch of suicide, routinely. Often, beneath this symphony of negativism and obfuscation rests a layer of dissociative pro-cesses that guard terrifying, essence-threatening, Not-Me thoughts, feelings, behaviors and physical sensations. We have to be willing to talk with the Not-Me self-states in our patients, and we have to help these self-states to become part of consciousness, part of what is consciously considered during moments of reflective awareness and decision making. Unless we ask our patients about dissociative experience, we are as lost as our patients. And we must challenge ourselves to become conscious of the Not-Me's in each of us that resonate and respond to the Not-Me's in our patients.

I would like to make a plea here for specificity in understanding these processes, many of which rely on dissociative mechanisms. To me, saying that someone 'dissociates' is not clinically useful unless it is used in the broad generic sense, such as 'she is so dissociative' or 'his dissociative symptoms became more prominent'. To say someone 'is dissociating' is to know little about a person. To say that the intensity of depersonalization experience increased, or she experienced herself drifting away from the room as a fog closed in, or she entered a spontaneous trance state, or she became confused about her identity, moves closer to the patient's actual experience. It also helps a person to understand the meaning of her experience as a marker of inner distress. We do well to track the extent of feelings of disorganization or disorientation as a result of provocative levels of emotional distress, and to use the specificity of words like 'depersonalization' or 'derealization'.

I do not want to give you the impression that I have been talking only about persons with dissociative identity disorder. Yes, it is true, I could be doing that, and doing that accurately. The truth is that I am talking about processes that always exist in all of us. We all have Not-Me self-states. Isn't that a basic premise of relational psychology? I am suggesting that states of mind are the building blocks of self-states. The association of states of mind into larger aggregations called self-states provides us a feeling of Self-ness, and a sense of coherence of this aggregate of self-states called 'Me', This very personal assessment relies on appraisals of the continuity, consistency, congruence and cohesion of our identities over time. I come back to this later.

How do you recognize the presence of a self-state in a patient who hides this Not-Me-ness from his or her consciousness in the first place? Stop, look, and listen. What do we see if we stop, and focus our attention on looking at our patients? We see that shifting from one set of thoughts and feelings to another is accompanied by a physiologic change of state that parallels the thoughts and feelings. Like the musical score of a movie, the memory of a thought or a feeling is encoded with contextual physiologic accompaniment. If we want to know about unconscious process, then we need to become keen observers of our patient's physiology and the associated bodily changes. Typical representative changes are: change in body position, shift in facial expression, shift in eye gaze, eye closure, swallowing, and skin flush. I include tears that flow onto cheeks and tears that well up but do not flow, finger, ankle, or other repetitive movement (both onset, and ending), rooms that suddenly get too hot or too cold, and so on. All of these are often readily observable, especially if you can see your patient. If you can't see your patient, then you won't see these icons of state change. You may be lucky, from time to time, to catch a change in the quality of your patient's voice or speech cadence. But you will never hear her 'goose bumps' stand up and say 'Look at me!' You may never notice that their yawn is dysphoric and representative of involuntary motor activity in response to terror. Your patient will have to report these things to you. You have to look at and see your patient's whole body to catch this information. If we are to observe the parade of self-states in our patients, then we must do more than rely on time-honored linguistic signs of intra-psychic conflict, beyond such events as 'slips of the tongue'. But even with more sophisticated attention to verbal double meanings, dream analysis, and so on, you will fail to bring into view a lot of Not-Me's if you ignore the basics of the experience of affect, bodily state and facial expression. The language of the body is the basis for speech. Damasio (1999) has written compellingly about the neurologic basis of conscious awareness and its reliance on the soma for its organization. So, the first step in discerning Not-Me states is to engage in a 'close-process' observation of your patient's bodily state.

If you do sit behind your patients, there is one other source of their physiologic state that you might notice: your own previously unconscious physiologic reaction. Call it the 'physiologic countertransference' if you like. If you can tolerate such scrutiny, then take the changes in the experience of your body as indicating that something in your thoughts and feelings has shifted in response to something happening in your patient – something about your Not-Me and their Not-Me. Would you be more comfortable thinking about projective identificatory processes? I can accept that. Be careful to remember that nothing was put into you, it was already there. Your own Not-Me simply became active in resonance with the unconscious recognition of a 'fellow' Not-Me in an Other. Get to know your Not-Me's. Some of my own Not-Me's have become very close friends, over time.

The second step in discerning a Not-Me state is to ask your patients about your observation of them. Ask things like: 'Something just went by on your face. Did you notice that too? Check in your body for sensation. What do you notice? Look with your Mind's sensing your Mind's eye. Is there an image, a sound, a sense of something different – a thought, an idea? What do you notice?' You don't need fancy techniques to do this, just a willingess to inquire. These kinds of questions are at the core of much of the cognitive technique in EMDR (Eye Movement Desensitization and Reprocessing) and hypnosis. You don't need fancy technical knowledge to ask about experience. If the patient is receptive to your question, if there is a good alliance, these questions are likely to be productive.

The third step takes place over many sessions. Fill in the narrative that goes along with the sensations, thoughts, affects, behaviors, and aggregate of states of mind that are consistent with the self-state. The only problem you will have is that the better you get at this with your patient, the more quickly the dis-aggregate becomes an aggregate. That makes it harder to recognize the separateness of the self-state, which is not a terrible problem because that is a sought-after goal.

The fourth step in discerning a Not-Me state is to develop reflective awareness for its appearance in everyday life. The self-state experience needs to be framed as it is, an important, useful, though perhaps antiquated aspect of self, relying on old, potentially inaccurate perceptions and conclusions about the world. Yes, this is a cognitive-psychoanalytic view. It does not preclude the analysis of transference or countertransference, and in many ways relies on this understanding to proceed.

The fifth step is to bring together the full context of the self-state, the physiologic sensation, emotion, knowledge, and behavior that describes the constellation of this part of the dis-aggregate Self. Patients who report their experience in a detached manner have not reached this step. Fear of affect may be a prominent impediment. Affects used as tools to avoid, distract, or preoccupy often block this achievement. This use of affect may be conscious or unconscious, and in any event, needs to be understood and appreciated for its self-defeating, creative protection from deeper states of intense, feared affect.

The sixth and final step is to appreciate the changes in self-state organization as a result of understanding and working through, and the effect this has on living a life. Appreciating the change, and noticing the effect, cements the previously disparate self-state to the rest of conscious awareness and self-identity. Not-Me has become Me.

Parallel to this experience in the patient is the experience, in the clinician, of change in Self in relation to the patient. What has this patient taught me about my Not-Me states? Do I feel differently now as I wait for them to attend their session? Do I negotiate my work with other patients differently because of what has happened with this patient? To be unaffected by our patients is not to have met them.

Isolated subjectivity

I want to add one more idea, so that those of you who like consistency of terminology will have something to take home with you that fits in your psychological tool kit. I simply want to notice that what we have been talking about, to a large extent, is alteration in subjectivity, Me and Not-Me. This is immediately obvious at face value. What is not so obvious is that when we use a word like subjectivity, we are thinking at a level of abstraction that involves the confluence of multiple self-states. When a self-state is in a Not-Me relation to Me, then just like affect that is isolated, the self-state (or states) has (or have) a quality of not being known. This is what I mean by isolated subjectivity.

If you can accept this idea of isolated subjectivity, then maybe you can also consider that this is what we see in the more extreme cases of robust dissociative processes: isolated subjectivity, personified. The personification is intensified by dissociative experience of depersonalization, derealization and amnesia. With this reinforcement there is not any experiential doubt about the Not-Me quality of Self, for instance, cutting the dissociatively numb arm of a Not-Me self-state (which raises the important point that there is always a *multiplicity* of Not-Me self-states). When there is isolated subjectivity, then just like the situation of isolated affect, the essence of Self is kept hidden, and the aggregate of self-states and subjectivities is less coherent. This incoherence is a fabulous unconscious tool for obscuring thoughts, feelings, sensations and behaviors! The mind becomes a repository for seemingly disparate parts of life's experience, a desperately rigid maze of hedges filled with psychic thorns that unconsciously poke, prod and consume so much mental energy that there is little left over for living each day. How sad. How exhausting! We can understand the ways in which isolated subjectivity contributes to impairing our ability to live by looking at some qualities of experience mentioned earlier: continuity, consistency, congruence and cohesion. Each of these qualities is associated with its opposite, as in 'congruentincongruent'. But we have a problem: 'cohesion' has no opposite, there is no 'incohesion'. This is more than a linguistic issue. 'Cohesion' actually describes a continuum, more or less cohesion. Some people use the word 'fragmentation' to explicate the lack of cohesion. But what fragments? This presupposes a 'wholeness'. If something lacks cohesion, then what are the elements that are separated? We have no good definition of a whole Self and no evidence for it, even though we have a wish to think of ourselves as whole. There is, however, a lot of evidence for states, leading me to suggest the term 'aggregation-disaggregation' as a much more parsimonious choice of language. This word-pairing, which emphasizes an active dialectic between states more than it does stasis and breakage, evokes imagery that Pierre Janet would find appealing. After all, it was Janet (1889, cited in Erdelyi 1994: 5) who originally described the appearance of dissociative states as a disaggregation of the personality – a description that has clear implications for the essence of Self being a lumpy, bumpy aggregate, rather than a cohesive, orderly entity.

The feeling of 'getting myself together' aggregation is accomplished when I have a memory that I am the same self I was yesterday: the same memories, thoughts, feelings and behaviors. With continuity and consistency for these elements of experience over time, there is a sense of being Me, having 'gotten myself together' congruence. Most importantly, because I no longer use dissociative or other 'diss-ing' operations (disavowal, distraction, disorder, denial, avoidance) to protect myself from the unspeakable, unthinkable and unknowable experiences of my life, my perceptions and the narrative of Me that results is coherent. Only after I achieve coherence can there be a sense of being the Me I know. The bottom line is the ability to make experience coherent. Processes that destroy coherence lead to a tendency to maintain disaggregation of whatever self-states might have otherwise gelled into a Self. We strive, in any psychotherapy, for understanding, coherence. But that is not enough. We must become coherent in Relation, or we are not truly human. It is this language of Relationship, so impaired by Diss-ing, that we negotiate anew, with each and every person we know, therapy or not. Read the words of a patient who is discovering she is a more complex person than she thought. See how she strives for coherence, checks on continuity and consistency. Once she establishes her orientation, she feels relieved, even though a listener with less isolated affect and subjectivity is left wondering how she can tolerate her situation.

Case vignette: 'J'

I have spent the last several hours as not-J. I don't know if I've ever felt exactly like I do right now. I just know I'm not me. I don't know who I might be, though. I feel like there's a tape player going on inside my head. Very noisy in there. Can't seem to stop it long enough to concentrate on anything at all. But not like I usually describe 'my head is going to explode.' No, different. More like, 'shut up shut up in there.' I'm trying to pull back, to ask inside where all of the energy is coming from. I ate ice cream for dinner tonight, which is only surprising since I am heavily dieting right now. Very uncharacteristic. Obviously someone wanted ice cream. I didn't have a bad day or anything like that. I got a ton of work done.

This is really scaring me. I don't have any control. It's like part of me is not happy I'm writing to you. Actually, when I ask about that I hear, 'Tell him to fuck off.' 'Sorry.'

I'm thinking of taking a second Klonopin. Right now I feel like I will never be able to go to sleep because there is so much activity. Earlier I had this strange visual of me slapping myself in the face repeatedly. Came out of nowhere. Or I just have to figure out where. I want to bang my head up against a wall to make the noise stop. I want to jump up and down and shout, 'no no no no no.' Like a little kid. Okay, took a second Klonopin. Thinking about a third and a fourth. Thinking about taking the whole goddamn bottle. Now I know where I am. I am in the space where I was when I was in the outpatient program at the hospital and the sheriff took me away. That's how I'm feeling. Have to ask myself about suicidal feelings. Okay, let's see . . . where am I . . . the part of me that's active is around an 8, pretty darned bad . . . but I still feel that I, J, have enough control to stop the part of me that wants to kill me. So, no real cause for concern. Okay, I think I'm done now.

From another time, six months earlier in her treatment:

Did you see this coming? Did you know this would happen? Or were you just sure that the happy period of contentment wouldn't last. You knew! I knew! You saw my body language change toward you as soon as you brought up E's name. I was praying that you wouldn't but you did. Why did you do it? I was doing okay. We were having a good conversation. At least I think we were, because now I can't remember a goddamn thing that happened prior to E coming out. Nothing! Do you know how frustrating that is? I don't have a fucking clue as to what we talked about for forty minutes. I'm just sitting here running my hands through my hair in complete disbelief. I don't believe this.

And from another session:

You know, what's happening to me is really quite incredible. I am really getting stronger. Thanks so much. I still have marks in my fingers where I was digging my nails into my hand. How did you know that's what I was doing? How come I stopped when you asked me to? What was that whole thing about? While E was . . . out? . . . I had severe burning pain in my vaginal area. Haven't figured this out yet. I'll let you know when I do.

Principles of treatment of isolated subjectivity (Not-Me self-states)

The treatment of the person who has isolated subjectivity and demonstrates Not-Me affect, knowledge, sensation and behavior (dissociated elements of experience) rests on an appreciation of five principles:

- affect: consciousness, tolerance, and integrity
- sadomasochism and other self-harming behaviors
- self as a flexible and resilient aggregation of self-states
- self as agent, object and locus
- self as capable negotiator with other.

Affect

'Affect consciousness' and 'affect tolerance' are self-evident terms, and the clinical work that leads to increasing competence in these areas is illustrated in the striving toward reflective awareness that is a major part of the clinical material presented below. 'Affect integrity' simply describes the notion that the emotions that are felt are understood in context, integrally, with the other elements of experience.

Sadomasochism

Sadomasochism is best defined as the use of one pain to muffle another. Understood in this context it explains the constellations of cutting, burning, bingeing, purging, head-banging and other behaviors that are designed to preserve self and regulate affect. There is a triumphant moment in the omnipotent fantasies associated with these behaviors as self hurts itself in a manner of its own choosing, preempting the possibility of another self doing the damage that is not so much anticipated or expected, but is a kind of given, a condition of living. Of course, self does not always recognize itself. Diss-ing achieves that level of incoherence, and aids in achieving the goal of relieving intense painful affect. The use of the pain is paradoxical. Pain induces a trancelike state, which relieves pain, a *petit morte*, a little death, a dissociation. As treatment proceeds, bold statements of enjoyment of cutting are replaced by an appreciation of the desperate need to see the self as an 'agent', even if it means competence at destroying the depersonalized body. The competence of Not-Me states to regulate affect paradoxically needs to be admired by the therapist and the Me state, if the Not-Me is going to feel respected rather than accused. The main objection to this therapeutic stance will come from the Me state of the patient, who will think of this strategy as a ploy to allow the Not-Me to control the Me. It is not. For example, the patient J has a Not-Me state that uses knifelike abdominal pain in a multiply determined and affect-regulatory manner. The pain causes dissociation of affect when it is intense, just like bingeing. The knife pain is related to a dream of the patient knifing her parents and killing them. The pain is used by the Not-Me state to control the Me state and force her to recognize what the Not-Me state feels is valid hatred of the parents. The Me state hates the Not-Me for causing her pain, controlling her, and harboring hate for the parents, an unacceptable feeling. The therapist talked about the desperateness of the Not-Me state to be recognized and accepted and its creativity in doing whatever it could to get Me's attention. While not supporting her methods, the therapist supported the effort and invited the patient to appreciate the Not-Me's longing for truth and openness, an admirable goal.

Self as aggregate

In successful treatments, this frame, in the form of the therapist's expectations, is applied long before the patient has achieved self as aggregation, and can be applied long before there is a fully coherent aggregate. It is an expectation that therapists keep in mind and is unconsciously communicated to their patients. It is also a matter of therapists understanding the activity of self-states in their own experience and modeling that level of reflective awareness for the patient with language that fits the experience. For example, a patient recently criticized me for saying something she believed was rude. After my initial silent denials and defensiveness, and my obvious lack of confirmation of the patient's point of view, the patient persisted. I finally discovered, with mixed feelings, how I had denied how frustrating the patient had been in her open defiance and disavowal of my observations of her. The 'mix' was in my concern over what felt like a need to disclose this to the patient rather than explore the patient's fantasies of what had happened, and not reveal my feelings to her – something that is often viewed as unacceptable in a psychoanalytically informed therapy. When I did decide to tell her that, on further reflection, she was correct, I told her I had not wanted to know how frustrated I was with her, and in disavowing and denying my own anger, I had diss'd my own angry Not-Me. I wondered out loud how I could expect her angry Not-Me to come to therapy, if I would not let mine. Her reply was simple: 'That's the smartest thing you've said in a while. Thanks.'

Self as agent, object and locus

No discussion of Self would be complete without including Schafer's (1968) idea of self-identity as consisting of the experience of a person as an agent (doer), object (in relation to others), and a locus (occupying space, having a location). In the extreme, the patient who experiences depersonalization loses much self-identity. The out-of-body experience means giving up agency. It may feel safer not to occupy the same space as my body, and exist to the side of others, so to speak, rather than directly in relation. Dissociative processes destroy selfhood. Disavowal and related psychic tools do similar damage to the potential for maintaining integrity of self.

Self as negotiator

If in the relationship with the therapist, the patient is not a real partner, who negotiates the course of the treatment and the therapeutically idio-syncratic 'language of significance' in the relationship with the therapist (language that only the two of them might understand in the context of their relatedness), then there is little hope for the patient's real growth. The therapist must be a real person who can engage the patient in an affectively alive conversation, achieving a mutuality in relationship. While brilliance in the therapist is not to be dissuaded, its appearance in conversation with patients may be threatening and destructive. Therapists need to find a way to be smart enough in their work, and also to recognize, admire and make use of the intelligence in their patients. Psychoanalytically informed treat-ments must contend with the observations of Not-Me aspects of self in patients and therapists. Therapists must model a reflective awareness of their Not-Me's if patients are to do the same. Respect for the essence of what it means to be human is to appreciate the organization of Mind as an aggregate of self-states that defines the experience of our subjectivity. Experience that is incoherent, inconsistent with expectation, incongruent with past experience, and lacks continuity with the rest of our lives pro-vokes organizations of states of mind that need to be experienced as Not-Me. The incoherence is intolerable for a Me. The creation of a Not-Me is requisite in the psychological survival of the Me until it gains the strength to tolerate intense affects that have been unbearable. The sacrifice of self, in the service of the preservation of self, is routinely observable. The central role of affect – its obligatory association with physiologic activity and its discernment through careful observation – is essential in working effectively with our patients. The isolation of subjectivity is an understandable adaptation in the service of the preservation of self. The construction of new narratives inclusive of behavior, bodily sensation, autobiographical knowledge, and intense affect bring healing to our patients when this is accompanied by the working through that occurs in the analysis of a transferencecountertransference constellation. The negotiation of the relationship between patient and therapist must include a model of reflective awareness in the therapist for the presence of both Me and Not-Me elements of self in the therapist too. To live in relation to others is to be truly alive. While we are indeed all much more alike than we are different, the extent to which we tolerate our own internal 'different thoughts and feelings' predicts the extent to which we either live with ourselves peacefully or at constant threat of war – a conflict that can lead to suicide. Whether our Not-Me's represent a different aspect of Self, or are projected onto different people, in a different culture, in another part of the world, we may all suffer greatly when we 'Diss' them.

VERBATIM TRANSCRIPT OF SEGMENTS OF A THERAPY SESSION WITH A PATIENT WITH DISSOCIATIVE IDENTITY DISORDER

Richard Chefetz's Preface

The following material is taken from a single session in which the conversation preceding this material had been about the degree of the patient's consciousness about her dissociative processes during the course of her life. Though the first and second segments of material are out of order, from the third segment on, the material appears in the same (unbroken) sequence in which it took place. Chefetz, the therapist, has inserted clarifications and brief explanatory comments meant to orient the reader and contextualize the 'surface action' of the material. Interpretation and understanding of clinical process are taken up in the commentaries that follow. The patient's words are in italics.

Case vignette: Nancy

*'I understand that it's all just me. With different aspects, or whatever the **hell** you want to call it, whatever you want to label it. But when you're from the inside looking*

out, it isn't me. That's somebody else. I'm not that person, I'm not this person, I'm not that person. **It's not the same!** *And that's where it's hard to. . . .'*

'Yes'

'Go out and do whatever you want to do with your life, because I never finish anything, I never accomplish anything, you know, it's like, all half started here, here, here, and eventually things get done, but you know, it's a hell of a route to get to everything. Okay?'

'Well, I'm looking forward to a time where you understand, you can count on yourself. Cause I know that's been missing for you.'

'Count on myself. That's like [made a sound conveying a not quite contemptuous dismissal of the idea and returned quickly to her previous tone], *thank you, yeah. I don't know. I think I trust that statement about as much as I trust counting on someone else. You know what I mean? It's like the inside doesn't have any more trust for the inside world than the outside world.'*

'Well, before you knew there was an inside, before you had consciousness for there being an inner world, in which a lot of these ways in which you feel like you're not you exist . . . waiting for an opportunity to take over, or do what needs to be done to get you through the day. Even before you knew that.'

'I understand that. But, and I might not have understood that's what it was. But I did know something was wrong. I mean, basically it was my sanity that I questioned.'

Dr. Chefetz comments: When I say that 'I'm looking forward to a time', I am setting an expectation for a future possibility. I am also acknowledging the current situation of disarray and lack of self-trust. This is a debilitating experience for our patients. I don't expect that she will agree that it's possible for her to achieve this state of confidence now, but I do let her know I believe it is possible. She confirms the gravity of the meaning of her lack of self-confidence, and of her switching behaviors, by indicating that it has caused her to question her sanity. I want to emphasize here that part of our job is to help our patients figure out what their experience of themselves actually is, to achieve a consciousness of being. In a typically dissociative, non-self-reflective person, this is quite an achievement. It is important that the language that describes this experience be as close to the patient's own language as possible, without the therapist imposing his own terminology. This language is often negotiated, so that both participants in the conversation know what they are talking about. The therapist assists the patient's inquiry and joins her quest for self-definition.

Segment 2

'Does it feel like it was you who did all these things? Or do you just sort of know the history of the week?'

'I was there. But sometimes, it was like, how do I explain it? It's like, while I was doing something, I know, I switched, and the Perfectionist came out and fixed something that I did, with the patch, the drywall patch around the marble, cause it was like, you know, I remember standing back going: Yeah, that looks better. That's what I was trying to do. Whatever. You know. But, it was like, I knew what was going on, you know, it's like all of a sudden, like Nancy said this, this big sigh like, you know [whooshing sound indicating transformation] and then switched hands and [same sound again] did it. Nancy goes like, in her mind: What just happened? So I know there was a switching there, cause, ya know, I got it better left-handed then I did right-handed. Which was kind of awkward, considering I was working on the right-hand side of the window. So I had to stand over to the side and you know its hard to work in a right-sided corner with your left hand.'

'Oh, yeah.'

'So, yeah. Stuff like that. And then it was like, I wasn't going to patch every hole in the room. And then boom [another whooshing transformation sound, magical in quality] everything was done. You know. Like all of a sudden there were spots all over the room going like: What color are you painting? What did you do? You had holes in the wall. So, um, hole painting today. [patient and therapist both laughing]. Anyway, you know, stuff like that.'

'Had to! Had to!'

'Yeah. Yeah. Oh yeah.'

Dr. Chefetz comments: Here the patient is talking about what it is like to notice the effects of her switching from one Not-Me state to another. Her laughter is anxious. I am trying to draw her out, to encourage her reflection. I stay away from interpretation or clarification. My emphasis is on matching her affect. Just like Beatrice Beebe (1997) matches the affective state of infants to calm them, I am matching her state of excited engagement. My spontaneous utterance of 'Had to! Had to!' is exactly the energy I must have been tracking. It is not the linguistic content, but the emotional content that teaches her she is understood. It is probably equivalent to Beebe cooing to one of her infants. The patient's 'Yeah. Yeah. Oh, yeah' reflects this attunement, a mutual pacing that is part of intimacy and builds trust. She knows I am 'with' her.

Segment 3

'Then there's the frustration of going to therapy and not knowing you've been in therapy for however long I've been coming here. So, it's been a while.'

'I guess so. How long have you been coming here?'

'I guess. What year is this? 2000? 2002? Okay. Um, late 90s somewhere. So, you know, 97, 98, 99, 98, 97?'

'Somewhere in there.'

'Somewhere in there. So it's been a long time. Doesn't seem like it. Isn't that weird?'

'Umhumm.'

'It doesn't seem like that.'

'It seems like we just met yesterday?'

'Well, not really, but kind of. Do you know what I mean? It's like all of a sudden I realize I am in therapy and it's me. Before that, it was like, the shell was going into this room and the shell was going out of the room. Do you understand what I mean?'

'You're conscious in a way that you weren't before.'

'Oh, yeah.'

'Really aware.'

'Oh, yeah. . . . And I was conscious that I was like going to therapy but not conscious as to what happened. And then there was that spell where, it's like, I don't know what that guy thinks, but, I know, that's not what's wrong with me. I just talk to myself. I don't know why you think this is, you know, whatever, but . . . then that kind of like changed. And then I go, reality sunk in.'

'You became conscious.'

'Well I, kind of.'

'In a different way.'

'In a different way. And then sometimes, it's like, I just stepped out of a boxing ring and, you know, it's like Heaven help me if I gotta slam the brakes on the way home because I don't think my legs would be actually strong enough to actually do that. I'm that weak.'

'Yeah.'

'Um, and then there's still the reluctance of uh, that, that little gut feeling that one of these days I'm going to have to say something I really don't want to talk about, knowing that it's a part of all of this. Probably a big part of all of this. And it's like, if I never say it, I don't know. Ay, ay, I, ay I. Anyhow, that's a subject that's not approachable.'

'Whatever that was. Was there something you were talking about even? I don't think so. Right?'

'I don't know. There is something I don't want to talk about.'

'What's it like for you to be conscious in this way?'

'What's it like?'

'Yeah, I mean how is it?'

[Laugh] 'Well, you know, I guess this is where I get my progress report. Gotta check in once in a while and see how everything's going.'

Dr. Chefetz comments: I continue to try and have her explore her awareness of her Mind. As she describes the change in her experience of working in therapy, she momentarily realizes that in a previous recent session she was severely distressed as she confronted thoughts and feelings that overwhelmed her then, and that she has still not openly spoken about. She has been increasingly suicidal, and I am not about to push her to talk about what she wants to hide. I join her by saying 'Whatever that was. Was there something you were talking about even?' Paradoxically, this gives her room to acknowledge that there is something that she doesn't want to talk about. I stay focused on the general, and avoid the specific, while aiming for increased self-reflection as I ask, 'What's it like for you to be conscious in this way?' The question is a 'fishing' question. I don't know what 'this way' is. I am hoping she will tell me. The particular language of the words above need some explanation:

'And it's like, if I never say it, I don't know. Ay, ay, I, ay I. Anyhow, that's a subject that's not approachable.' For you, the reader, it is probably difficult, not being able to hear the words or to see the person uttering them, to grasp the quick succession of self-states that took place in this sentence. First the voice tones of a person feeling somewhat baffled about what she was trying to communicate, then the suggestion that she was about to say something pithy, and finally, all in the same sentence, a person who acts as if she is being stopped from speaking by being yanked off the stage with a vaudevillian stage hook! People with dissociative disorders may exhibit what is called 'interference phenomena'. In this experience, patients report feeling as if their voices were suddenly controlled by someone else, or their thoughts 'stolen' from their minds. This hypnotic experience is similar to what is described in the hypnosis literature as 'made thoughts' or 'made feelings'. A good resource for understanding these kinds of experiences is Loewenstein (1991).

Segment 4 (continuous)

'We've been talking a little bit about how your life has changed in terms of like the church and stuff.'

I'm a different person. There's no doubt about it. I mean everyone around me notices it. And it's like. . . . And the people I let around me now, it's like, you know, if it's a hassle or whatever, Bye. I don't want any part of it. Instead of just . . . I guess I'm strong enough to know what I'm comfortable with or what I'm not comfortable with, or saying. Before, it would have been like, who am I to say? But it makes, you know, I don't tolerate, and I'm not even sure what it is I don't tolerate. If you know, I'm around someone who yells a lot, I won't go round them any more, I don't want to hear it. If someone's yelling a lot and I have no choice, I'm like, you know, making sure they understand they're not acceptable or whatever. Or, I have this habit of shutting out things around me that I'm not into or something, I don't know. Or. . . .'

'How do you shut it out? What do you do?'

'I don't know. But I don't hear it. I don't see it. I'm in, you know . . . I'll go through whatever I'm doing in whatever situation it is, it's like listening to my father scream at me. You know. Turn the switch down, and finally turn it off. I could have been in the same room with him while he went on for an hour and never heard a word he said. I can still do that.'

'But would you feel something of it?'

'Do I feel something of it?'

'Yeah. I mean you might not have heard the words, but was there something?'

'Oh . . . yeah. Look around and there he is. His mouth is still moving and you could tell that he was getting madder and madder, but I didn't hear.'

'Would you feel the threat?'

'No. Nope.'

'Would you know about the threat?'

'Yes.'

'You'd kind of know about it.'

'Yeah.'

'Like a headline, but it wasn't about you?'

'Even if attack was imminent, it was like go ahead, it doesn't affect me. I'm just going to sit just exactly what I'm doing, where I'm at, doesn't matter. I still have that ability to just put myself, staying in one position, but put myself totally away from what's going on around me. If I don't like what I'm seeing or hearing or what's going on, I don't participate, maybe that's what it is. I check out. Then it becomes a foggy memory. And then sometimes it's like . . . most of the time I walk around, it's like there's no hap- happy sad, unhappy, whatever, and then sometimes the emotions and stuff are so raw, I can't handle listening to the news, watching a commercial, read a book. I can't do anything.'

'What do you think about?'

'What do I think about?'

'Yeah. What do you think is happening?'

'What do I think has happened? I don't know. I'm not DOING your job.'

'You want me to do my job?'

'You want me to do your job too?'

'Come on! [laughing emphatically together]'

Dr. Chefetz comments: I keep pressing ahead to identify feelings. I joke with my patients about the 'F' word – feelings. Affect consciousness is the goal. Affect provides context and meaning. Get rid of affect, and she can watch her father's mouth move, but not appreciate any threat. Still, she somehow, implicitly rather than explicitly, is aware of a threat. I want to help her fill in the blanks, to associate. I use humor when possible. It helps me too. The last few lines of this segment might have sounded like a rehearsed comedy routine. Both she and I enjoyed the action.

Segment 5 (continuous)

'What do I think has happened? I think I touched on something, or something's triggered something like a memory or I mean a lot of times when that happened, there's like flashbacks. You know, the flash cards or the silent movies, or something go on and off in the brain.'

'And do you react to those while they're going on and off?'

'No.'

'You don't?'

'No. I know they exist. I know there're happening. It's like that's when I don't feel anything.'

'Is it happening to you?'

'Is it happening to me? Heck no. It's a black-and-white movie I'm watching. You know, the old news flash in front of the movies. Sixty seconds . . . coming, next the cartoon. Steamboat Willy, I don't know.'

'These are scenes from your past?'

'Well, I hope so. I wish they weren't, but yeah, they are. Scenes I know. Scenes I've been to, and stuff. I mean. . . . know.'

'What's it like for you to be talking about it right now?'

'As long as you don't ask for the subtitles, I guess it's okay [with a chuckle].'

'But when I asked you my question, if you're faced with. . . .'

'What question?'

'What's it like for you? Your face wrote a whole novel.'

'Did it?'

'Yeah. In about five seconds of twitching.'

'Ah.'

'A lot of movement in that face.'

'Okay, but . . .'

'A lot of feeling.'

'Okay, well, I think that, sure [laugh] I feel numb. That's the easy answer.'

'You notice what the legs are doing?'

'Yeah. I know that. Antsy, is that the term for this?'

'So, it's very uncomfortable talking about it?'

'Well, that's bordering on the . . . you know it's always like I always gotta skirt that edge of talking about what I don't want to talk about.'

'Whatever that is.'

'Cause intellectually I know I have to.'

'Eventually.'

'Sooner or later it's all got to be worked out. And I can skirt it all I want, and it's not going to come out. It's just . . . but, this is it. Okay? That's what this is. This is that.'
'Yeah, always moving.'
'Getting toward that goal, you know, you gotta talk about this one of these days, and it's going to be a while.'

Dr. Chefetz comments: This was a convenient ending for this transcript, but it was not the actual end of the session. We are still in the middle of an effort to raise consciousness for her experience. She notices the meaning and jokes about it, as if I am the one who is not sure what is real or not real. She also notices the meaning that I address: some of the things she might be expected to own as her actual life experiences are held in a Not-Me place, and rarely does she own these as part of her life. It's OK to know, if we don't add the subtitles. Translation: I can see these scenes in my mind, but it doesn't affect me when there are no words to hint at the meaning of what I see. These are just scenes in my life. I draw attention to her face so that she becomes more aware that she has a face that has expression, conveying affect and clarifying meaning. Frontal lobe and limbic circuits that generate emotional expression receive feedback from facial sensation. When someone smiles as he talks about his anger, these feedback circuits get confused, and it is easier for someone not to know about his feelings. In her wisdom, my patient finishes this scene by saying that she knows that at some point she needs to understand her life. She's right: after almost exactly five years, it's still going to be a while.

COMMENTARY ON CHEFETZ'S CLINICAL MATERIAL

Philip Bromberg

I want to thank Rich for his generosity in sharing things so private and personal. I'm particularly grateful, because I could have been left out on a very long limb. It's always risky telling someone you hear an enactment taking place in his work, because he might not have the slightest idea what you are talking about, so to hear Rich, in the next session, not only agree but also describe what the enactment was *about*, is very satisfying. As I listened to the tape of Rich's session with Nancy I heard the beginning of an enactment involving mistrust, and I'm going to try to recreate what took place inside me as I listened that led me to that formulation. I began to hear what had clearly started as a 'discussion' about Nancy's dissociation subtly develop an enacted subtext. A part of Nancy seemed to be experiencing Rich's effort to give her hope about the future *at that moment*, as a way of his not having to listen to her frustration and anger – that her life continues to be just too damned hard, because all he gives her is insight into the fact that she has a lot of different parts. But *she's* the one that that has to live with them, and still suffers from the fact that it hasn't changed. Nancy is highly dissociative, which I obviously knew in advance of listening to the tape; the fact that she is dissociative is what the conference is about. But I also could *hear* it, not just in their discussions *about* dissociation and her multiple selves, but in the self-state shifts that seemed to be evoked by the affective complexity of her relationship with Rich – the kind of complexity that can feel suddenly destabilizing to both patient and therapist. Rich brings to a relationship a blend of personal qualities that aren't often found together in a therapist – a seriousness of purpose, a deep affective reson-ance with his patient's internal life, a spontaneous playfulness, and a mind that is always thinking. You've all gotten a taste of what I mean just by being with him here today. It's a blend of real qualities, not an analytic posture. As a therapist, Rich's blend of professional skill and personal relatednesss makes him a dream come true, but for a dissociative patient such as Nancy, it is precisely for that reason he is also dangerous – not a dream come true, but her worst nightmare; certain parts of Nancy can easily trust Rich and start to hope there is more to life than trauma waiting to happen just when you think you are safe. A dissociative mental structure functions essentially as an 'early warning system'. It is geared to disrupt the growth of trust and hope, thus preserving the patient's vigilant readiness for disaster. Any perception that a relationship may be trustworthy com-promises the vigilance a patient relies on to maintain control over the dissociative system. Each island of self has its own internally defined func-tion, and each dissociated self becomes its own island of 'truth'. If such a patient forgets, even briefly, that feeling secure and connected to her ther-apist can lead to unforeseen betrayal, she threatens her own hard-won 'fail-safe' system. This is why there is often a bewilderingly abrupt shift in the interactional field at the very moment a dissociative patient starts to feel close – a switch to a state of consciousness in which she will find or evoke something she can use as a danger signal associated with the hope of continued closeness. And there is never a shortage of things that a patient can find in a therapist to use in derailing the hope of sustained and satis-fying connection. The therapist invariably provides them, simply because no matter how much a therapist cares about his patient, he is not an empathy machine. There's always that damned fact that in any relationship, you have a mind of your own, anxieties of your own, and needs of your own, and that goes for therapists too. The nature of human relatedness includes one's 'otherness'. The essential core of therapeutic growth for any patient is in the negotiation between self-interest and secure attachment to an 'other' in those areas of personality where this negotiation has either been compromised or has never taken place. Aspects of any therapist's subjectivity – his own selfhood – will inevitably be disjunctive with his patient's subjective experience at certain moments, and will be *felt* by his patient as 'off', 'intrusive', 'wrong', 'threatening', and so on, even when (perhaps *mostly* when) those parts of each person's self that are in collision are dissociated, not represented in conscious thought by *either* person: that is, when they are 'not-me'.

I became aware of a shift in Nancy's state of consciousness to one where she seemed to find needed proof that Rich, like everyone else, has to be watched carefully. It had the feel to me of what is sometimes the start of an enactment involving mistrust. 'Trust' is not a word that is easily applied to the personality structure of patients such as Nancy. What looks like trust is often the unreflective adaptiveness of a still dissociated part of the patient's self that cannot hold self-interest and attachment to the other in the same relational context.

Other dissociated parts of the self are functioning as on-call watchdogs, vigilantly ready to intervene and protect the patient from 'certain' disaster, if she seems about to place her trust in someone. I heard some of what I've just described in a segment of the tape, the part where Nancy gives a little speech, beginning 'I *understand* that it's all just me . . .' and Rich says, '*Well*, I'm looking forward to a time . . . etc. . . . etc. . . . etc.' I heard a 'not-me' part of Nancy who reacted, not with hopefulness to what Rich said, but with mistrust, as if he were saying, 'The Nancy you are *right now* is making me feel bad about *myself*, and I prefer to think about who you *will* be in the future – a time when I will feel like a great therapist.' My own self-states were very active while I was listening to this. For example, a part of me that became responsive to what I later conjectured was a 'not-me' aspect of Rich, led me to feel a vague discomfort that Rich was working too hard, and I was aware of feeling a little grouchy with Nancy. I've observed that when this sort of thing takes place in my own work, my dissociation is most frequently in response to shame – a warded-off blow to my momentary stability as a therapist. There have even been times with certain patients that I've questioned whether I *ever* knew what I am doing. I can remember one situation where an old *New Yorker* cartoon popped into my mind. A female patient was on the couch, and her male analyst, wearing his hat and coat and carrying a briefcase, was standing up next to her, saying 'Excuse me, Mrs. Smith, but I've decided to retire.' What made this drawing particularly funny is that the expression on the analyst's face was totally serious and unperturbed as he is about to give up his profession in the middle of an analytic session. You don't have to *be* an analyst to recognize that the analyst's professional-self in the cartoon had become so completly destabilized by the relationship with his patient that he didn't have a clue he had been taken over by *not-me*. This cartoon, in less dramatic form, happens routinely in every therapist-patient relationship.

In what was going on between Rich and Nancy, I could feel the presence of a subtext that transformed what was a topic being discussed into an affective reliving of it in the here and now. A shift in my own self-state allowed a direct contact between aspects of *my* 'not-me' experience and aspects of Nancy's. My attention switched from thinking *about* Nancy from the outside, to feeling Nancy's presence from within an intersubjective field of which I, momentarily, had become a part. Had I been her therapist, and experienced in that context what I experienced listening to the tape, would I in fact have used this shift in my self-experience as 'material' with that patient at that moment? If so, how? If not, why not? I don't know, and I can't know, because it would depend on what went into organizing the totality of my experience at that moment, not on a clinical choice based on the objective application of a principle of technique. Had I been her therapist, I would have my particular knowledge of Nancy and my own experience of what our relationship felt like at that point in treatment. Would using my experience of the enactment *openly* with her come as a shock, because it would be a huge departure from what she otherwise anticipates from me? If yes, wouldn't my unanticipated behavior be most likely dissociated by her, and sucked into the enactment, becoming just more proof to Nancy that she can't trust anyone? Let's imagine it did happen exactly in that way. Is it an 'error'? Can the moment of her dissociation, if it is observed by the analyst, be itself used as a potential window into a therapeutic outcome? I believe that what happens at that point depends in part on the treatment model that supports an analyst's clinical approach. Rich as an analyst is dedicated to a thoughtful and judicious concern for his patient's affective safety and communicates this through his ongoing behavior with her. A part of Nancy knows that he cares and thinks about her emotional welfare, even at those moments when another part of her recognizes that his effort to give her 'encouragement', rather than hanging-in with her pain, is most responsive to his own needs. Some part of her knows that he cares about helping her more than he cares about preserving his self-image as a 'good analyst', even though, at that moment, his own needs have the greater priority. As long as an analyst's responses to his patient do not represent an unreflective 'anything goes' attitude, the possibility is remote that he is going to pointlessly retraumatize his patient when she is feeling most vulnerable. In other words, from the clinical vantage point that Rich and I share, we don't believe there is a 'rightness' or 'wrongness' contained in one's clinical choices, as long as the patient is not being misused. What matters is being as attuned as possible to the impact of the choices you *do* make. This means being committed to recognizing your patient's dissociated responses to your participation as well as her more conscious responses. It doesn't mean always being *successful* at it. Using enacted experience in this way, dissociated parts of a patient's self, such as the part that holds mistrust of someone to whom she is attached, can come to be voiced and recognized as a healthy part of 'me', through a therapy relationship in which the past is relived in a 'safe-enough' way.

I decided to organize my thoughts about Rich's clinical material around one theme, the issue that most made us want to do this conference together: that is, there are always pieces of dissociated self-experience that have weak or nonexistent links to the experience of 'me', and with certain of these inaccessible 'not-me' self-states, before they can become aspects of 'me', available to internal conflict, they must first become available to self-reflection. Until this happens, they can only be talked 'about' over and over, without self-change, because they are not felt, experientially, as belonging to 'me'. I now concentrate on the final segment of Rich's tape, because I think it provides a particularly good illustration of this issue as it develops in richness (no pun intended) through the linking of two related moments in time. My hope is to show how talking with 'Me and Not-Me' has the same basic treatment goal for Rich as it does for me – the goal of facilitating a patient's ability to increasingly take her own mind as an object of reflection (which for most psychoanalysts, regardless of theoretical persuasion, is the signature of an analytic process). Let me set the stage for my commentary. When an analyst wishes to help a patient deepen her emotional experience of an event she is describing – for example, an event that the patient states had been upsetting, but is reported without much affective immediacy – the intervention that is most typically offered is some variation of the question 'What did you feel?' or 'What was the upset-feeling like?' This, to me, is a great improvement over the more traditional 'What comes to mind?' But an analyst can do even more, as for instance, asking 'What is it like for you to feel upset?' This question addresses a more complex reality than even 'What was the upset-feeling like?' (which is a request simply to describe the upset feeling). An answer to 'What is it like for you to feel upset?' requires, not only accessing the experience of the (upset) feeling itself, but also simultaneously trying to access the experience of the experience (a request to reflect on what being upset itself is like). Fonagy and Target (1996) refer to this as the ability to represent a mental representation, the underpinning of mentalization, and the foundation for what analysts have traditionally called 'the observing ego'. The question that Rich asked, as you might imagine, is not an easy one for a dissociative patient to cope with. It requires her to emerge from her dissociative cocoon, at least momentarily, in order to try to answer it. This challenge to the dissociative mental structure will often evoke a switch to a different dissociated self-state or sometimes lead to a dissociative *symptom* (such as a headache, a glazed look, or a flickering of the eyelids), which can then become an object of attention in itself. The question, 'what is it like at this moment to . . . blah blah blah,' is not a request to simply deal with the experience cognitively, but an invitation to the patient to try to do something that is, for her, quite complex – to access the dissociated aspect of herself that holds the perceptual experience of her own upset mind and contain it consciously as part of the here-and-now reality of talking *about* it with her therapist. Nancy is being asked to *perceive*, in the here and now, a past experiential moment, not a narrative to be described from a distance, not a 'story to be told', but a space to be reentered experientially – a nonlinear reality where past and present, linked by cognitive reflection, coexist. It is a moment such as this that links my clinical vantage point with Rich's especially closely. I'm going to try to illustrate this through what I heard taking place between Rich and his patient in the last section of his tape – an example of what I've just called 'the process of facilitating a patient's ability to increasingly take her own mind as an object of reflection.' It is a way of expressing, in the language of clinical process, what I've described in more conceptual language as a link being made in the here and now between the mental representation of an event that resides in short-term or working memory, and a mental representation of the self as the agent or experiencer.

Rich has just asked Nancy how long she's been coming to therapy, and she starts counting, with only a vague sense of time orientation. The patient's words are in italics.

'What year is this? 2000? 2002? Okay. Um, late 90s somewhere. So, you know, 97, 98, 99, 98, 97?'

'Somewhere in there.'

'Somewhere in there. So it's been a long time. Doesn't seem like it. Isn't that weird?'

'Umhumm.'

'It doesn't seem like that.'

'It seems like we just met yesterday?' Rich offers.

'Well, not really, but kind of. Do you know what I mean? It's like all of a sudden I realize I am in therapy and it's me. Before that, it was like, the shell was going into this room and the shell was going out of the room. Do you understand what I mean?'

'You're conscious in a way that you weren't before.'

'Oh, yeah.'

'Really aware.'

'Oh yeah . . . And I was conscious that I was like going to therapy but not conscious as to what happened. And then there was that spell where, it's like, I don't know what that guy thinks, but, I know, that's not what's wrong with me. I just talk to myself. I don't know why you think this is, you know, whatever, but . . . then that kind of like changed. And then I go, reality sunk in.'

'You became conscious.'

'Well I, kind of.' [not really agreeing]

'In a different way.' [he amends it]

'In a different way. And then sometimes, it's like, I just stepped out of a boxing ring and, you know, it's like Heaven help me if I gotta slam the brakes on the way home

because I don't think my legs would be actually strong enough to actually do that.
I'm that weak.'
'Yeah.'
Um, and then there's still the reluctance of uh, that, that gut feeling that one of
these days I'm going to have to say something I really don't want to talk about,
knowing that it's a part of all of this. Probably a big part of all of this. And it's like,
if I never say it, I don't know. Ay, ay, I, ay I. Anyhow, that's a subject that's not
approachable.'
'Whatever that was. Was there something you were talking about even? I
don't think so. Right?'
'I don't know. There is something I don't want to talk about.'
'What's it like for you to be conscious in this way?'

To reiterate, I believe that Rich's question, 'What's it like for you to be
conscious in this way?' is one of the most powerful interventions a therapist
can make. It increases communication between different parts of the self by
co-constructing an intersubjective space (in which the therapist's mind and
the patient's can coexist) and increases her capacity for mentalization.
The first part of the question enhances her capacity for self-reflectiveness
('What's it like?'), while the second part ('. . . to be conscious in this way')
asks her to stay *in* the experience she is reflecting on. The more her mind
can do that, the less she needs to dissociate. Nancy replies, puzzled,

'What's it like?'
'Yeah, I mean how is it?'
[Laugh] *'Well, you know, I guess this is where I get my progress report. Gotta check*
in once in a while and see how everything's going.'

I believe that what Nancy means by 'check-in' is checking-in with another
part of *herself*. One can see here how frightening it is for her to self-reflect
with Rich in the moment, so she holds tight to her dissociative mental
structure, and instead of responding to his intended meaning – 'What's the
experience like for you *right now* to be conscious in this way?' – she
responds (with a nervous laugh) as if he had asked her for a cognitive
evaluation of her progress (How do you think you are doing?). I hear this
moment between Rich and Nancy resonating with my own vignette
described earlier, where my patient's girlfriend 'checked out' and replied
'sort of' when asked to reflect in the moment on her own mental processes.
It's the kind of moment that I think often provides a great window of
opportunity, if you can catch it and if there has been enough groundwork
laid to work together with the experience of her checking out, right then as
it is happening. I think this is an important point, because it underlines the

fact that the value of Rich's intervention doesn't depend on whether it 'works' in the linear meaning of the word. By allowing some intersubjective space to open up *at that moment*, her shutting down and dissociating can itself become increasingly available as a shared event. 'Not-me' is a self-state that because it is dissociated, is not directly accessible to symbolization by offering new meaning to the self that existsin the here and now – a process that has been referred to over the years as 'interpretation'. In order for new meaning to have 'meaning', a patient needs first to feel her 'not-me' state being recognized and responded to relationally, and this can happen only through 'not-me' feeling real and alive to the therapist at that moment. Unless the patient's 'not-me' state of mind is fully recognized by the therapist, any new level of meaning, no matter how significant it may appear to the therapist, is to the patient just one more fiction *about* her. Until 'not-me' feels relationally alive, the patient is being asked to inhabit meaning that isn't hers and to accept some new words or concepts as a substitute for feeling real. Okay. Let's look at what happens next! Well, not exactly 'next' but very shortly. Nancy has been talking about her flashbacks, but from a very removed place – as movies, cartoons, or flash cards, and Rich suddenly asks:

'These are scenes from your past?'
'Well, I hope so. I wish they weren't, but yeah, they are. Scenes I know. Scenes I've been to, and stuff. . . .'

Rich then does it again:

'What's it like for you to be talking about it right now?'
'As long as you don't ask for the subtitles, I guess it's okay.'

That's so lovely! Nancy almost says directly that she will talk about anything as long as she doesn't have to reflect on what she is talking about while she is experiencing it. So, this time, as distinct from the time before, she openly (but metaphorically) acknowledges her dissociative defense.

Rich continues to pursue her:

'But when I asked you my question, if you're faced with. . . .'
Nancy replies: 'What question?'

Here is where you will hear Rich talking *to* 'not-me' (not just *about* 'not-me') at the same time he is talking to 'me'. It is the body that holds the dissociated 'not-me' experience, so listen to how he speaks *to* and *about* her body at the same time. Rich asks, as he did earlier:

'What's it like for you?'
(but this time, he goes further):
'Your face wrote a whole novel.'
'Did it?'
'Yeah. In about five seconds of twitching.'
'Ah.'
'A lot of movement in that face.'
'Okay, but. . . .'
'A lot of feeling.'
'Okay, well, I think that, sure [laugh] I feel numb. That's the easy answer.'

Nancy has said to Rich, 'There is something I don't want to talk about.' But Rich knows that another part of Nancy is 'listening' and he wants to let her know he is aware of its presence. It's the part holding the experience that Nancy (as 'me') doesn't want to access, much less reflect upon – the process she calls 'subtitles'. Rich, talking to both 'me' and 'not-me' at the same time, is in effect saying to Nancy:

> 'I know there's something you don't want to talk about, and I also know that you *can't* talk about it, because it's not really yours to talk about yet. But there's another part of you who I can see from your face is trying to get our attention – a part of you who probably does know what that "something" is, and doesn't want to keep being so alone with it. Maybe she hopes you will let her speak to you, so that little by little you will know what *she* knows, and then you and I can talk about it together, so she won't have to be so alone and you won't have to be so afraid of her. It sure is scary, though, to have her "in your face", and to know I see her there, and why wouldn't it be? After all, what's *always* most frightening is the possibility that something you're not ready for might hit you all at once, and it could be too much for your mind.'

As Rich is speaking to Nancy, he knows that the 'not-me' part of her that he sees in her face is listening too, and he wants her to know that he is aware of his role in protecting Nancy's emotional safety if she *does* share with Nancy's mind the affective experience of the 'something' that happened to her. As a result, Nancy becomes *aware* of her numbness and is even somewhat able to reflect on it as shown by her laugh. In other words, she's able to experience herself using dissociation to escape from the moment, and even calls it the 'easy answer'. This gradual process of making a patient aware, in the moment, of her own dissociative reactions – especially when the awareness comes about through shared processing of here-and-now experience – allows her thought processes to mentally represent experience that had previously been affectively unregulatable, and this, in turn, reduces her reliance on dissociation as an automatically 'triggered' response. *Until the unspoken self is engaged, speaking to the self that is already engaged eventually reaches its limit of usefulness.* How do we know when that limit is reached? We don't actually 'know', but often we can feel or see 'something else' happening while we are talking *about* the patient. The 'something else' we feel or see is what alerts us to the wordless voice of a 'not-me' trying to be heard – a voice that *can* be heard and eventually engaged, providing our experience of the 'something else' reaches the threshhold of our somatopsychic awareness.

SPEAKING FOR NOT-ME

Richard Chefetz's Preface

The reader is advised that the speaker who delivered the next commentary spoke in the Southern accent of a country doctor from the Blue Ridge Mountains of Virginia. This is not a thick accent, but it was clearly present to those in attendance. While Dr. Chefetz practiced medicine for ten years in such a locale, it was not his intention to start speaking in this tone during the presentation. It sort of just happened. You can believe what you like, but that is the truth. Yes, it surprised him, and it also kind of delighted him. The truth is, Philip has told you only one of his reactions to this clinical material. He and Rich talked, and decided that the version you've read made the most sense for this discussion. But it was the second version Philip wrote, the one you didn't read, that made the most sense to Not-Me. I am an old friend of Rich's, though I haven't always been so friendly. And as long as they were talking about Not-Me, it is worth noting that there is more than one Not-Me. No surprise, huh! So, let's get on with what Philip heard, and see what you think about it. I'll tell you what I have figured out, and if Rich is lucky, he'll get a chance to speak at the end, but not before I'm done. This is my time. Philip noted, in the other version of his response to Rich, that he thought he heard the beginnings of an enactment regarding mistrust. Rich wasn't aware then that *I* was active again in the background, though he is aware now. I'm a version of Rich about whom you are going to learn a lot more than *he* ever wanted to know.

Here's the text where I show up, twice no less. You have it in front of you, right from the getgo, the first line in the audiotape as Nancy spoke. Remember what I told you about her voice tones? Remember how she felt? She was making a point, wasn't she? It had to have been in response to something Rich said.

*'I understand that it's all just me. With different aspects, or whatever the **hell** you want to call it, whatever you want to label it. But when you're from the inside looking*

out, it isn't me. That's somebody else. I'm not that person, I'm not this person, I'm not that person. **It's not the same!** *And that's where it's hard to . . . go out and do whatever you want to do with your life, because I never finish anything, I never accomplish anything, you know, it's like, all half started . . . and eventually things get done, but you know, it's a hell of a route to get to everything. Okay?'*

'Well, I'm looking forward to a time where you understand you can count on yourself. Cause I know that's been missing for you.'

'Count on myself. That's like . . . thank you, yeah. . . . I think I trust that statement about as much as I trust counting on someone else. You know what I mean? . . .'

[Rich starts out and tries again] 'Well, before you knew there was an inside. . . .'

[Nancy repeats] *'I understand that. But, . . .'*

What has happened here? Philip noticed something about this exchange. He did what he does so well, he used his feelings to hear what happened. In Philip's own words:

> I felt a part of Nancy needing to mistrust Rich, and in his own piece of it, I could feel Rich not wanting to be mistrusted. As in every enactment, the therapist is participating in his own dissociative process, and slowly *becomes* the person he is perceived as being.

Philip doesn't ask who Rich becomes, but I will tell you. He becomes like all the other people in Nancy's life who didn't listen or see that she was living in Hell. She didn't know who she was, or how she was, and Rich ignores her passionate statement and sticks with his own agenda. He must not have known he wasn't listening, because it is like he is arguing with her point of view: you might feel that way, but I'm looking forward. He, in fact, says: 'Well, I'm looking forward to a time where you understand you can count on yourself. Cause I know that's been missing for you.' I know he's a good therapist. So, why did he say that? He ought to know that when he uses the word 'Well', he is disagreeing and might not be listening. He wasn't getting it. It's kind of a mild form of Diss-ing, isn't it? Whose reality are we in here, after all? And he also didn't know *I* was there. He didn't listen to me either! He just *acted* like I feel. That's what always happens. See, I don't want to know what living in Hell is like either. He thinks he is the good therapist, wise, thoughtful, compassionate, all that stuff. But when he starts talking like Cassandra, the immortal who could see the future, then he suffers her same fate, nobody listens to him either. Good therapists don't necessarily need to do good things. Sometimes they need to tolerate thinking and feeling about what it is like to live in their own private hell if they are going to understand and respond to their patients. Are you still listening, Rich? So, Philip heard a Not-Me in Rich, organized around trust.

Nancy heard it too, and challenged him. She doesn't trust Rich's statement that she will be able to count on herself. And, as yet, she can't trust him to listen to what she is saying, though she keeps on trying to get it across to him. I think it's especially important when, in the final paragraph of that section, Nancy uses the word 'but'. (I'll reprint what Nancy said just below, so you can see what I mean.) She uses it twice, maybe for emphasis, after Rich asks her to reflect on the time when she wasn't conscious of having an inside. The word 'but,' just like the word 'well,' heralds a contradiction, a disagreement, a challenge to another view. The view that is challenged is the view of a second Not-Me, a cousin of mine, one who's not about trust. Listen, the theme is hidden, though not too deeply. Nancy says:

> 'I understand that. But, and I might not have understood that's what it was. But I did know something was wrong. I mean, basically it was my sanity that I questioned.'

In response to Rich's first Not-Me, Nancy basically tells Rich to stop dreaming about her being able to trust herself and work with the fact that she doesn't trust. She's living in Hell and needs some help with it. She tries to tell him that he is not listening to her, but he keeps not listening. The second Not-Me is related to Rich's fear of feeling that he is not sane. She wants to put aside understanding dissociation and learning about dissociative mechanisms and focus on the question of what really worries her: is Nancy insane?

Rich has a problem in this session. His patient just spent four sessions in a row working on heavy-duty, trauma-related feelings and has gotten increasingly suicidal. He's not happy about that, but he's used to it, at least that's what he likes to think. Lots of luck, Rich. How did you ever think you could get used to that? You must be the King of Wishful Thinking, you know, like the song from a few years back. So Rich, you know, as long as you maintain this view that suicidal patients don't really bother you because you are used to it, you are at risk for not listening to them, and that is risky. You *know* that. Why aren't you listening here? You had convinced yourself that you could speak in everyday hypnotic language, referencing a time in the future to which the patient could look forward. You forgot a few things. First, in the face of your patient's suicidality, you decided to solve her problems by proclamation, rather than to give her what she really needed, to be understood. That would make you a hero, but not a very good listener. Nobody ever listened to Nancy. She needs that more than she needs you to be so smart. OK, yeah Rich, I'm being pretty blunt, but if you are going to learn something from this, then you need to tolerate the truth. Rich has another problem here, and his name is Not-Me. If he tunes into Not-Me, then he locates his own pain, and if he doesn't tune in, he is liable to repeat this scene again with this patient and others. If I can keep his attention, then maybe he can learn something from me. All you have to do, Rich, is ask yourself a simple question: Why do you believe I might have shown up in this scene, at this time, with this patient? Now Rich, don't dump on yourself about little ole' Not-Me making you conscious again of something you prefer not to think about. Remember, I am not here to torture you, just to protect you from what you find you can't tolerate feeling, or find unknowable, or unspeakable. Ask yourself: What makes it possible for Not-Me to be active now? What do you prefer not to sense, know, or feel? Does this have anything to do with what is going on in Nancy, that she doesn't want to know or feel? Is anything going on in your life, or even with another patient, that is affecting what is going on here with Nancy? What gave me the opening, Rich, to show up in this emotional script, right now? That's right, Rich. Make a list. It's OK to be a little obsessive. So, before you saw Nancy, you had just finished seeing one of the two most challenging patients in your practice. Chronically suicidal, you meet with her every week, just before Nancy. Go on. OK, Nancy also has been suicidal, and she does not always trust herself to be safe, promises to call if she is in trouble, but never calls. You often find out about suicidal intent by a so-called slip on Nancy's part, after the fact. So, you must be anxious about her. No, you haven't forgotten about the patient who killed herself while you were in medical practice. Why would you? Suicide is not just an idea. You know all about the reality, don't you? Who could really forget? You've worked through that long ago, but it doesn't mean you have forgotten, even if you'd like to. The scar is healed, but it's still there, if you will just look and notice. So, yes, there is a trust issue, and it's not just about whether or not you will listen. You are not sure if you can trust Nancy's safety, and you're not sure if you can trust your judgment about her safety. The thing is, Rich, in the interaction we're looking at, you don't seem to want to know that she doesn't trust what you are saying. If you did, then you would have heard her say that she understands *but*. . . . And you would have asked her about it. Sounds like you couldn't tolerate knowing. Why? Oh, OK, you can't tolerate knowing how scared you are that she or one of your many other suicidal patients might actually kill herself. But think about your being intolerant of knowing you are scared. If you are scared that she might kill herself, then how is she likely feeling? Right, she's scared too, but hasn't said so. That's the other piece of you not listening to her concern about whether or not she is sane. People sometimes kill themselves if they think they are going insane and will never recover. Now you understand me, too, Rich. You understand Not-Me. You don't want to know those feelings in yourself. Who would? I won't hold that against you, if you won't hold it against Not-me. Deal? Remember what you know, Rich: Nancy will do best if she feels she has a connection with you, even if it is understanding her helpless despair, if that's what's cooking in her. You know you don't need to cheer her up to help her survive; she needs to make sense out of her experience, to know she is sane, coherent. If she is in Hell, acknowledge it, tune in to it. At least then she won't be confused, and she won't feel so alone because you join her when you understand. Remember what you said earlier? Coherence. Right? Even if you can't stop her pain, she is better off being understood, in pain, but not so alone.

What else is on your list, Rich? Oh. Well, why should that be a surprise? You're tired of tuning in, being empathic, you need a break? Sounds like rocket science to me! OK, if you can't change the scheduling of your patients, then maybe you could give yourself the mental space of being aware that you are tired. Remember, I'm the one who steps up to the plate when you don't want to know. I will protect you, but my kind of protection comes at a price. If you are not aware, then the fatigue will warp your perceptions. Yes, work on your schedule, screen your new patients well, but know how you feel.

So why do *you*, my readers, think Rich avoids dealing with Nancy's statement that her issue is about feeling sane or not? Yeah, right. All of *you* out there may be getting a little reality fatigue yourself, just reading a Not-Me's paper. Surprised? This is part of what is so challenging about listening to dissociative process. You just can't do it all the time. Nobody has the brain power to do that. Sounds pretty cut and dry, doesn't it? But then you would make the same mistake that Rich was making, being rational about this. He doesn't want to tune into feeling disoriented. He can do it, but as I am saying this, he is realizing for the first time that there is something about Nancy's story that is so painful, something about the pain in her face and body that is so compelling, that he is having a hard time with it. Rich prides himself on being thoughtful, organized, intuitive, incisive. Tuning in to the experience of feeling so distant from his actions that he could watch himself doing drywall spackling and have no control over how his body was behaving must be a little unnerving for him. How are you doing thinking about that? Yes, Nancy is not exactly comfortable with it either. You know that she didn't first depersonalize because she didn't like drywall dust. She knows that too.

After Philip heard your paper, Rich, he said that Nancy *thinks* this is not sane, so she doesn't have to *feel* it's not sane. She can use the thought to distract from the feeling. I think that you, Rich, do the same thing with suicide feelings. Rich thinks he manages the suicidality in his patients well, so that he doesn't have to feel the impact of their wish to die or his own experiences of humiliation and despair. It's not pretty, but it is what it is. This is just more of Not-Me who doesn't want to feel scared but does.

This depersonalization experience, watching yourself do things that you don't intend to do, like doing drywall patching, sounds crazy, doesn't it? It's not. It is not psychotic, it is dissociative. It is just an extension of depersonalization and derealization experience, being not in my body and seeing the world as if there is something not real about it. Add a little isolated subjectivity, and there it is, experience that is hard to make coherent, and hard to trust. Depersonalization is an experience that preserves the essence of Self.

Rich has something he is just chomping at the bit to say, and he has been listening to me, so I'm going to give him a chance to speak. Thanks for listening. That is the biggest gift to a Not-Me. I appreciate it. OK.

Hi. It's nice to be back. There is only a brief time left, and I want to add some thoughts about a problem that psychoanalytic theory hasn't been able to manage yet. It is the problem of a person like Nancy who has amnesia for things she says and does, depending on which self-state is present. The problem gets trickier when a self-state spends much of its time sitting back and observing the traffic of one self-state after another, doing their thing in the world, and doing things differently, so differently that it is as if they are different people. Sometimes that self-state keeps track of what is happening by assigning different names or other signifiers to these observable experiences – names like The Kid, the Protector, The Whore, The Dummy, Mary, Jack. If that is what our patient reports to us, then how are we to respond to that report? If I am sitting with a patient who appears to be behaving like a child, speaking like a child, and she begins to cry, wouldn't it be natural for me to say, with some tenderness in my voice, 'Nancy, what would these tears say if they could speak?' Sure. But what if my patient replies to that by saying, 'I'm not Nancy. She has gone away. She doesn't like to feel sad. Now I'm all alone.' How would you respond? Would you ask, 'What is your name? Who are you? Has this happened before? What happened the last time Nancy left you with the sadness? How did that work out?' If we stick with the intention of moving toward coherence, then these questions seem reasonable. What if I were to say, 'Nancy has to be here, you and Nancy are the same person, you don't understand.' How would the patient respond to your dismissal of her experience? Philip and I have had a number of discussions about the importance of our original audience, and now our readers, thinking about multiple self-states as a normative process. Each of us believes that, and works with that view. Both of us are concerned that two outcomes might happen as you read this. First, we were worried you would think we were writing about self-states only in the context of dissociative identity disorder. Second, we worried that you would stop looking for Not-Me states in yourselves, because you might think that if this were only about DID, then it didn't apply to you. I think there is also some risk in raising the question about amnesia and identity alteration. One kind of risk I have noted. The other is that to not *take* (the emphasis is more effective on the word 'not', I think, than on the word 'take'), the risk of noticing would mean I'd have been untrue to myself, and my patients, in bringing to you only part of what they bring to me to understand. So, I am making a plea for all of us to think and learn together, to not assume that we know. Identity alteration is a pseudo-delusion. Eventually, as my patients with dissociative identity alteration come to understand the full range of their lived experience, affect, sensation, behavior and knowledge, the opaque divisions between self-states become transparent, dissolve, and are no more. I cannot convince them that they don't experience what they experience any more than I could convince Nancy that in the future she could trust herself. Each altered identity is overflowing with a richness of meaning that must be understood before healing can take place. Winnicott admonished us not to analyze the transitional object. To me, that means avoiding statements like, 'You know Nancy, that is just a regular wool blanket, there is nothing special about it, in reality, you just believe there is.' If Nancy has a Not-Me associated with a childhood experience, it makes no clinical sense to me to tell that Not-Me, 'Look at the size of your feet, and the rings on your fingers, you are an adult, you just believe you are a child.' It does, however, make sense for me to say, 'You know, I have been noticing the rings on your fingers. I've been wondering what you know about those. Why do you wear them? What does it mean that you have them on your fingers?' Identity alteration is very important in working with suicidal thoughts and feelings in our most disturbed patients. Depersonalization and derealization are robust findings in eating disorders, borderline personality disorder, and persons with substance abuse and addiction histories. Selfdestructive acts are often experienced as occurring in a Not-Me manner. 'I didn't feel it. It was like I was cutting someone else.' 'When I cut the skin, it was numb, but when I saw the blood, I felt a sense of relief, as if this arm that seems to have no meaning for me, not even to be connected, might, after all, have some proof that something in me is alive' *or* 'I ate, and ate, and ate. I couldn't stop myself. I watched myself eat pizza after pizza, until the pain became so big that it blocked out everything else, and then I went away. I just don't know what happened after that. The next morning I woke up on the floor of the bathroom. I don't know how I got there.' How do we understand these experiences and help our patients? You have heard from two clinicians who bring somewhat different backgrounds together to work on problems created by dissociative processes that seem designed to protect the essence of our Selves, but when taken to excess exact a steep price. We all have multiple self-states. And just like all of us being equal, sometimes some self-states seem to think they are more equal than others. (Well, at least that's how Me left Not-Me feeling. Bet you thought, just like Rich, that you might never hear from Not-Me again!)

Notes

1 I am particularly indebted to Robert Bosnak whose 1996 book, *Tracks in the Wilderness of Dreaming*, provided me with the inspiration and courage to adapt his thinking to my own style of working (also see Bosnak 2003; Bromberg 2003c).

2 Daniel J. Siegel (1999), in a powerful and lucid synthesis of subjective experience, neuroscience, and the interpersonal context of self-development, dramatically supports this view of the mind as a multiplicity of internally cohesive self-states that in any given individual defines its own pathology by its relative inability to access its full range of relational flexibility (Siegel 1999: 229–30, 237–8).

References

Beebe, B. (1997) Developmental factors of hatred: Co-constructing mother–infant distress. Presented at 'Hatred and its Rewards', a meeting of the Institute of Contemporary Psychotherapy and Psychoanalysis, Bethesda, MD, 12 April.

Bosnak, R. (1996) *Tracks in the Wilderness of Dreaming*. New York: Delacorte.

Bosnak, R. (2003) Embodied imagination. *Contemporary Psychoanalysis*, 39: 683–95.

Bromberg, P.M. (1993) Shadow and substance: A relational perspective on clinical process. In Bromberg (1998) *Standing in the Spaces: Essays on Clinical Process, Trauma, and Dissociation*. Hillsdale, NJ: Analytic Press.

Bromberg, P.M. (1998) *Standing in the Spaces: Essays on Clinical Process, Trauma, and Dissociation*. Hillsdale, NJ: Analytic Press.

Bromberg, P.M. (2000) Bringing in the dreamer: Some reflections on dreamwork, surprise, and analytic process. *Contemporary Psychoanalysis*, 36: 685–705.

Bromberg, P.M. (2003a) 'Something wicked this way comes': Trauma, dissociation, and conflict – the space where psychoanalysis, cognitive science, and neuroscience overlap. *Psychoanalytic Psychology*, 20: 558–74.

Bromberg, P.M. (2003b) One need not be a house to be haunted: On enactment, dissociation, and the dread of 'not-me' – a case study. *Psychoanalytic Dialogues*, 13 (5): 689–709.

Bromberg, P.M. (2003c) On being one's dream: Some reflections on Robert Bosnak's 'Embodied Imagination'. *Contemporary Psychoanalysis*, 39: 697–710.

Bucci, W. (1997) *Psychoanalysis and Cognitive Science: A Multiple Code Theory*. New York: Guilford.

Bucci, W. (2002) The referential process, consciousness, and sense of self. *Psychoanalytic Inquiry*, 22: 766–93.

Bucci, W. (2003) Varieties of dissociative experience: A multiple code account and a discussion of Bromberg's case of 'William'. *Psychoanalytic Psychology*, 20: 542–57.

Damasio, A.R. (1999) *The Feeling of What Happens: Body and Emotion in the Making of Consciousness*. New York: Harcourt Brace.

Erdelyi, M.H. (1994) Dissociation, defense, and the unconscious. In D. Spiegel (ed.) *Dissociation: Culture, Mind, and Body*. Washington, DC: American Psychiatric Press.

Fonagy, P. and Target, M. (1996) Playing with reality. I: Theory of mind and the normal development of psychic reality. *International Journal of Psychoanalysis*, 77: 217–33.

Havens, L. (1976) *Participant Observation*. New York: Aronson.

Hilgard, E. (1977) *Divided Consciousness: Multiple Controls in Human Thought and Action*. New York: Wiley.

Janet, P. (1889) *L'Automatisme psychologique*. Paris: Felix Alcan.

LeDoux, J.E. (1996) *The Emotional Brain.* New York: Touchstone.

LeDoux, J.E. (2002) *The Synaptic Self.* New York: Viking.

Lichtenberg, J.D. (2003) Communication in infancy. *Psychoanalytic Inquiry*, 23: 498–520.

Linklater, K. (1997) Thoughts on theatre, therapy, and the art of voice. In M. Hampton and B. Acker (eds) *The Vocal Vision: Views on Voice.* New York: Applause Books.

Loewenstein, R.J. (1991) An office mental status examination for complex chronic dissociative symptoms and multiple personality disorder. *Psychiatric Clinics of North America*, 14 (3): 567–604.

Lyons-Ruth, K. and Boston Change Process Study Group (2001) The emergence of new experiences: Relational improvisation, recognition process, and non-linear change in psychoanalytic therapy. *Psychologist-Psychoanalyst*, 21: 13–17.

Putnam, F.W. (1988) The switch process in multiple personality disorder and other state-change disorders. *Dissociation*, 1: 24–32.

Putnam, F.W. (1992) Discussion: Are alter personalities fragments or figments? *Psychoanalytic Inquiry*, 12: 95–111.

Sands, S.H. (1994) What is dissociated? *Dissociation*, 7: 145–52.

Schafer, R. (1968) *Aspects of Internalization.* New York: International Universities Press.

Schore, A.N. (2003) Summary of panel on 'Trauma and neuroscience: Bringing the body more deeply into psychoanalysis'. *Psychologist-Psychoanalyst*, 23: 42–3.

Siegel, D.J. (1999) *The Developing Mind: Toward a Neurobiology of Interpersonal Experience.* New York: Guilford.

Sullivan, H.S. (1940) *Conceptions of Modern Psychiatry.* New York: Norton.

Sullivan, H.S. (1953) *The Interpersonal Theory of Psychiatry.* New York: Norton.

Sullivan, H.S. (1954) *The Psychiatric Interview.* New York: Norton.

van der Kolk, B.A. (1987) The psychobiology of the trauma response: Hyper-arousal, constriction, and addiction to traumatic reexposure. In B.A. van der Kolk (ed.) *Psychological Trauma.* Washington, DC: American Psychiatric Press.

Index